FIRE BIRD

THE PHOENIX PROPHECY
BOOK SIX

CARA CLARE

ARCANE

THE PHOENIX PROPHECY SERIES

Books 1-6 can be read as a complete story arc.
Books 7-9 follow Nova and the guys as they face a new threat.

When above turns to darkness
And below breaks free
A witch born to humans
Salvation shall bring
Fated to five who are not what they seem
The Phoenix will rise and become Earth's Queen
Into the embers
One
Two
Three
Devoured by Flame
The Phoenix is She

KOLE

My face burns, but I can't turn away. The flames dance higher and higher, stretching from the basin of the fountain up toward the ever-darkening sky.

I'm aware of Eve and Ragnor shouting at one another. She's waving her arms, he's putting his hands on her shoulders and shaking her, but I can't bring myself to look at them.

All I can see is Nova. Her arm hanging over the edge of the fountain. Her face when she said goodbye. But she is no longer there.

Devoured by flame.

She is leaving me. Leaving *us*. With every flicker of the bright orange fire, she slips further away. My chest tightens and my gut twists violently. I lurch forward and grab the nearest tree so I don't fall to my knees. What if I was wrong?

What if she doesn't come back? What if I just sent the woman I love to her death?

* * *

THE MOON IS high in the sky by the time the flames die down. I am still holding onto the large oak tree beside me. It feels my pain. Thin, winding branches have wrapped themselves around my arm, holding me upright. The oak's heartbeat matches my own. Only earth mages feel the rhythm of the trees. Usually it is comforting. Now, here, it brings no solace; just a reminder that I am still breathing, and Nova is not. Despite the hours that have passed, she is still not here. She has not risen. She did not stand and walk through the flames back into my arms.

The Phoenix has not returned.

A crowd has gathered around the fountain. Werewolves in their human form stand, salivating over what is happening before them.

It took Ragnor and Eve only seconds to turn their confusion at what was happening into victory. "We did it, Ragnor," she cooed. "We did what he asked. We captured The Phoenix. We bottled her blood, and now..." She turned and splayed her arms out to her sides, "she is no more."

"We should put them out," Ragnor replied, his dark eyes reflecting the dance of Nova's final flames.

"No." Eve hugged herself, smiling. "Let the witch burn."

Finally the flames seem to be putting themselves out. Stopping their relentless attack on Nova's beautiful body. Leaving her in peace. Ragnor claps his hands and calls for silence. He strides toward the fountain. As he draws nearer, blood rushes to my ears and throbs in my veins. The thought of him touching her brings white-hot bile to the back of my throat. I swallow it down. At the same time, I try to squash the magick inside me; I want to rip up the ground beneath Ragnor's feet. I want to hang him upside down from the oak above my head and choke the life from his sick, ruthless body with my bare hands.

He grips the rim of the basin and peers down into it. I can barely breathe. I want to see her, but I'm not sure if I can. This part, I'm not sure if I can watch.

For several long, quivering moments, Ragnor is still. His shoulders rise and fall with the movement of his breath. I narrow my eyes and tug my arm free from the branch that has been holding me up; I need to get closer.

Stepping sideways, I move into the shadow just inside the treeline. Still out of sight, but only just. Ragnor dips a hand into the fountain, then rights himself slowly. Eve is watching him too, ticking her head from side to side and bobbing on the soles of her feet as if she can barely stand the anticipation.

"Ragnor?" she asks when he turns to face her.

Everyone else is silent. Ragnor looks down at his closed hand, then a smile twitches his lips. It stretches across his face. Eyes sparkling, he raises his fist. When he opens it, ashes fall to the ground.

"She's gone," he barks loudly. "The Phoenix is no more!" He looks up at the moon and raises his hands toward it as if he is praying. "In five days' time, when the moon is full, we will use the Phoenix's blood to raise The Shadow King." His voice grows darker and louder. "We will end humanity! Supers will reign supreme! We. Will. Rule!"

Cheers break out. The werewolves start baying and howling, even though they're still in their human forms. Ragnor throws what's left in his hand up into the air and I watch as Nova's ashes catch in the moonlight.

I want to lunge for them, gather them, save them, save her.

But they drift away on a breeze I didn't even know was there; Nova drifts away from me.

"Time to celebrate!" Ragnor puts his arm around Eve, but she breaks away and starts dancing. She pulls him with her. He refuses to dance but allows her to skip circles around him while the others continue to shout and cheer.

I fall to my knees. My chest swells as if it's going to break open. I can barely breathe. I scrape my fingers through my hair and look back at the fountain. "She was supposed to come back," I whisper, digging my fingernails into the cold earth beneath me. "She can't be gone... she was supposed to come back."

Nova... I search for her with my voice. If she's out there, and she can hear me, she'll let me know. She'll find a way to reach me. *Nova, Little Star, please... don't leave me.*

I glance back into the darkness of the woods. It is the first time I have taken my eyes from the fountain since Nova left my side, but all I can think of now is the others. Are they waiting or did they return to the lake? Did they see the smoke? Are they comforting one another at this very moment, whispering to each other that it will all be okay because *I* promised it would be?

I look back when I realize the noise around the fountain has quietened. Everyone is staring at the house. On the steps, a figure has appeared. A woman dressed in white with long, black hair and a willowy frame. As she descends, eyes fixed on Ragnor, I notice her feet are bare. She is so fragile; she looks like she might snap at any moment.

When Ragnor opens his arms and smiles at her, I realize who she is. I am staring at Sam's mother, Elena—the woman Ragnor loved so much he would destroy the world to bring her back.

Like a frightened child, she shrinks into herself as she weaves through the crowd of werewolves to find Ragnor.

When she reaches him, he pulls her to his chest, then cups her face in his hands and strokes her hair from her cheeks. She whispers something I can't hear. His expression changes to one of deep concern. Still staring at Elena, he shouts, "Back inside, everyone! My wife wishes to celebrate somewhere a little warmer."

There is a murmur of discontent, but it quickly dissipates when Ragnor snaps his head up and marches forward, arm fixed firmly around Elena's shoulders.

When they reach the steps, Eve catches Ragnor's arm and mutters something in his ear. He shakes his head and waves a dismissive hand at the fountain. Eve nods, looks furtively back at it, then follows Ragnor inside.

I wait until the beat of loud, angry music drifts from the house, then I break my cover. I stride quickly to the fountain but pause a few feet away from it. I flex my fingers at my sides; my palms are hot, and my hands are shaking.

Part of me wants to turn away so I don't have to see, but the part of my blood that is bonded to Nova's can still sense her. It does not understand that she is gone. It vibrates and hums beneath my skin, pulling me toward what is left of The Phoenix's body.

When I reach the basin, I brace my hand on the large concrete column at its center. I breathe heavily as blood pulses in my ears, then I force myself to look down.

Inside, there is nothing but a pile of ashes. Ashes, and five wooden rings.

2

MACK

S now is growling at me. He's pissed that we're just standing here in the woods. He's pissed we let Nova walk away from us, and he's heartbroken thinking about the possibility of losing her. He wants me to shift. My skin itches from the inside out. My muscles twitch with the urge to grow, and harden; to become something bigger and stronger. Something capable of ripping trees from the ground and roaring at the sky so everyone knows the anguish we're feeling.

As my thoughts spiral downward, inevitably returning to The Hollow and all the awful things that place has witnessed over the years, Luther approaches and puts a stoic hand on my shoulder.

"You okay, Baloo?" He's using my nickname but he's not smiling.

"Are any of us okay?" I look around the group. We are huddled beneath the cover of the trees right where Kole and Nova left us. We haven't moved since they walked away.

"It's been hours," he says, looking up at the dark canopy above our heads. We can't even see the stars from here.

"We should go look for them." Sam has been sitting with Tanner, but now he stands and walks into the center of the group. I'm on the floor, back against a tree, trying to resist the urge to pace like a caged animal. "It's been too long," Sam adds. "Hasn't it?"

Suddenly, I realize they're all looking at me. Expecting *me* to make a decision, but what the fuck do I know? There was a time when I thought I was in control of all this. A time I thought I knew what was coming and how to prepare for it. But now? All I know now is that if Kole was wrong and Nova doesn't return to us, the world can burn for all I care because my life won't be worth anything without her in it.

I'm about to answer Sam when we both, at the exact same moment, smell something on the breeze. Smoke. Remnants of smoke, and…the Viking.

"Kole?" I spring to my feet as he appears through the trees. He's cast a small green light in front of him to illuminate the way and it's painting his features in an eerie glow.

"You waited," he says, striding into the small clearing.

Instead of rushing forward and bombarding him with questions, the four of us stand quivering with nervous energy, staring, trying to read his face. Snow releases a grumble of tortured anticipation that makes my skin prickle. "We waited," I repeat, my mouth so dry I can barely get any words out.

I glance at the others. Tanner is the one to ask, "Where is she?" He looks behind Kole as if this all might be some elaborate joke and Nova's about to jump out from the bushes and yell, *Surprise!*

"What happened?" Sam says, scraping his fingers through his curly hair.

"You didn't see the smoke?" Kole's shoulders have dropped. He looks exhausted.

I shake my head and exchange a knowing look with Sam. "We smelled it, just now when the wind changed direction. Before that…" I swallow hard then repeat Sam's question. "What happened, Kole?"

Kole lets his arms hang by his sides, shakes them and holds them in front of his stomach instead, then unfolds them again. Even when he was coming off F.H.B. I never saw him this agitated. "She let Ragnor and Eve capture her as we planned. They—" He closes his eyes and pinches the bridge of his nose. Watching him, my heart plummets to the bottom of my stomach. "They put her in the fountain and drained her blood." He's speaking quickly now, eyes still closed. "They filled a vial. They said it was for The Shadow King. They were about to fill more when the flames started."

"They set her on fire?" Tanner's eyes widen. He shivers and rubs his forearms.

Kole shakes his head solemnly. "No. The fire just… *was*." He looks at me. "You really didn't see the smoke?"

"We really didn't see," I tell him.

"She burned for hours." Kole suddenly wavers and looks like he's going to fall. Tanner lurches to catch him. Sam helps, and they ease him to the ground. "I didn't take my eyes off her. I stayed with her until the end." Kole looks up at us. "When they left—the wolves and Ragnor—I went to her. I wanted to bring her back to you—" He chokes on his words and a guttural sob escapes his lips. "I thought if we buried her, maybe that's how she'd return but—"

He is not holding a body. Was she too badly burned? Did he try to save us from having to see her like that? I'm about to tell him I don't care, that I can handle it, that I just need to see her, when he reaches into his pocket. His fist is bunched tight, knuckles whitening.

"There was nothing left." He looks up. When he catches Tanner's gaze, Tanner sinks to the ground too, holding his chest as if he can *feel* what Kole saw. "Nothing but ashes. I tried to carry them, but they slipped through my fingers." He holds out his hand and slowly unfurls his fist. "These were all I could bring."

When I take my eyes from his face and look at his palm, a heavy, jagged breath rushes from my lungs. He's holding her rings. Five wooden rings.

"They're all that was left," Kole says, brushing his large thumb over the small, charred bands. "Just these. I don't know how they survived when she didn't..."

There is silence for a moment. Snow is quiet, but his anguish throbs in my limbs. He felt this way when Layla died. I swore he'd never feel that pain again, but this time I couldn't protect him. I couldn't protect us. We fell too hard, too fast.

"You said she'd come back." Luther strides over, picks his ring from Kole's hand and clenches it tightly. "When? When does it happen?"

Kole shakes his head. "I don't know."

"What do you mean you don't know?" Luther barks. "This was *your* plan. You told us she'd return. How? When there's no body? How is she supposed to come back? What's she supposed to come back to?"

"Don't say that—" Sam interrupts him.

"Don't say what?" Luther rounds on Sam instantly, eyes flashing with red-hot fury.

"*Body*—as if it's separate from her. It's *Nova*. We're talking about Nova."

"You don't think I know that?" Luther squares up to Sam. He looks like he wants to slam his fist into Sam's face. Not because he hates Sam or even because he hates what Sam just said to him, but because what the fuck else is he supposed to do with all the pain he's feeling?

Springing to his feet, Tanner steps between them. "Stop," he whispers. "Nova told us to look after each other. What would she say if she found you two fighting five minutes after she…" He stops before the word *died* crosses his lips.

I know I should be doing something. I know I should be playing the peacekeeper and stopping them from being at each other's throats. I should persuade them to go back to the lake, wait like we promised, trust Kole, trust Nova. But my heart hurts so much I can barely see straight.

Kole stands then reaches out a hand and pulls me to my feet. He has pocketed the remaining four rings. Luther has slipped his onto the tip of his ring finger.

"We should return to the lake," Kole says what I was thinking. "We told Nova that's where we'd be. When she returns, we should be waiting."

I look at Luther. Sweat has broken out on his forehead. His eyes are dark and full of fire at the same time. "We should keep watch over The Hollow. Take shifts."

"We can't," Kole replies. "It's too dangerous, Luther. If Eve releases the hounds, or if the wolves find us, Nova could come back and discover she's a fated mate down." He tries to offer Luther a wry smile but it doesn't look right on his face. "And she'd be mighty pissed if that happened."

Luther narrows his eyes then, without saying a word, turns and stalks back in the lake's direction. Wisps of smoke drift up from his shoulders; he is quite literally burning with grief.

I let Tanner and Sam follow Luther, then step in line next to Kole. "Do you still believe she's coming back?" I ask him, praying he smiles at me too. Convincingly this time. "After everything you just saw, do you still believe?"

Kole doesn't answer.

3

TANNER

To me, the lake has always been the epitome of beauty and peace. Swimming here even in my darkest times, offered relief and solace. The fierceness of the falls juxtaposed with the silky-smooth water of the lake did something to my soul that no other place could.

When we return, however, a little before midnight with the moon hanging brightly in the sky, the lake looks different. She is darker and choppier. Instead of healing me, I feel like she wants to drown me—pull me down to her deepest depths and let me die among the weeds.

Luther doesn't stop to look at the falls or remember our last moments here with Nova. Instead, he storms toward the caves and disappears inside. Kole and Mack go after him, but I need to be outside.

Slightly frantically, I take off my shoes and walk to the water's edge. *Please, release me.* I let my gaze drift out toward the dark heart of the lake. *Please, release me. It hurts too much without her. Make it stop.*

I'm about to wade in and plunge beneath the surface of the water, allow the lake to swallow me up if that's what she wants, when Sam steps up next to me. He's barefoot too, his toes nestling into the sandy earth beneath the shallow water. "She's coming back," he says firmly. "I don't feel like she's gone. So, she has to be coming back."

I exhale heavily and smile. He really does believe it; his faith shimmers around him. "You're an optimist."

Sam shakes his head. "No, I'm a realist. If I can be rescued from a hell dimension, then Nova can be brought back from wherever she is right now. We just have to be patient."

"Kole's rattled," I tell him as we walk back to the beach and sit down.

"He saw her die. Of course, he's rattled." Sam rubs his knees and looks up at the moon. Most wolves *look* wolf even when they're human, but Sam is different. I'd never have known he was a werewolf if he hadn't shifted in front of me. If anything, his face is more cat than wolf—but I wouldn't dare tell him that. "This is the third time I've lost her," Sam says, "and fate has brought us back together twice already. I have to believe it will happen this time too."

"Four times," I mutter, my skin bristling as a cool breeze drifts across the lake. "If you include our ancestors. Our history."

Sam nods slowly. He nudges me with his upper arm. "Fated to five," he says, quoting the prophecy. "Fate has been meddling with us from the start. It won't let us down now."

Pressing my lips together, I look at the falls and follow the sheets of water down to where they create a pool of bubbling foam and froth. "I never really believed in fate," I say quietly. "At least, not until those three came into my life." I jerk my head toward the caves, half-wondering what Kole, Mack, and Luther are doing in there. If they're fighting or consoling one another.

"How did they?" Sam asks, angling himself so he can see my face a little better. "Come into your life?"

"Sam, I don't really feel like talking."

"Right now, talking's the only thing we can do. So, tell me… I know Mack taught Kole and Luther at the Academy. But you never told me how you became part of their group." His forehead creases a little as he watches my expression. When he dips his head to catch my eyes, his dark, curly hair falls across his face and he's forced to sweep it away with the back of his hand.

"It's a long story," I tell him, my mind already tugging with the urge to take me back to memories I've tried so hard to erase.

"Right." Sam nods.

"I haven't even told Nova all of it," I say, resting my forearms on my knees.

"Sorry, Tanner. You're right. I shouldn't have asked. Not now." Sam puts his hand on my back and pats it lightly. "It's not the time."

Despite the heavy thudding in my stomach, perhaps because I need the distraction, perhaps because I know Sam's truth so he should know mine, I draw my shoulders back and take a deep breath. "I was a hopeless water mage. Always found being an empath easier. It came naturally. I didn't have to force it or *learn* how to control it." I shudder as memories start to dance across the lake in front of me. "I was seventeen, not far off from taking my exams, when The League took me."

I glance at Sam and see him watching me with a steady expression. If he's hearing the echoes of his own past in mine, he doesn't let it show on his face.

"They had a theory that if a mage's elemental affinity is restricted, their secondary affinity will flourish."

"Restricted?" Sam frowns—despite being a werewolf, he's

almost as lacking as Nova in magickal knowledge and clearly thinks this is a common terminology that he's missed out on learning.

"It had never been done before and, to my knowledge, hasn't been done since." I shiver and notice Sam move a little closer. His warmth helps me to carry on. I brace myself, then say quickly, "They deprived me of water. For years, not a drop crossed my lips. They hydrated me with an IV." I rub my palms together as the memory of the needle scratches at my skin.

"You were seventeen when you were taken, so you're in your thirties now?" Sam's lips curve downward a little as he tilts his head. He looks impressed. "I thought you were my age. Nova's age."

"Empaths are notoriously youthful," I tell him. "But you're kinda missing the point, Sam."

"Sorry." He frowns at himself. "What happened? Did it work? Is that why you're able to do what you do?" He taps his temple. "With peoples' heads?"

I breathe out heavily and straighten my legs, moving my arms so I'm leaning back on my hands. "Yeah," I tell him. "It worked. A lot of the time I was in the dark. Alone. My senses became heightened. Including the way I was able to read people. I started *feeling* them when they weren't even in the room with me. Maybe a few feet away, maybe in the next room or the one above. At first, just one at a time. Then anyone who was nearby. I tried not to let them see—the ones who watched me—but it became impossible to hide. As soon as they knew it was working, they doubled down." I swallow hard as my mind fills with darkness. I push it back and anchor myself on Sam. He's not disgusted, or afraid, or pitying me. He's just listening.

"They're the ones who taught me how to jump." I meet his eyes quickly, then look down at my toes wriggling in the cold sand. "At first, they just had me locate people for them. They'd give me a picture, and something that belonged to the person, then ask me to seek them out. Honestly, I still don't understand how it works. But it did. And the more time went on, the better I got at it." I turn to Sam and, this time, hold his gaze. "Toward the end, they made me jump into peoples' heads. Control them. Manipulate them..." I keep staring into his eyes because I need to see what's there; I need to see if I have horrified him yet. When he doesn't look away, I say, "You're not the only one with a dark past, Sam. The difference is you had things done to you. Me? I was the perpetrator. I hurt people. I made people hurt *other* people."

"What kind of *people?*" Sam asks softly.

"Humans, usually, with connections to the A.M.A."

"What did you make them do?"

I close my eyes and moisten my lower lip. A shiver of sickening guilt creeps up my spine. I can't believe I'm about to say this out loud. "I made them kill supers."

I can't look at Sam. My cheeks are burning with shame.

"Why? I don't understand why they'd make you do that? The League is all about protecting supers, isn't it?"

"No," I snap. "The League wants to fuel hatred. To prove that humans and supers shouldn't coexist. And they'd do anything to make that happen. Even sacrifice their own."

I hear Sam release a heavy sigh. "It's not your fault, Tanner, they manipulated you."

"I haven't told you that," I say. "What makes you so sure they *made* me do it?"

"Because they kept you captive for over a decade, and because I know you." Sam taps my knuckles gently with his index finger. "I know you, Tanner, and Nova does too. She might not know all the details, but she wouldn't love you the way she does if you were a bad person."

I clear my throat. The threat of tears surges like bile, but I swallow it down. "They told me they'd kill my parents if I didn't do what they asked. They showed me videos taken outside the house. Photos of my mom at work, my dad playing golf, my cousins…" I dig my nails into my thighs to stop their faces coming back.

"So, you did it to keep your family safe." Sam wraps his fingers around mine and squeezes.

"Yeah."

"And it worked? They're safe?"

"Yeah, they're safe." I look down at my hand and at Sam's.

"Then you should tell Nova. She'll understand. And secrets…they eat you up eventually."

The strength of Sam's conviction—both that Nova will forgive me and that she'll come back and be *able* to forgive me—makes my heart swell in my chest. He is naïve and haunted at the same time. He reminds me of Nova when she first came to Phoenix Falls, but also of me.

"My parents didn't understand," I mutter. When I look up, tears are in my eyes, and I have no idea why I'm allowing these emotions to come to the surface now of all times. It's like a floodgate has been opened and I can't slam it shut.

"When I finally returned home, I thought they'd be the ones to tell me it wasn't my fault. I thought they'd see I did it to keep them safe, so I told them everything. All of it. All the gory details."

Sam inches closer and wraps his arm around my shoulders. He doesn't say anything, just sits next to me, breathing slowly.

"They told me they were ashamed. That they'd rather die than have a son who did those things. I haven't seen them since."

"Tanner, I'm sorry." Sam's palm moves across my back. "I'm sorry they hurt you like that, but Nova's different. She'd never turn away from you."

I sniff loudly and wipe my face on my arm. "I hope you're right."

"I know I'm right." Sam nudges me with his shoulder, then there's a pause before he says, "Kole, Luther, and Mack? They rescued you?"

"Kole had a vision about me. He came back to Phoenix Falls, found Mack and Luther, and told them they needed to save me. That I was important."

Sam's eyebrows tweak upward. "And he was right." A smile spreads across his face. "So, chances are, he's right about Nova too."

"You really do believe that don't you?"

"I do."

"I wish I did." Taking my hand back, I rub my temples again and lower my head.

"It's okay," Sam says. "I can believe hard enough for both of us."

4

LUTHER

The image that keeps coming back to me is the way Nova looked in the woods. Not when she said goodbye—before that. When we'd just been released from Thessaly's vision and I'd stumbled away into the undergrowth. At that moment, when she appeared in front of me, everything fell into place. I knew why I loved her, and why I was angry with her, and that it had nothing to do with whether she was a human or a witch.

I loved her because it was in my blood to love her, and I was angry with her because that same bloodline had carried the pain of losing her for hundreds of years. And I was terrified of it happening again.

Now, it has. I said goodbye, and she walked away. Just like that, I'm alone again. All I have of her is the ring she was wearing on her finger when she died.

Inside the cave, I sit in the dark and rub my thumb over the ring. I trace its curves again, and again, and again.

She died.

Nova died.

"Luther?" Mack's voice drifts through from the first cave behind the falls. I wave my hand and cast a small fire. It floats in front of me until I lower it to the ground. "Luther," Mack repeats when he sees me, striding over and crouching next to the fire. "We're all feeling it," he says, putting a firm hand on my shoulder.

Behind him, Kole has appeared. He lingers in the entrance; arms folded, tall and dark and brooding. His hair is loose over his shoulders, which means he must be really screwed up right now. Usually, the only times he shakes it free are right before he goes to sleep or when he's trying to release the tension in his head.

"Is this how it was supposed to happen?" I ask him, still clutching Nova's ring. "What now? How long until she returns?"

"I don't know." Kole's muscles twitch. Whatever he's feeling, he's locking it down tight, keeping it beneath the surface, trying to act as if he's *okay*.

"You still believe she's coming back?" I ask, standing up.

"Yes." Kole looks at Mack. Something unspoken passes between them.

"Kole," I growl, stepping forward. "Did you fuck up? Is she coming back?!" Now, I'm yelling. The fire surges and my voice rebounds off the cave walls.

I was angry with Nova when we first met. Terrified because if I fell in love with her and she left, I'd be broken. To my surprise, I'm not mad at her anymore, but I am angry with Kole. Just looking at him brings a fire to my belly that I can barely hold down.

I'm not so out of touch with psychology that I think he deserves it; I know I'm channeling my rage toward him because if I don't, I'll set the whole fucking forest on fire; then stand here and watch it burn. But all the same, I don't

21

stop myself striding over and slamming my hand around his throat.

He could easily throw me off. He's taller than me, bigger than me, and—if I'm honest—his magick has always been more powerful. But he doesn't.

"Tell me, *seer*, when is she coming back?" I yell in his face as I send heat to my palm.

I feel Mack moving toward us, but he doesn't intervene. Not yet.

Kole puts his hand on mine. His neck is growing red beneath my touch. "I don't know, Luther. I don't know when." He inhales shakily, my fingers still squeezing his neck. "But I still feel the blood bond. I still believe she will return."

As Kole finishes speaking, Mack puts his hand on my shoulder. "Luther, we need to stick together." He tugs a little and, finally, I let go.

My hand has left a deep red mark on the snatches of Kole's skin that are visible between his tattoos. He rubs his throat and steps round me to sit by the fire. Staring at it, he says, "I didn't see Nova returning. I just knew she would, and she knew it too." He reaches out and warms his palms. "The visions have been right so far. There is no reason they would fail us now."

"Have they been right? Or have they been causing all this?" I stand above him, arms folded.

Kole looks up at me.

"The prophecy, the visions… how do we know we're not *making* them come true? How do we know they're not just—"

Kole's eyes flash with a darkness I haven't seen for a long time. He stands slowly, and something about the way he moves toward me makes the hairs on my arms stand up. "Because that is *not* how it works, Luther."

I am dangerously close to insulting everything Kole believes in and everything his family believes in. I'm on the cusp of telling him to prove to me how it fucking works, for once, when Mack's hand appears between us.

"Here," he says. "We can wear her rings until she comes back for them."

He's holding a piece of blue rope in his hand. Looking at it makes me wince as I remember how it looked against her skin, and how it felt when I tightened the knots. When Mack starts unpicking a thread, the memory fades.

"Do you have them?" Mack asks Kole.

Kole dips his hand into his pocket and takes out the remaining four. Mine is still in my hand. I pass it to Mack and, one by one, he creates five blue-thread necklaces. When I slip mine over my head, the ring comes to rest on my chest right above my heart. I breathe out slowly and close my eyes.

"We are all hurting." Mack's tone is dark and solemn. "Right now, all I want to do is shift and run." When I open my eyes, he's staring at me. "But we have to stick together." He sits down and gestures for me to do the same. "We've been in this from the start, the three of us."

Kole sits down, too, on the opposite side of the flames.

"From the day I first recruited you both, we were brothers. Not a professor and his students, or a boss and his employees. We were family. This is the biggest test we've had —bigger than when Kole went missing, bigger than when you burned that village to the ground..." Mack meets my eyes.

My stomach lurches and I clench my fists. "How do you know about that? Kole was the only one—" My cheeks burn. Did he tell Mack? All these years, he let me think he'd kept my secret.

"You were caught on camera. No one could tell it was you, but I knew. As soon as I saw the name of the village, I knew."

The look on Kole's face tells me this is fresh information

for him too. Clearly, he believed he was the only one who knew my secret.

"They killed your parents, Luther, I understand you wanting revenge. But it could have destroyed everything if you were caught. You'd have been thrown out of the S.D.B. I'd have been arrested for aiding and abetting. Kole too."

"Why are you bringing this up now?" I meet the professor's eyes. Amber flickers in them.

"Because I'm trying to remind you that we've been to hell and back together. The three of us. We can't turn on each other now." He pauses then adds, "Plus, like Kole said, Nova will kick our sorry butts if she comes back and finds us at each other's throats. And I don't want an angry girlfriend *or* an all-powerful witch coming after me. Do you?"

5

SAM

The others are freaking out. I can see it in their faces, and you don't need to be an empath to figure out they're torn between overwhelming grief at the thought of losing Nova completely and anger at themselves for doubting she'll come back to us.

Perhaps I should be freaking out too. I'll admit, when Kole appeared in the woods looking like he'd just seen the worst horror of his life, I felt sick to my stomach. The idea of her being gone, and the thought of her burning like that, made me want to vomit.

But I can't feel what they're feeling because I *know* she's okay.

Maybe it's because I went to hell and came back. Maybe it's because this entire thing—the prophecy, and the visions, and the rising of the underworld—is so crazy it has to be true. Maybe it's because I lived twenty years waiting to be reunited with her, believing she was alive even when I should have believed she was dead.

Whatever the reason, I feel calm. All we have to do is be patient. She *will* come back.

I'm staring out at the lake, standing with my toes in the shallow water when Tanner appears at my side. He's holding two pieces of blue string and offers one to me. "Mack made these."

I hold it up. The ring I gave Nova dangles in front of me. At the same time, Tanner and I fasten our necklaces. "The others are going to try and get some sleep," he says. "You want to come inside?"

"Not yet." I look at Tanner sideways then—despite it being freezing cold and the middle of the night—I tug off my shirt and drop it to the ground.

"You want to swim? Right now? Really?"

"No," I tell him. "But you need to." I reach down and unfasten my belt. "You need to clear your head."

"I can't, Sam, not now." He looks out at the water and his face creases strangely at the sides. Usually, when he looks at the lake, I see relief in his eyes. Now, there's nothing but darkness.

"She wouldn't want you to suffer like this." I stand in front of him, blocking his view of the water.

Tanner's eyes drift to my chest. My scars catch the muted moonlight. The silvery skin glistens. He reaches out and presses his thumb to the one just below my collarbone. "Alright." He steps back and, finally, starts to undress.

Quickly, we both pull our pants over our ankles and wade in. The lake is freezing. Without Nova to warm it, my teeth start chattering straight away but Tanner seems immune.

"How are you not shivering?" I ask, moving my arms and legs quickly through the water in an effort to keep myself turning blue with the cold.

"Thick skin," Tanner says. "Water mage perk." He looks at

me and chuckles. "Come on," he says. "That's enough. You'll freeze to death if we stay in here."

"But you—"

"I already feel better," he says, lying through his non-chattering teeth. "Job done, so come on." He turns and swims back to shore. I follow pathetically slowly.

"You know," I tell him as we stride up onto the beach, "I'm surprised I still know how to swim."

Tanner scoops up his clothes and turns to me, raising an eyebrow.

"I spent years in captivity, too, Tanner. Last time I went swimming properly, before fooling about in the lake with you all, I was four years old."

"I still owe Nova some lessons," Tanner says. "I'll give you a discount if you book a double session."

"How could I refuse an offer like that?" I'm flirting with him, but perhaps that's what we both need. I move a little closer.

Tanner looks at me for a moment. A smile murmurs on his lips, but it disappears when he says, "Sam, I get that you're 'zen' about Nova coming back. But are you really okay with everything else too?" He pauses, his eyes softening a little. "I feel like, maybe, you're not letting yourself absorb it all. It happened so quickly."

I laugh and look away from him. Something bubbles in the pit of my stomach. The blanket of calm that was hugging me has loosened. A breeze is drifting in. I try to shake it, but the way Tanner is looking at me is making it almost impossible. "I'm not sure what you're talking about." I try to laugh again but this time it catches in my throat.

"Sam, we haven't talked about your mom or about Nico." Tanner meets my eyes. "You can't just bury it. It'll come to the surface eventually. What was it you said about secrets?"

"I can't. Not now." I push my fingers through my hair and head for the caves.

"When?" Tanner catches my elbow. "You're doing a good job of hiding it, Sam, even from yourself but—"

I stop and brace my hands on the small of my back. When Tanner steps in front of me, I fix my gaze on his. "I can talk about Nova because I believe it's going to be okay. I'm not faking it, Tanner. I *know* we'll see her again."

"I know," he says, a confused frown on his face.

"But I can't talk about Nico, and I can't talk about my—" I can't say the word. It disintegrates in my mouth. "I can't talk about them because, for them, it's not going to be *okay*."

Tanner inhales slowly. He doesn't correct me or try to comfort me. Instead, we just stand together for a while in the darkness.

6

THREE DAYS LATER
MACK

Snow grumbles at me, but I tell him to shake it off. Literally. *It's only rain, buddy.*

He hates the rain. Cold weather? Yep, he can deal. He's a polar bear, of course he can. But rain? He hates it, and I have to admit I'm not the biggest fan either. It's already penetrating our thick pelt. By the time we get back to the lake, our fur will be sodden and murky. The color of shallow puddles and dirty dishwater.

We stop and sniff the air. For three days, we've been patrolling the woods for a sign, or scent, or whisper of Nova. For the third day running, we have come across nothing more than the occasional dead rabbit.

Sam emerges from a thicket nearby. As a wolf, he is remarkably similar in composition to his human self; lithe but muscular, dark fur, dark eyes.

He sniffs the air too, then looks up at us. He finds it odd that he can't communicate with us the way he can with other weres. I tried explaining that polars are different from weres, but a vacant look filled his eyes. A look that my students used to get when what I was saying was too difficult to truly understand.

Although Sam has grown up as a werewolf, he shares so many traits with Nova that I'm starting to crave his presence. He knows little of the supernatural world beyond what he was exposed to in the club and doesn't have the first idea how magick really works. To him, other supers have always been nothing more than shadows in the dark. Glinting eyes and writhing bodies watching him suffer for their own enjoyment.

Now, he tips his head in an eastern direction, and trots off into the undergrowth. We follow him, a lot less discretely; where Snow and I go, a very obvious trail usually follows.

Ahead, Sam has stopped. He's sniffing the ground and glances over his shoulder to indicate we should come closer. We dip our head and examine what he's found; another rabbit, except this one is just a skeleton. Something has eaten the rest of it.

Wolf, I tell Snow. He growls in agreement.

Sam has recognized the scent, too, and his heckles are standing on end. I don't need to read his mind to know he's wondering whether Ragnor has finally sent his werewolves to track us down.

The lack of activity at The Hollow over the past few days has been alarming. Each day, one of us has ventured as close as we dare and reported back. None of us have seen signs of life inside the building. In fact, Luther was so convinced Ragnor had left that he insisted this morning we should try to get inside.

"Eve's barrier's still in place," Kole had growled. "Which means they're inside. They won't leave until the ritual is complete."

At that point, for perhaps the hundredth time, the two of them had begun to argue about whether or not we should be doing more than just waiting. Luther thinks we should try to break in and retrieve Nova's blood. Kole disagrees. He believes we should wait.

So far, I've been keeping the peace by telling Luther we will wait a little longer. But I'm starting to wonder just how long that will be. How long until we have to admit that Kole might have been wrong?

Snow huffs at me. He hates it when I think like this. His faith is as unwavering as Sam's; as far as he's concerned, Nova is *going* to come back. No question. No doubt.

Next to me, Sam nudges the rabbit with his nose, then he stops. His muscles tense, his shoulders drop into a hunting position. A low grumble leaves his jaws. Then he pounces. Just like that, he hurls himself into the bushes.

There's a bark, then a growl, then a yelp. In two steps, we are there and pushing the branches aside. Sam tumbles out. Another wolf follows. It is on top of Sam, going for his throat, but he manages to gain the upper paw and flips their positions. He's on top of the other wolf, jaws around its throat, when it shifts.

Our blood turns to lava in our veins. *Kayla.*

Nico's mother presses herself flat to the ground. Sam releases his jaws but doesn't take his foot from her chest. "Please," she mutters, "don't."

When Sam lets her go, Snow grumbles again. He doesn't want me to shift back; he wants to rip her head from her shoulders and drag her carcass back to the others. But I need to know why she's here.

It takes a lot of strength to overpower him. When he's determined like this, it's a matter of willpower. Except, it's like I'm battling with my own mind. It has taken a lot of practice to get to the point where I can win.

Butt naked, I stride toward Kayla and grab her shoulders. She doesn't resist as I slam her against the nearest tree. "What the fuck are you doing here, wolf?"

Behind me, while Kayla struggles to answer my question, Sam shifts back. Being that he's a wolf not a bear, he's fully clothed and grabs Kayla's wrist, pinning it above her head.

"He asked you what you're doing here?" Sam snarls.

Kayla's eyes widen as she takes in Sam's face. "You…" she breathes. "How…?"

"We're asking the questions," Sam replies. "What are you doing here, Kayla?"

For a moment, Kayla simply stares at Sam as if she can't quite believe what she's seeing; like she might have gone mad out here in the woods and be hallucinating. When he tightens his grip on her wrist, her eyes flicker. "Let go," she says, looking from Sam to me, "and I'll tell you."

Eyes flashing, Snow's anger rumbling in my gut, I let go of her and step back.

"Hard to take you seriously when you're…" Kayla looks pointedly at my unclothed body. "*Au natural*," she adds.

"Talk," I tell her. "Why are you here?"

"Because I have nowhere else to go." Kayla straightens herself up, as if looking *okay* will make up for the fact her skin is carrying a thin layer of dirt and she smells like she hasn't washed in weeks.

"You should have left town when you had the chance," I tell her.

I'm about to grab her again when Sam says, "It's you who's been killing the rabbits?"

I frown at him. The rabbits? Who gives a shit about some dead rabbits?

Kayla meets his eyes. Hers narrow while she looks at him. Then she shudders and shakes her head. "Why would I leave a trail of dead, uneaten rabbits? Nothing to do with me."

"You ate that one," Sam snaps, ticking his head back in the direction of the skeleton we found.

"Because I *found* it," she says. "I don't make a habit of hunting other animals for sport. Food, yes. Playthings, no."

Sam raises his eyebrows. "If you didn't kill them, where did they all come from?"

I want to ask why the fuck Sam is asking her about rabbits instead of ripping her throat out for what she did to him, but now he's mentioned it, it does seem odd. Cats kills for the enjoyment of killing, but most of the creatures in these woods kill for food. Not for the buzz of the hunt.

Kayla presses her lips together. For a moment, she looks like she's about to tell him to get screwed, but then she sighs heavily. Scraping her hands through her short, black hair, she says, "The Hellhounds. They don't need to eat, but they like to play. They've been hunting in these woods for a few days now."

"Hellhounds? Bullshit," Sam says. "We haven't—"

"Smelled them? No, you wouldn't. They don't leave a scent." Kayla brushes down her shirt and folds her arms. "And they only hunt at night."

Sam glances at me; whether we like it or not, Kayla just gave us information that might have saved our lives. If we ventured beyond our barrier after nightfall and came across them, especially if one of us was alone, there's no way we'd be able to fight them off.

"And now I've answered your question, you can answer mine." Her tone changes as she says, "How are you here? I saw you fall. I sent you to hell."

"With Nico," Sam says. "You sent me to hell with your son."

"*I* didn't send him there. He was trying to save you," Kayla growls. Her lips curl into a snarl and she's about to lurch forward when I step behind her and grab her upper arms. She strains against me, then goes limp beneath my hands.

"You used him his entire life," Sam spits. "You manipulated him. You made him do things he *never* wanted to do. You were his mother. He trusted you, and you betrayed him."

"And then you betrayed him again by trying to murder the brother he gave his life to save," I whisper darkly in her ear.

A small sob escapes Kayla's mouth. She hangs her head, and her body starts to shake. She takes a deep breath. Silence hangs thick between us. Then she says, barely audibly, "I'm sorry." She looks up at Sam. "Please, tell me, how did you come back? Is he here? Is he with you?"

I loosen my grip a little. She's a monster, but she's also a mother. Her pain is real, even if she caused it herself. Even if she deserves it.

Sam breathes in deeply. He hasn't spoken to any of us about Nico since he returned. Even Tanner hasn't been able to encourage him to share what happened.

"He's not with me," Sam says, tilting his chin up and swallowing hard. "He died in my arms. He's gone."

Kayla's knees buckle. As if she's losing her son all over again, she drops to the ground. I let her kneel and release my grip on her arms. Hugging her belly, she sobs, shaking her head and rocking back and forth like a child.

"Are you telling the truth?" she looks up, eyes full of tears.

"Yes." Sam folds his arms. His voice shakes a little as he adds, "I tried to save him, but I failed. He's gone."

I step away from Kayla and put my hand on Sam's shoulder. His muscles are taut, his features are too. He doesn't move, just stands stoically still and stares at Kayla.

From the ground, she looks up at us. "Kill me," she whispers.

I exchange a long glance with Sam.

"Kill me," she repeats, the scar on her face glinting as a ray of sunlight breaks through the canopy above us. "There is no point in me being here now. Not without my son. Please, kill me."

"Your call," I tell Sam.

He crouches down in front of her and squeezes her face between his thumb and forefinger. "I won't kill you," he says slowly. "Do you know why?"

"Because I deserve to suffer?" A tear runs down Kayla's cheek, following the groove of the scar Kole gave her many, many years ago.

Sam almost smiles. He shakes his head and sighs. "No, because Nico was my brother and he loved you. Despite everything, he loved you. And *I* respect that bond enough to put his feelings before my own." Slowly, Sam stands up again. "I knew him a few days. You knew him his whole life, and you weren't a good enough mother to do that."

As Kayla staggers to her feet, Sam turns away from her. He stops, shoulders rising and falling slowly with his breath. Then he says, "Don't let us see you here again," and walks away.

7

SAM

I wait until I'm back behind the barrier before truly breathing. One hundred emotions swirl in the basement of my stomach. Memories scratch at the backs of my eyes. Memories I've been trying to keep at bay.

Mack puts a steadying hand on my back. "You okay, kid?" he asks.

"I'm not a kid," I shrug away from him. "I'm Nova's age. Twenty-five, Mack."

"I know," he says, an apologetic frown creasing his forehead. "I just meant—"

"I know what you meant. I'm sorry. I'm being an asshole." I turn to lean back against the pine tree that marks the start of the protection spell which has been shielding us from view for the past few weeks.

"It was a brave choice, letting her live." Mack is standing in front of me. He's completely naked. I probably should have gotten used to it by now, but it still surprises me. Looking at him, I can see why it would be inevitable that Nova would fall for him. Seeing him in *all* his glory every time he completes a shift does something to the brain. After the twentieth-or-so time, you start to get up the confidence to look. *Really* look. And when that happens, thoughts start to happen.

I snap my eyes back to his face and clear my throat. I shouldn't be looking *or* thinking, but for a moment—that brief moment when I was admiring the shape of Mack's thighs instead of thinking about my brother—the pain wasn't as painful anymore. The memories faded.

"Fuck," I mutter, scraping my fingers through my hair. "I wish Nova was here."

"I'm sorry," he says, "I'm not much of a substitute. Tanner's a good listener. You should talk to him. Or reach out to Sarah. She doesn't even know you're back—"

"It's not listening that I need," I tell him. "I don't need to talk about what happened. I need to forget it. Drown it out."

"Nova's good at that," Mack says. "Drowning things out."

"She did that for you?"

"Being with her..." Mack pauses, rubbing his neat gray beard. "The things from my past that haunted me disappeared when I was with her." His cock twitches and I can't help noticing. What is he remembering? "I had all sorts of hang-ups," Mack laughs. "I thought I was too old for her. I thought I'd end up hurting her because, well, most people who get close to me end up hurt one way or another. I thought I didn't deserve to feel good." He pauses as if he thinks he's said too much.

"But she made you see that you do?" We seem to be standing closer now, and the space between us quivers a little.

"Yes," Mack says, his voice strained. "She did."

37

"How?" I meet his eyes. He doesn't have to tell me. He could shrug and turn away, and we could continue our walk back to the lake. But something flickers in his face and suddenly I know he's not going to do that.

Leaning forward, Mack rests his arm beside my head so he's curved above my body. His face is close to mine. His naked *dick* is close to mine. "The first time I really understood what it was like to have that kind of release was when she and Tanner tied me to a chair."

I breathe in, then release a small sigh as the image forms in my mind.

"She sat on my lap and opened her legs for Tanner. He made her come, but I couldn't touch her. I couldn't move."

A shiver of arousal creeps down my spine and tugs at my balls. "Fuck," I mutter.

"When I finally came, while she and Tanner sat there watching me, it was the sweetest release I'd ever felt."

I put a tentative hand on Mack's hip. There's still time for him to pull away, but he doesn't; he tilts his pelvis toward me. "I need that," I whisper.

"Need what?" Mack fixes me with a dark stare that makes my cock pulse.

"Release," I reply, barely able to speak.

"Do you think Nova would want me to help you?" Mack's eyes flash amber as he reaches for my jeans and begins to unfasten them.

A smile flutters on my lips. "Are you kidding?" I laugh, breaking the seriousness of the moment with a chuckle I can't hold back. "She'd think it was *crazy* hot."

Mack's lips twitch too. He's pressing his crotch against mine and tugging at the waistband of my jeans. "I agree," he says, moving his mouth so close to my ear that I feel his hot breath on my neck. "I'm going to help you, Sam, on one condition."

A small groan rumbles in my throat as Mack's hand finds my cock. "Anything," I whisper, my voice thready.

"We tell her every *single* detail when we see her again."

"Yes," I answer instantly. "Everything. We'll tell her everything, Professor. I swear."

"Alright then." Mack takes his hand away and drops to his knees in front of me. Seeing him like that—an older guy, on the ground, mouth open, ready to please me—sends a wave of electricity to my core. He's the daddy of the group. The one in control. The one who has his shit together, and he's about to do this for me. The sudden reversal of the power dynamic between us has made me breathless. My dick stiffens as Mack runs his tongue from its base to its tip.

"I didn't know you… liked it like this," I whisper, barely able to get the words out.

Mack stops. I want to pull his mouth back to where it was, but I also want him to answer me because, even though he's been part of our group activities, I've never seen him do anything with the other guys. "I'm not sure Nova does either," Mack says, frowning as if it's an interesting question. "Usually, with the others, I enjoy watching. But you're different." He runs his hands up my thighs.

"Different?" Somehow, I get the word out.

Mack's lips are tantalizingly close to my tip. A bead of pre-cum glistens. He swipes his tongue over it, and I'm almost driven wild with the need to be inside his mouth. "You remind me of Nova." Mack slips his hands beneath my shirt and runs his strong palms over my stomach. "Your energy. Your strength, despite all the darkness."

"You don't remind me of her one bit," I chuckle, reaching down to stroke his beard.

"Quiet now, Sam." Mack holds my gaze. "Pay attention, so we can give Nova a live replay when she returns."

The thought of Nova watching Mack suck my cock

makes me tilt my head back and mutter, "Holy stars." I lace my fingers together behind my head and close my eyes as Mack's lips seal around my shaft.

Expertly, like somehow he knows exactly how to drive me wild, he takes my entire length in his mouth. He gags, and the sound is heaven. Guttural. Deep. Animalistic. He applies pressure with his lips, then grips the base of my cock with both hands as he plunges his mouth onto me again and again.

When he stops and stands up, I stumble a little and put my hands on his shoulders. "Keep doing that," I beg. "Please, Professor."

But Mack just takes me in his hand. He offers several long, torturous strokes with his tightly closed fist, which feels so different to Nova's and Tanner's. Bigger, stronger, rougher. My cock is wet from his mouth, and his fingers slide easily up and down.

With his free hand, he roughly pushes his fingers through my hair. Then I feel something else pressing against me. I can't look down, because he's holding my head in place, but it doesn't take many seconds for me to realize he's now wrapped his hand around *both* of us. His cock is being squeezed against mine.

Mack releases a low growl as he strokes slowly, then faster, then harder. He meets my gaze and holds it, keeping my head steady, too, so I can't look away from him.

"Fuck, Mack, I'm going to—"

"Not until I say you can," he growls at me without breaking his rhythm. "Got it?"

I nod, my body tightening like a coiled spring, filling with heat and electricity. I'm on the cusp of an orgasm. I bite my lower lip, straining to keep it at bay. When I think I'm about to lose it, Mack releases his grip. The pressure fades. Panting, I beg him not to stop.

"Are you going to come?" he asks darkly.

"Not until you tell me to. I promise."

He starts again. Building the rhythm, using both hands now, his own dick suffering the same painful delay in release as—every time we are close—he stops. Finally, when I can't take it anymore, instead of stopping, he whispers, "Now."

Before the word has even left his lips, I yell and brace my hand on his shoulder. My fingernails dig into his skin as my hot cum spills over his hand. When I look down, he's using my cum to moisten his own dick, still holding them close, not letting me go.

Instead of fading, the fireworks inside me keep going, and going. Then Mack comes too. His creamy liquid merges with mine as he slowly, languidly, brings his fist to a stop.

We're both breathless and flushed. Mack's chest is sweaty, dimpled with the imprints of my fingernails, and his neck is pink. Laughing a little, he shakes his head and looks down at his hand. "Didn't really think about how I'd clean this up," he mutters.

"I can help you with that," I tell him, bringing his cum-soaked hand to my lips.

Mack's eyes widen. "Sam..."

I shake my head and run my tongue around his index finger, licking it clean. "Shhh... Nova will *love* this part."

8

KOLE

I don't know where the others are. Sam and Mack said they'd patrol the perimeter of the barrier. Luther didn't say where he was going, and Tanner? Usually, I'd say he's swimming, but since we got back, he's been avoiding the water. It's almost as if he doesn't want to feel better. He doesn't want it to heal him or soothe him because, with Nova gone, the only thing he should feel is emptiness.

There was a time when we distracted one another when things were bad like this.

When our demons threatened to overwhelm us, he submitted to me and I let him, and it was a delicious diversion. Now, it doesn't seem right. We've both thought about it; Tanner knows there's a darkness growing inside me. He can feel it the way he always feels it. But without Nova between us, anything we could offer each other would be... not enough.

At night, my mind has been drifting back to the times we've spent together. Especially the three of us. My favorite memory is of chasing her through the living room at the cabin, turning her upside down, then filling her up at the same time as Tanner. I miss the expressions on her face when we're pleasing her. I miss the way she looks at me. I miss her voice in my head. I miss her warmth and the curve of her body when it's tucked against mine. I miss her strength, and her devilish smile, and the way she's the only woman who's ever made me feel confident enough to fall in love. I miss the way she both stokes and soothes me. Makes me want her but holds me back from going to the part of myself I hate.

I miss *her*. And I'm still praying to the stars that I was right; that she will come back. I should be the one who is standing firm but, after what I saw at The Hollow, I'm wavering and the others can see it. Only Sam seems utterly convinced, without a doubt, that he will see her again, and I hate that I can't force myself to feel the same.

With the others out of the way, I settle myself in front of the fire Luther left burning and take a small leather pouch from my pocket. I've carried it since we left the colony and was hoping I'd never have to use it.

Gently, I shake its contents into my palm. Sparkling black dust. The feel of it in my hand reminds me instantly of the moment I plunged my fingers into the fountain and tried to carry Nova's ashes with me from The Hollow. I remember them slipping from my grasp, watching them fall to the ground and disappear between the blades of grass as if they never existed.

I close my eyes and try to swallow down the feeling. The Hunger stirs in my veins. It has been gnawing at my insides ever since she disappeared, as if she was the only thing satiating me.

It would be so easy to give in and fall back to where I was all those years ago. But maybe that's the point. Maybe this is some kind of test, and fate is waiting to see whether I am truly worthy of her.

With the thought bringing some comfort, I throw the dust into the fire and mutter the incantation that will summon my mother. Almost instantly, her face appears in the flames.

"Kole?" her voice fills the cave. I can't tell whether she's inside or outside. She peers at me, then her face drops. "What happened?"

"She's gone." I close my eyes and lower my head. My hair is loose. I tuck it behind my ear as I glance back at her. "She sacrificed herself as the vision told her to."

My mother nods slowly. "We knew this was the way," she says. "The way it had to be."

"She hasn't returned." I sit up on my knees and move closer to the flames so their heat licks my face.

My mother tilts her head. "She will. You saw it."

"I saw her dying." I pinch the bridge of my nose. I'm finding it hard to separate my dreams from my visions. What I *want* to happen from what I *foresaw* happening. "What if my interpretation was wrong?" The question leaves my lips as nothing more than a whisper.

The illusion of my mother's hand reaches out from the flames. It is shimmering and warm, and it strokes the curve of my face. "It doesn't work like that. We're not the kind of seers who look at tea leaves and draw conclusions. We *know* what the visions show us. It is delivered to us by fate herself." My mother takes back her hand. She is staring at me with utter conviction in her eyes. "You saw her dying and *knew* she would return."

She's not asking me a question, but I answer all the same. "Yes, Nova knew it too."

"Then she *will* return. Maybe a week, maybe a month, maybe a year from now. But it will happen, Kole."

"You have such faith in me."

"Because I saw it too." The words leave her mouth quickly. When I look up, her eyes have softened. She's watching me carefully.

"You…?" I rub my thighs. My skin prickles with an emotion I can't label. "You saw Nova's death? When?" I cast my mind back. She told me about accessing the prophecy, knowing we were important to each other, but she did not mention Nova's passing.

My mother draws in a long, steady breath. Her usually stoic expression has changed. Her jaw twitches. "I had a vision. When you were in Europe." She smooths her hand over her forehead, bracelets jangling on her wrist. "I never told you. I should have, but…" She trails off.

"What vision? What did you see?" I want to reach into the fire and grab her shoulders. "Why didn't you tell me?"

"I saw Nova, and you. Luther, Tanner, Mack, Sam. I saw all of you. I saw her being beaten and abused by that terrible man she was living with. I saw flames. I saw her coming to you, finding you. I saw the six of you being reunited." She rubs her palm over her face, then fixes her gaze on mine. "And I saw her dying. But—like you—I *knew* she would return."

"You knew all of it? From the beginning? And you left us to figure it out on our own?" If I wasn't speaking to my mother, I'd be yelling, punching the cave wall, clutching my gut to squash the betrayal throbbing deep inside it.

"You know the rules, Kole. I couldn't tell you. I bent them as far as I could by—" She stops. A visible shudder makes her shoulders tremble. Her image grows blurry and dark.

"Stop, Mother. Wait. What did you do?"

She shakes her head slowly. Her large, brightly colored earrings dangle softly against her neck. She offers me a slow, tearful smile. And as her image fades to darkness, I hear those three familiar words... *Something is coming.*

9

LUTHER

I'm sitting by the falls on a rock so slick with water it's going to leave my ass cheeks soaking wet, throwing pebbles into the swirling white foam. I can't hear the pebbles when they fall, but the way they're dragged under is weirdly soothing.

The spray, too, is helping cool the unrelenting heat which has plagued my skin since Nova left. It's like every emotion I ever had has risen to the surface and is being played out again, and again, stoking a fire so violent I can barely contain it.

If we were at the cabin, I might have burned it down by now. But we're not, so I've settled for throwing pebbles and letting the roar of the falls drown out the thoughts in my head.

When Kole emerges from the cave behind the waterfall, my first instinct is to get up and leave. We've barely been in each other's company for more than a few seconds since we returned from The Hollow. I know I have to stop blaming him eventually but, despite Mack's best efforts, I'm not ready yet. Not sure when I will be. I guess when—because it has to be *when* not *if*—Nova comes back to us.

I stand up and pull my damp pants fabric away from my thighs. I allow a wave of heat to surge through my legs and, almost instantly, the patch—and my skin—dries.

"Luther..." Kole is standing next to me.

"You okay?" He looks pale, and his voice is even more gravelly than normal.

"My mother—" He stops. My stomach lurches. Fuck, what happened to his mother?

"Come over here. Sit down." I guide him away from the rocks. When we reach the sandy section of beach nearest the caves, he lowers himself to the ground and crosses his legs like he's about to meditate.

For now, my anger has dissipated; the look on Kole's face has seen to that. I might be mad at him, but he's still my brother. So, I sit and wait for him to talk.

"She knew," he whispers.

"Knew what?"

"About Nova. About us."

I frown at him.

"She knew *all* of it, Luther. She saw Nova's past, and our future. She saw her death. She..."

I'm still not getting it. When Thessaly showed us the Original Six, she told us she knew about our connection and that she'd known since Kole was born. Is it really so much of a stretch that she knew the rest too?

"It was her. She was the voice."

"The voice?"

"The one we heard. The one who told us something was coming, the one who told us to find Sam. *Find the werewolf.*"

"You guys aren't supposed to do that," I tell him. "Right?"

Kole shakes his head. "No, we're not."

"So, what does this mean?"

"It means she broke ancient laws to help us." Kole meets my eyes. "It means there will be consequences."

"What kind of consequences?"

Kole lowers his face into his palms, but he doesn't answer me.

* * *

IT'S LATE when the others return. Kole is still shaken. I have no idea what *consequences* he's talking about, and it feels a little insensitive—even for me—to ask whether he means consequences for us or for his mom. It also seems insensitive to point out that if she broke the rules anyway, she might as well have gone the whole nine yards and told us what was going on rather than sending creepy voice notes on the spiritual airwaves. But I'm sure, if I did, Kole would remind me it's 'complicated' and that I don't understand the first thing about *his* people.

Maybe Mack will have some answers.

As he and Sam enter the caves, bringing with them a whisper of cold air from outside, they exchange a look I can't interpret.

"Find anything?" I ask.

"Kayla." Sam's reply is terse and laced with emotion. He sits down and takes the cup of coffee Tanner offers him.

Exhausted from his three-hour swimming marathon, Tanner looks pale and has already poured himself a second cup. He takes a long sip, offering Sam a sympathetic glance over the rim of his coffee mug.

"What is she doing here?" Kole growls, offering Mack a coffee too.

Mack takes one and sits down, wrapping his large hands around it. Sam doesn't seem in the mood to answer, so Mack does it for him. "Scavenging for food. She told us Hellhounds have been hunting in the woods at night. Just beyond the barrier."

"Hellhounds?" I look at Sam and he nods. "Shit."

"You let her go?" Tanner lowers his mug and tilts his head, examining Sam's expression.

Sam nods curtly, not offering an explanation. "I let her go."

"Okay, listen…" I tap my coffee cup like it's a mic on a lectern. "We need a plan. We can't just sit here waiting, being angry, and sad, and *fucked up*."

"I thought that was what we were supposed to do… wait." Sam looks at Kole. Everyone is looking at Kole.

He breathes a deep, pained breath, then says, "Honestly? I don't know what we're supposed to do. I haven't had any more visions. I contacted my mother but…" He trails off, his jaw twitching. "She can't help either."

Listening to him admit he doesn't have a clue what we're supposed to do next causes anger to swirl in my belly. The coffee in my cup bubbles with heat, so I set it down on the floor and say, "If we don't know, then we're going to have to trust our own instincts. Are we the kind of mages who just sit around waiting?" As the others look at me, I clarify, "I don't mean that we shouldn't wait for Nova." My voice tightens. "I will *never* stop waiting for her, and I know the four of you won't either. But Eve has Nova's blood. In two days' time, she and Ragnor will use it to bring back The King and hell will *literally* be unleashed.

"So, we need to put our own fucked up feelings to one side, and we need a plan." I lace my fingers together in my lap. "That's all I'm saying… we need a plan."

"Luther's right." Kole pulls his hair back and ties it loosely at the nape of his neck. "We don't know when Nova is coming back. But we know that if Ragnor's ritual succeeds, it's going to be harder for her to win when she does return."

"I thought The Phoenix was supposed to stop The King?" Sam interrupts. For the first time since she left us, uncertainty is in his voice. "If Nova's coming back, why do we need a plan?"

Silence descends, thickening in the gaps between us. We are all thinking the same thing, even though we're praying it doesn't come to it, we're thinking we need a plan in case Kole was wrong. In case we have to fight this battle on our own.

TANNER

When I wake, and the dark cave ceiling fills my field of vision, I suddenly and viciously hate it. I hate this place. This hole we've been stuck in for days.

I spring to my feet and, by the time I'm on the rocks outside, my shirt is off and I'm diving into the thick, vicious foam beneath the falls. Its furious weight swirls around me, moving my limbs is like trying to move blocks of concrete through a vat of treacle. But I don't want this to be easy. I need the resistance before the release.

When I finally pull free from the swell, I swim to the center of the lake. I come up for air then dive to her darkest depths. Fragments of light make it past the surface and the reeds, to touch my face. Everything else is dark.

I picture Nova in the water. The way she felt when she was sandwiched between me and Sam, her skin soft and radiant. As I head back to the surface, still dreaming of her, it occurs to me that I've never felt so confused in my whole life.

Other peoples' feelings often complicate my own thoughts, but usually I find a way through. I unpick their essence from my own and manage to see clearly. Now, however, I don't know what I'm feeling. I'm completely unable to pull what I think and feel apart from what the others are feeling because I have no idea if I'm confident like Sam, terrified like Luther, or somewhere in between like Mack and Kole.

When Luther suggested forming a plan, it seemed sensible. I tried to be objective about it; he wasn't suggesting Kole was wrong, or that Nova wouldn't come back; he was just being smart. A backup plan is always a good idea. Right?

Except, it doesn't feel like a backup plan. As the hours slip by, and she still doesn't appear in front of us, our hope fades and our fears magnify. Even Sam's.

Last night, I saw the first flicker of doubt in his eyes. I'm praying it will be gone when he wakes up this morning because, right now, he's the glue holding us together. His firm belief that Kole was right, and that we *will* have Nova in our arms again, is giving us the strength to keep breathing.

When I emerge from the water, Sam is there. On the beach. He's barefoot and standing in the shallow water, letting the cold bite his toes. He raises a hand to wave at me, but waits until I'm within earshot before saying, "Morning."

"I had to get out of there." I push my fingers through my hair to shake out some of the moisture, then perform the party trick that impressed Nova so much when we met. Sam watches as the water soaking my clothes and skin disappears. He's curious but doesn't ask how I do it.

"You're not a fan of cave living anymore?" he asks, smiling.

I shake my head. "With Nova here, it was like a cool, sexy camping trip. Without her, it's..." I search for the right description. "Oppressive."

"Camping is sexy?" Sam asks, raising an eyebrow.

"It is when it's mostly-naked, fooling-about-in-the-lake camping," I reply.

Sam chuckles, then sits down on the sand.

I sit next to him and draw my knees up to my chest. "You okay with Luther's idea?" I ask eventually because perhaps if I know how Sam feels about it, I'll be able to decipher how I really feel.

He shrugs and flexes his toes. "I think it's pointless," he says. "But also, harmless."

"Pointless but harmless?" I repeat.

With his index finger, Sam starts to draw circles in the sand. "Nova is coming back to defeat The Shadow King, so it seems pointless us concocting an elaborate plan to do it for her. *But* I can't see the harm in it so…"

"So, you're playing along?" I search his aura. Usually when someone is this steadfast in their opinion, deep down, they're hiding something. I'll find a whisper of uncertainty or a nugget of fear. In Sam, I see neither of those things. If his faith wavered last night, it has rebounded tenfold.

"I guess," he says.

I pick at a loose thread on my jeans. Is Sam in complete denial? Or is he the only one of us who has the guts not to try and prepare himself for the worst?

"I had an idea," he continues. "We couldn't figure out how we were going to get into The Hollow, past Eve's barrier."

"Luther suggested hitting it with a million spells," I say, rubbing the back of my neck.

"Last time you tried that, they just bounced back at you," Sam says. "And then you were captured, and I was murdered."

"So, you're saying it didn't turn out great last time?" My lips curl into a sarcastic smile.

Sam shakes his head. "You could say that."

"Okay then, oh faithful one, what's your idea?" I angle myself toward him and wait for an answer.

For several long seconds, Sam stares out at the lake. The trees on the other side seem so far away, and yet I know I could reach them in minutes if I swam out there. Finally, he says, "Kayla."

"Kayla?" At first, I think I might have heard him wrong.

Sam shakes his arms, a movement that reminds me of the wolf inside him. "Yes, Kayla. She could be our way in."

"Sam, really? The woman pushed you into a literal hellhole."

Laughing wryly, Sam brushes his thick curly hair from his face. "Because she was angry, Tanner. But she's not just angry with me. Ragnor cast her out. He put Nico in danger, he *stabbed* him, then abandoned her. I'm no empath, but I'm pretty sure there are some unresolved feelings there we could use to our advantage."

I let the idea tick in my head for a moment. I hate to admit it, but Sam could be right.

* * *

WE'VE JUST FINISHED REPEATING Sam's idea to the others while drinking lukewarm coffee and eating yet another round of protein bars, when Luther says, "I'm not convinced." He wipes his mouth and scowls at the protein bar. "You're saying we ask Kayla to kill Ragnor?"

"No," Sam says, "not exactly." He shrugs and tries to relax his shoulders. He's not used to being the one to speak up, and his new role is clearly rattling him a little. "I'm saying, I'm not sure how the barrier spells work, but isn't it possible that Kayla can still just walk right through it? Straight up to The Hollow?"

Mack breathes out through pursed lips. "That's a stretch,

Sam. Eve could just have easily cast Kayla *out* of the spell as she could have left her in."

"Okay, so Option A: Kayla *can* still walk through. She gets in, kills Eve, and the shield drops. We go in and finish Ragnor."

"And Option B?" Luther asks.

"Option B: Kayla begs Ragnor to let her back in. He relents because some kernel of decency inside him feels sorry for her. Kayla kills Eve. Rinse and repeat."

Luther looks down at his coffee, then stirs it with his finger. It's a gross habit, but also one I envy; the ability to make any drink steaming hot with just a touch. I *should* be able to do it myself. A lot of water mages can manipulate water particles enough to heat them, but I've never been able to master it. Ice, yeah. Heat, not so much.

Noticing me staring, Luther leans over and sticks his index finger into my coffee too. "There," he says. "Don't say I never do anything nice."

I frown at his dripping finger, but I want the coffee too much to object.

"Sam, both of these are risky ideas," Mack says.

"Anyone have anything better?" I ask.

On the other side of the fire, staring at the trees as if he thinks they might deliver an answer to our problem, Kole is silent. Conflict rolls through him in waves. He doesn't want to be doing any of this. He doesn't want to prepare for the eventuality that he was wrong, and Nova is gone. He certainly doesn't want to ask Kayla for help.

"I don't see any other way of getting in," he says. "Not in the timeframe we're working with. We have less than forty-eight hours."

Mack nods thoughtfully and scrunches his protein bar wrapper in his fist. "Alright," he says. "No arguing. We vote. Those in favor of seeking Kayla's help."

Sam raises his hand. Tentatively, I raise mine too. Mack, Kole, and Luther follow.

"Okay," Mack says firmly. "It's unanimous. Which means we have a she-wolf to track."

* * *

"You're sure you're okay with this?" I catch Kole's eye as the others start clearing up after breakfast, and gesture for him to step away from the group with me.

"If we need her, we need her." He folds his arms. He's wearing a black tee that exposes the tattoos on his upper arms. It's not warm. In fact, early mornings and late evenings are becoming increasingly cold as we inch toward fall. But Kole never seems to feel the cold. Never has.

"You and Kayla…" I feel his aura quiver when I mention her name. "You have history, Kole. You've never told me the details of your time together in The League, and I've only gathered snippets of what happened when she held you and Nova captive. But I know enough to know she caused you pain, and lots of it. So, are you sure you can stand her being a part of this?"

Kole's biceps twitch, but his arms remain crossed. "You're right. She hurt me in many ways. She hurt Nova, too, and Sam. But if we truly need her, I'll put that aside and refrain from ripping her heart out."

Not a glimmer of amusement crosses Kole's face; he's serious. Deadly serious. If he'd been the one to come across Kayla in the forest, she'd probably be lying dead in the woods right now.

The image of her bloodied body splayed on the forest floor fills my head, and I know it's filling Kole's too. He presses his lips together and moistens them. His jaw is tightly clenched like the rest of his muscles.

"Are you feeling it?" I ask quietly. "The Hunger. Is it back?"

"It never went away." He looks down into my face, and a familiar darkness settles in his eyes. "Nova changed it into something else. She tamed it. She *satiated* it. Without her, I'm not sure how I'll—"

"You won't have to, though, will you?" I hold his gaze. "Because we'll see her again soon."

Kole opens his mouth to speak, but whatever he's about to say dies on his lips. Instead, he tips his head in the others' direction. "I'm going to go to the cabin with Luther while Mack and Sam locate Kayla. She might be more willing to help if I'm not there when you ask for it." He taps his cheek with his index finger. "I hurt her too, remember?"

I nod, but the truth is, I don't remember. When I was with The League, I never saw Kayla's face. If she ever spoke to me, I don't recall her voice or her essence. Kole told me he confronted her when he broke me out with Mack and Luther, told me he half sliced her face open with a blade of broken glass, but I have no memory of that night at all.

I remember noises outside my cell. I remember rage, and fear, and anger coursing toward me like a swirling cyclone or a tsunami. I remember battering the door with my fists and yelling for someone, anyone, to tell me what was happening. And then I remember light pouring in, hurting my eyes. I saw Kole's silhouette in the doorframe. I heard the words, "We're here to get you out, Tanner." Then everything went dark. The next clear memory I have is of waking up in The Hollow and wondering how the hell I went from being The League's pet empath to lying on a couch in a mansion with a Viking-like mage towering over me.

"Tanner?" Mack interrupts my train of thought.

At some point in the last few seconds, Kole turned and headed back over to Luther. They're talking quietly while

Sam pulls on his sneakers and a dark blue hoodie. Not for the first time, I wish someone could draw me a diagram of how the heck it works when he turns wolf. Where do the clothes *go*? How do they not get ripped to pieces like Mack's?

"Sorry." I blink myself back into the moment and look at the professor. "My head was somewhere else."

Mack seems like he's about to ask me if I'm okay, but then —maybe because he's decided none of us are okay—changes his mind and says, "Can you accompany Sam to find Kayla?"

I frown. Bears aren't wolves, but they're better at tracking than empaths. "Sure, but—"

"Sam's nose is better than mine. He'll find her and, when he does, it might help to have a sympathetic ear."

"You mean it might help to have someone who can tell if she's lying or intending to double-cross us?"

Mack shrugs a little. His beard has become more unruly in the past few days, and it must be irritating him because he rubs it with his palm. "Something like that, yes," he says. "So, will you? Go with Sam?"

"Of course, but what will you be doing?"

"I have an errand to run," Mack replies. "I'll tell you about it if it results in anything useful."

11

SAM

"Where did you find her?" Tanner asks as we break away from the beach and head into the woods.

"Not far from the barrier. She'd been eating Hellhound leftovers," I tell him, my stomach lurching at the thought of eating raw meat; despite being part wolf, it's one thing I never quite got used to. Preparing to shift, I add, "They used to feed us rabbits in the club."

Tanner pushes a branch out of his way and keeps looking ahead.

"Couldn't stomach them. It was only when they noticed I was losing weight that they finally gave in and started feeding me something else." I pause. "Madame insisted."

I feel Tanner's eyes flick toward me. I haven't spoken about Madame very much since I arrived with them, although I'm not sure how much Nova told him.

I try to laugh, but it comes out a little forced. "She didn't want me losing muscle mass." I flex my upper arms and wriggle my eyebrows. "Gotta keep the crowds happy."

"Sam—" Tanner stops and looks like he's about to give me one of his *I'm here to talk* lines.

Before he can say anything at all, I point to a tree up ahead. "It was about here," I say, noticing the rabbit's skeleton is no longer on the ground.

We push through the undergrowth, and the spot where the professor and I had our 'moment' comes into view. My cheeks flush even though I'm trying not to think about it.

"You okay?" Tanner frowns at me. He's noticed the blushing, and probably the swirling tug of arousal in my body. I try to disguise it, but it's too late; he's already sensed it.

Perhaps he thinks I'm feeling it because of him, because he steps a little closer and lowers his voice. "Sam, is there something you want to tell me?"

Casually, I brush my fingers through my hair and shrug. "Not really the time, Tanner."

"You sure? Seems like there's something you need to get off your chest." There's a twinkling cheekiness in his eyes that I haven't seen since Nova disappeared. He looked at her that way *all* the time. Even when shit was bad, and in amidst all the crazy stuff that went down, he still couldn't help being turned on by her. Now I know he was kept in a concrete box for fifteen years, I guess that explains some of it. He missed his adolescence the way I missed my twenties, so perhaps he's been playing catch up with Nova.

I roll my tongue over my teeth and contemplate whether I should answer his question. Hesitantly, testing the waters, I say, "Have you and Mack ever...?"

Tanner cants his head to one side. "Fucked? No. He's been part of the *group* since we got with Nova, but he's never gone there with any of us. Other guys? Maybe. I dunno. Never thought about it." He's still looking at me with a perplexed look on his face. "Why? You have a crush on the professor? Must run in the family." He laughs and says, "Did I ever tell you about the time me and Nova tied him to a chair? He'd got all up in his own head about being older than her so we—"

"You didn't tell me, but Mack did." I let the words sink in for a moment.

Tanner's eyes flash with curiosity. "He told you?"

"Right before he took my pants off and—"

"You and *Mack?*" Tanner looks as if his mind has quite literally just been blown. He rubs his reddening neck and breathes out hard. I can't tell if he's turned on or just totally confused. "When?"

"After we found Kayla."

"How?"

"You need me to explain the choreography?" I ask, shaking my arms because the urge to shift is becoming too much.

"No, but... Mack? You and Mack? Now? With every-thing..." Tanner trails off. He doesn't *sound* like he's judging me but, all the same, his questions make the hairs on my arms prickle.

"I needed a distraction. Not from Nova. From everything else. Kayla had asked about Nico, and it brought back..." I pause and push my hair from my face. "Stuff."

Tanner bites his lower lip. "Right." His tone has softened. "I get it. No judgement."

"I figured Nova wouldn't mind. She likes it when you and I—" I raise my eyebrow at him.

"Yeah," Tanner smiles. "She does."

Shaking my head, I say, "Look, I'll give you more details later. But we should—"

"Go ahead." Tanner waves at me. "Break out your wolf superpowers."

I laugh at him and nod. Somehow, knowing everything he went through, and how hard it must have been to come back from it, his carefree demeanor has become even more attractive. I can see why he was the first one Nova fell for. I can see why he was the first one *I* felt truly comfortable with.

"Wolf Boy, coming up," I tell him.

In a few cracking, straining, stretching seconds, I'm on all fours and covered in fur. A wave of adrenaline courses through me. I shake it off and focus on the task at hand—tracking Nico's mother.

At first, it's hard to catch her scent. It's masked by something I didn't notice before. When Mack and I patrolled the woods, I kept catching a whisper of it but thought it was a plant or weed I hadn't encountered before; it certainly didn't smell like an animal of any kind. Now, I know exactly what it was—the trail left behind by the Hellhounds. Just a trace, but enough to remind me of darkness, and damp, and rotting flesh.

Pushing through it, I search for wolf instead. I catch my own scent, and Snow's. I can smell the remnants of my encounter with Mack, where some of it spilled onto the ground between us. It sends an animalistic shudder through me, but I turn away and head deeper into the woods.

I move faster than Tanner. He has to run to keep up with me, clumsily pushing branches aside and yelping whenever he scratches himself on one. Occasionally, I turn and offer him a withering stare that says, *By the stars, Tanner, be quiet or she'll hear us before we find her.*

We're almost at the edge of the woods, close to a street on the edge of town which is full of quaint white houses. I stop and notice my tail stiffen. I raise my head and sniff the air.

"You got her?" Tanner asks, crouching down beside me.

I meet his eyes, then turn and move slowly through the pine trees. The space between them is wider now, and we could easily be spotted. I'm staring at a fenced-off backyard in front of us. It is overgrown, and the house itself looks abandoned.

"She's in there?" Tanner asks.

A low growl rumbles in my throat. *Yes, she's in there.*

* * *

A HOLE IN THE FENCE, obscured by freakishly tall weeds, tells me I'm right. I sniff a piece of fur caught on the cut wire. Tanner crouches down and examines it, then nods at me.

Silently we creep forward together until we reach the backdoor. It's ajar, so Tanner pushes it open. As we enter, a million scents assault my nose. Rotting food, mold, damp, people, and wolf.

With a shudder, I shift back. My muscles twitch for several seconds after a shift, as they reacclimatize to their human form. It's an odd sensation, but slightly pleasurable at the same time.

"Kayla?" I call out. Tanner looks at me like I'm crazy, but I ignore him. "It's Sam and Tanner. We need to talk to you."

There's silence, then a floorboard creaks and she appears in the doorway. "You tracked me here?" she asks, even though she must already know the answer.

"Like I said, we need to talk to you."

Kayla's eyes flash toward Tanner. "Oh good," she snarls. "You brought the empath."

"I could have killed you, but I didn't. I think that deserves a few minutes of your time," I tell her, perching on the edge of a cluttered kitchen table.

"Whose house is this?" Tanner asks. His face has darkened, and he's looking around at the walls as if they're haunted. For him, they probably are; Tanner senses the ghosts of emotions like I sense the ghosts of smells.

"No idea." Kayla folds her arms. "Found it like this. Figured I might as well use it." She looks down at her fingernails as if she's horribly bored by the conversation already. "You said you want to talk, so talk, then get out. Because last time we spoke, you were telling me you never wanted to see me again."

"Nico is dead because of Ragnor." I stride closer. "He betrayed you and your son, then he rejected you."

Kayla's entire face becomes pinched as she says, "He did *not* reject me. I left."

"I can smell it on you," I growl, wrinkling my nose. "The stench hovers round you like flies."

I feel Tanner shoot me a look that says, *Aren't we supposed to be getting her on side?* But I ignore him.

"He rejected you long before Nico died. He chose Elena. My mother."

"Sam…" Tanner warns.

"All of this—everyone's pain—mine, yours, Nico's, my mother's. It's all because of him. Are you really telling me you don't want to see him punished for what he did?" I square my shoulders and move so I'm standing within an inch of her face. Her scar is deep, pale, and pinched at either end. "It was his blade that pierced Nico's flesh."

"Because he jumped in front of *you*," Kayla cries.

"And do you think Ragnor felt bad? Did he try to save Nico? He could have, but he didn't. All he cared about was—" I swallow down what I'm about to say. I can't talk about what he did to my mother or think about her body lying in his arms.

"Enough," Kayla growls. "I don't want to hear her name. Just tell me what you want."

Tanner holds my elbow and steps forward. "We want to kill Ragnor, and we want you to help us."

12

LUTHER

"You're sure we need to go back?" Kole asks as we follow the stream that winds from the falls to the cabin.

"If Kayla refuses to help us, we need a back-up plan."

"You have a bunch of grenades hidden back here?" Kole growls. Somehow, even when he's sarcastic, he manages to sound like he's pissed off.

"No, but I have my laptop and a Wi-Fi connection." A branch catches on my hoodie and causes a thread to ping free from the dark gray fabric.

Kole waits for me to explain how either of those things can help us.

"We need to figure out how to defeat Eve."

Kole's jaw twitches. "She's powerful. Nothing we've tried so far has worked."

"But *why* is she so powerful?"

"She's taken a lot of F.H.B.," Kole says darkly. "Could be a part of it."

I shake my head. "There's a reason Ragnor chose her. Do you remember her from your time with them? Was she around back then?"

Kole visibly flinches. We never talk about the time he spent undercover with the League. We don't ask questions, and he doesn't volunteer answers. "The only person whose name I knew was Kayla's," Kole replies through tightly clenched teeth. "But that doesn't mean Eve wasn't around. I was Kayla's project. I never met Ragnor, never even knew his name, but he was still a big part of it. So, just because I didn't hear the name *Eve*, doesn't mean she wasn't hovering in the background." Kole frowns, and his pace slows a little. He chews his lip for a second before saying, "Although… something in the way she spoke when she was in the van with me —" He glances in my direction. "When they took me from the warehouse to the hotel in Redrock."

I nod; I knew what he meant.

"She said she'd heard a lot about me. That I was a legend." He closes his eyes as if he's trying to remember more details. "I can't be certain, but I got the impression everything she'd learned about what happened had been second-hand—after the event." He pauses, then adds, "How does that help, Luther?"

"I have a gut feeling that if we can find out who Eve is, and where she came from, we might figure out how to defeat her." I smooth my palm over my head. "I don't like the idea of relying on Kayla."

Kole nods. "I agree. I just think you're asking a lot for such a small timeframe."

I shove my hands into my pockets and take a deep breath to steady the sloshing nerves in my stomach. "Which is why I'm hoping mine and Mack's replacements forgot to revoke my access to the Sheriff's database. Someone like Eve? She must be in there somewhere."

I'm feeling confident. Perhaps because I have to or I'd go mad with nerves, and sadness, and whatever else is going on in my fucked-up head right now. But when Kole remains silent, the vein in his neck noticeably pulsing, doubt starts to creep in.

Am I just doing this to waste time? So I don't have to think about what will happen if Nova doesn't come back in time? Or at all?

* * *

AHEAD, the cabin is dark. There were no shields or barriers in place, and there are no signs of life inside. Just as they promised, Rev and Sarah must have returned to town.

"We should have reached out to them," I mutter. "We didn't even tell Sarah that Sam was back."

Kole hums his agreement under his breath. "It happened too quickly," he says. "All of it."

A sigh shakes my shoulders. How can a place that once brought us so much peace now bring so much sadness?

As if he's thinking the same thoughts, Kole says, "Building this cabin with you was my salvation, Luther. I don't think I ever thanked you for it."

I shrug; strong, unfamiliar emotions pulsing beneath my ribs. "It helped all of us," I tell him.

"I'm sorry it's been tainted for you. I know it was always your safe haven."

We've started walking toward the steps. Kole's sudden openness has surprised me; neither of us are known for wearing our hearts on our sleeves.

"When Nova comes back, it will be a happy place again." I stop at the bottom of the steps and look back toward the lake. At the end of the jetty, the light catches on the water and—for just a moment—I almost believe I can see Nova. Soft, and naked.

69

Wrapped in a blanket while I sit behind her, watching the water together while we explore each other's bodies properly for the first time since we admitted how we felt about one another.

I turn away and take the steps two at a time. The door isn't locked. Inside, everything is as we left it.

Although it's only been a short time since we were last here, somehow, I expected it to be covered in dust, weeds creeping up through the floor, birds nesting in the roof.

It feels like a lifetime has passed, and yet the cabin is proof it has barely been more than the blink of an eye.

Kole is staring at the corner of the room just behind the couch. He swallows hard and unties his hair.

Both of us look at the ceiling. I'm glad the laptop is downstairs. Already, the memories we created here are almost killing me. If I had to venture into the bedroom, I might implode.

It's bad enough standing in the living room. Every inch of it reminds me of her; the way she looked dressed in my tee, parading around with that confident grin on her face, so different to when we first met her. The way she teased us all, made us hungry for her, then soothed us with her body and her brilliance. The way I tortured myself for all those weeks before finally admitting how I felt about her. The time I wasted. The moments I lost because I was too stubborn and fucked-up to face it.

All those things are bad enough; the thought of going upstairs and seeing the bed we shared with her is too much.

"I'll fire up the laptop. You see if you can find any coffee." I gesture to the kitchen, and Kole nods at me.

As he starts clattering around in the cupboards, I sit at the large oak table and open the computer. It's old and far too slow but, eventually, it wakes up.

"No coffee," Kole says, standing behind me. "But I did find

these." He puts a half-empty bottle of whiskey and two glasses down on the table.

"Make mine a double," I tell him as he starts to pour.

* * *

"Fuck!" I yell as I slam the laptop shut. "Nothing. Not a fucking thing."

"Luther, it was always a long shot. We don't even know if Eve is her real name." Kole pours us another drink. "Let alone a surname."

I down mine in one then stand up, bracing my hands behind my head. "I searched every person with links to the League. Everyone we had on file. Eve's face didn't crop up once. I put her description into the database, too, in case there was a link to some skanky F.H.B. dealer. Nothing. Tried the witch register for this state and the next. Nothing. It's like she didn't exist before she met Ragnor."

"Luther," Kole says again, "you've only got access to the local databases. The Bureau has way more files. Locked down files. Plus, the register is voluntary. Do you think someone like Eve would—"

"Fuck!" I yell again. My heart is pounding, my head too. Like I've got a hangover already.

As Kole grows silent and stares into his drink, I stride to the bathroom and slam the door behind me. It rattles the barely-there pieces of mirror on the wall. I stare at them, breathing hard, my face reflected in the fractured glass.

I close my eyes. Of course, I wasn't going to find Eve on the police database. Or any other database. Even if I had, what good would it have done?

But I needed to feel like I was doing something. I couldn't sit around all day, while Sam and Tanner went off to find

Kayla and Mack did whatever the fuck he needed to do so urgently, waiting.

Behind me, the door opens then closes again. "All we do is wait," I mutter. "Since she disappeared, all we've done is wait. I can't wait any longer, Kole. It's killing me. If she's gone—forever—I need to know so I can…"

Kole puts his hands on my arms. They're large and warm, and fit snuggly round my biceps. "So you can what?"

"I can't be here if she's not." My voice is barely a whisper. "The vision your mother put in our heads felt real. Like it really was me. I remember all of it. I *remember* losing her. I can't take it a second time."

"You haven't lost her." Kole's grip tightens. He's a little taller than me. In the shards of mirror left on the wall, I can see him watching my face.

"You know how that happened?" I gesture to the glass.

Kole doesn't reply.

"It was when I first fucked her. She found me in here jerking off into her panties, and we…" I trail off. I was trying to laugh at myself, but it hasn't worked. Visions of Nova flash through my head, and I screw my eyes shut again. "I feel the way I did then. I want her so much I can hardly think straight. Except, back then all I needed to do was open my mouth and tell her how I felt. Now, there's nothing I can do to bring her back quicker and nothing I can do to ease this fucking *ache* in my chest."

Kole's hair is hanging loosely over his shoulders. It brushes against my neck as he leans closer. "Show me what you were doing when she found you."

I blink at his reflection. He doesn't repeat himself, just stares me down.

My skin prickles with heat.

He plays this game with Tanner. I've heard them in the mansion more times than I've admitted. But Kole and I?

We've fucked twice. Both times were angry, and confused, and full of pent-up tension that needed to be released. We've never done *this*.

A shudder runs down my arms. My fingers twitch. The pressure of Kole's hands on me doesn't change. He's stock still, waiting.

Still holding his gaze, I release a gravelly sigh and flick open my jeans. I push them roughly over my hips and pull out my cock. It's soft but thick in my hand. Guilt trickles through me. I close my eyes but, as I'm about to take my hand away, Kole's fingers land on my throat. They stretch up to hold my chin, cupping my jaw tightly. "Open your eyes," he commands.

Something about his tone of voice makes every muscle in my body sigh with relief. He's taking control. I don't need to think. All I need to do is follow what he tells me.

"Show me," Kole repeats, tightening his grip just enough to release a small groan from my lips.

Leaning forward, I brace one hand on the sink, so I don't have to look at myself, then move the other up and down my shaft. My palm slides roughly over my piercings, and the tugging sensation is the cue my dick needs. It swells in my grasp. As it hardens, and pulses of arousal vibrate in my balls, I collect the bead of pre-cum from its tip.

"In your mouth," Kole says.

I hesitate and look up. No one has *ever* spoken to me like this before.

"Taste yourself," he tells me.

As I obey him, he watches closely. When my finger enters my mouth, he hums darkly and licks his lower lip.

"Keep going," he says, pulling off his shirt so I catch glimpses of his inked torso in the broken mirror. There's the sound of a belt snapping open, then pants dropping to the floor. I glance over my shoulder to see Kole's erection quivering behind my ass.

I've never truly looked at his cock before and, even though he hasn't told me to, I turn around. Kole's eyes narrow questioningly. For a moment, I think he's going to tell me to turn away, but he doesn't; he steps closer and braces a hand on my shoulder.

He isn't touching himself. He just looks down and stares at my hand as it moves in long, languid strokes over my shaft. Rolling his tongue around his mouth, he spits on it and hums as the lubrication allows me to go faster.

I groan loudly and rub my thumb over my pierced tip, trying to fight the rising surge of electricity in my core. "Are you going to fuck me?" I ask, meeting his eyes. "Or are you just a spectator?"

"I'm not going to fuck you, Luther," Kole growls. "Not until Nova returns." He moves his hand to the back of my neck, then presses his forehead to mine. "When she does, you're going to fuck *me* and she's going to watch."

My eyes widen. I'm fisting myself furiously now, desperate for release.

"You're going to show me what those chunks of metal feel like in my ass."

With my free hand, I reach for Kole's dick, but he swats it away. Instead, I press my palm on his chest.

"You're going to fuck me while I fuck her. You're going to fuck me while I'm inside her." Kole tightens his grip on my neck. I make a fist and thump him hard. I'm so close it's almost painful. "Or perhaps you'd rather fuck Nova's ass while I'm inside her? Show her what it's like to be completely full. Feel her tight little hole squeezing you while you come. Do you think she could take it? Your metal? Would it make her—"

"Fuck..." With a shudder, an orgasm rocks through me

like a tidal wave. It peaks quickly and subsides just as fast, leaving me unsteady on my feet and gasping for breath.

Still hard, Kole pulls his pants back up and fastens his belt.

"Torturing yourself?" I ask, reaching back to grip the sink and stop myself from falling. "I can—"

"When she's back." Kole meets my eyes. "I'm saving it for when she's back." He turns and pulls on his shirt as he opens the door. "When she is, you can take charge."

Despite just having come all over myself, the filthy words coming from Kole's mouth make my dick twitch. "I'll hold you to that promise," I tell him.

Kole stops in the doorway and looks over his shoulder at me. "I hope so."

13

EVE

She's a strange, willowy thing. *Elena.* The photograph Ragnor carries in his wallet shows her in a very different light. In a wedding gown with cherry-red lips and dark flowing hair, smiling up at him; she looks radiant and strong.

I wonder which version is the illusion; the woman who has been floating like a phantom through the mansion since she returned—too nervous and skittish to speak to anyone but Ragnor—or the one with the bright red lips.

I suppose it was naïve of us to think she would be anything other than alarmed by her return. Who knows what her poor little mind is like after coming all this way?

I stare at her often, but I can't decipher what she's thinking or whether she understands where she is. She doesn't seem to have noticed that Ragnor is twenty-five years older than when she last saw him. And wolves don't age like vamps; they *look* their years.

She trails around after Ragnor as if she's a child. Occasionally, she remembers she had a baby, and asks him for it. Every time, Ragnor gives her the same answer; it is being taken care of. You can see it when you're well.

This seems to quiet her. She presses her pale lips together and wrings her hands in her lap. But after a few hours, she asks the same question again. And again. And again, until the mewing sounds coming from her delicate throat make me want to rip out her insides and dance with them.

I've been studying Ragnor too. At first, he was enamored. Overwhelmed with joy. As the days wear on, however, he looks at her differently. He pities her and he's frustrated by her. She's too fixated on the child, and not interested enough in him. She's so fragile he daren't touch her for fear she'll break. He thought they would have a romantic reunion. He thought there would be gushing declarations of love and lust-filled fucking out on the lawn under the stars.

She has given him neither.

Kayla was a better choice for him. A better *fit*. I never liked the woman, but she was strong, and fierce, and loyal. She had fire in her belly and in her eyes, and she smelled of stars and charcoal.

Elena smells of mist and squashed river reeds, and that's not what Ragnor needs. He needs more.

He also needs to remember where his own loyalty lies. Elena has distracted him. She has pulled a thin white veil over his eyes and wrapped it around his head, and she's suffocating him with it.

His love for her is pulling the breath from his lungs and the fight from his soul. He is allowing himself to be dampened by a human, and it is making me very, very sad to watch it. Especially because I know The King will not be pleased.

When he returns, he will smell it on Ragnor, and then Ragnor will be no more. Which is a shame because I did *so* want us to be a happy little family. Even if *she* had to be in it, too.

But she is not the woman he said she was. She is no different to the rest of them. In fact, she might be the most pathetic example of a human I've ever encountered. Even more pathetic than that sniveling boyfriend the Fire Bird dispatched.

Thinking of the Fire Bird, my heart begins to sing. It flutters in my ribcage as if it has wings.

She was so beautiful when she burned.

When we drained her, I saw Ragnor's light come flickering back. The lust that runs in his veins. The lust for power, and control, and blood. While her body became charred and shriveled in front of our eyes, he remembered our plan. He remembered he wanted to tear her limb from limb, and bring The King back to Earth, and rule over humanity. He remembered just how superior we are, and that we *are* on the right path.

Because if we weren't, she would have fought back, wouldn't she? The Phoenix would have set free her almighty powers and destroyed us.

But the prophecy was wrong. Maybe she could have been powerful if she had the chance, but we stopped her. *We* stopped her.

Not that I ever paid much heed to prophecies, anyway. Ragnor believes in them but, when I was a girl, my mother told me they were nothing more than the inventions of scared, lonely women who were desperate to prove their worth. So desperate they made up a talent—an ability to *see* what no one else could. They made themselves vessels of the future and wrote laws which decreed that only *they* could speak the truth and only *they* could determine what truth they told and how much of it they revealed.

They allowed the gift of foresight to pass to their male heirs, but only women kept the power of prophecy. It was the one thing they had that men could not take away from them.

They thought they were being clever, imbuing themselves with some kind of almighty power. But then legend became truth, and truth became *fate*, and fate—sadly—is the most dogmatic master of them all.

The seers refer to fate as a woman. They say things like *she* has sent us a vision. *She* sent us a prophecy. But I know better; fate is a man, and he is as cruel a master as any.

I reject fate. I reject prophecy. I reject anything and anyone who tells me that what is meant to be *has* to be, and that I cannot change it.

We changed it. We looked fate in his burning eyes and declared we would not let him win.

Ragnor believed in the prophecy. He believed that a pathetic half-blood child could destroy us. Even when she lay burning in front of us, I felt him waiting for her to open her eyes.

But she didn't.

She is gone.

It is time for Him to return, and time for Ragnor to put down his pet human and play his part.

"Eve?" Ragnor's footsteps shake the floorboards as he strides through the mansion. It is a dark place now. Blood stains the walls. Quite literally; I am not imagining it. Wolves being wolves, fights are inevitable. Especially when they've been doing nothing but drinking and fucking for days. Celebrating the end of The Phoenix.

Although I hear him calling me, I don't reply. He knows where I am. I'm in the professor's study. I like it here. Words dance out of his books and into my head, and paint pictures that dance in the fire of my mind. I like the desk, too. Big and sturdy. Like him—the bear.

I've only known one other bear shifter in my lifetime. A huge, scarred, brown bear from a colony near Jasper. He fucked like he fought; hard and unrelenting. I was sad when I killed him, but only for a little while.

By the window, which frames a pretty picture of the fountain and the grounds in the pinkish-orange sunlight, I hold up the vial.

It has been hanging around my neck ever since we filled it with her blood. Ragnor tried to snatch it from me—because he doesn't trust that I will be strong enough to resist it.

"This is my last and greatest test," I told him, gripping it tight and feeling the energy pulse through the glass and into my palm. "I will keep it safe until He needs it."

"Fine, but it's on your head if you fuck this up, Eve," Ragnor growled.

I've barely seen him since then. He's been stalking up and down the halls of the upper floors, waiting for his human to recover and service his needs.

"Eve?!" He is bellowing now.

I hum to myself and turn the vial upside down, watching the congealed blood drip slowly down its sides. I moisten my lower lip. The black veins that decorate my face pulse with hunger. One taste, just one...

I screw my eyes shut and clench the vial, then I slip its chain back around my throat and tuck it into the neckline of my dress.

"I will be strong for you, my King."

The door to the study clatters open on its hinges. "Those

fucking hounds of yours have escaped again. Don't you have a spell that would—"

"My babies cannot be controlled by spells," I laugh, shaking my head. "They are not from our dimension, Ragnor. They are hell beasts, demon dogs, evil in canine form—"

"Alright," Ragnor waves his hand to shut me up, "just make sure they don't stray into town again. We can't have them drawing attention to us. Not now."

I tilt my head sideways and smile. Ragnor's body is tense. His muscles are taut. I walk over and slide myself behind him, floating up to put my hands on his shoulders. "Is your little human not giving you what you need?" I whisper.

"Fuck you, Eve," Ragnor barks, but I ignore him. His words lie. His body doesn't.

"It's not good for you," I say softly. "I can help." I slide my hands down his sides and tuck them into the front of his pants.

Sometimes, when I play this game, he grabs my wrists and jerks away from me. Today, he stays completely still.

I let my palm rest on the bulge of his cock. He tilts his hips, ever so slightly, and presses himself into my hand. "Do it," he growls.

But I take my hand away and skip around him. Hopping onto the professor's desk, I sweep his papers to the floor and open my legs. "No," I shake my head. "Do *me.*"

Ragnor assesses me with dark eyes. I pull my skirt up around my waist and show him my cunt.

Then I reach into my pocket and take out a different vial. I drink down its contents in one, and hum as the F.H.B. burns my throat.

Ragnor strides over and takes a fistful of my hair. He pulls my head back and his pants down. He is fucking me hard, and loudly, when I hear her. The little mouse. Elena. I dig my nails into his back, so he groans as she enters the room.

"Ragnor?" his name drips from her lips like honey floating on a winter breeze. "What are you doing?"

Ragnor freezes between my legs. His dick twitches. I grind my hips against him, and he shoves me away. Zipping up his pants, he turns around. I can see the sweat glistening on his forearms.

"Elena, it's not what it looks like. You were so tired, still recovering, I didn't want to press you for…" He trails off. She is sobbing. She's not angry, or shouting, or running away. She's just standing there sobbing. Her small body trembling.

When Ragnor runs to her and folds her into his arms, she lets him comfort her and lead her from the room.

No wonder he grew to hate humans. No wonder she died giving birth to that wretched half-breed child of theirs; she is so weak. The walking epitome of what I despise about humanity.

I pull my skirt back down and hop from the desk.

I could call Andre and make him finish what Ragnor started, but it is nearly sunset. The ritual will begin in a few short hours, so perhaps it is fitting I should wait for my king.

A violent shudder rocks my entire body. At first, I think it's the F.H.B. making my heart swell in my chest. Then my eyes snap to the window. Someone has breached my spell.

14

MACK

"Are you sure she is willing to do this?" I ask, pacing as Kayla disappears into the trees up ahead.

It is almost sunset. The sky is a strange, violent pink splashed with orange. There are no clouds, and the air is unusually cold.

"She was telling the truth," Tanner says.

"Wolves are good at masking their thoughts," I reply. "Nico—" I stop and look furtively at Sam. At the mention of his brother's name, he closes his eyes and looks away. I tilt my head and lower my voice, but it needs to be said. "Nico hid his true identity from us."

"And I still knew he wasn't to be trusted," Tanner says. "I might not have known *why* but I knew he was hiding something." He folds his arms and pushes his shoulders back. "I'm right about her, Mack. She hates Ragnor and Eve as much as we do. She wants to do this. She wants to avenge her son."

"I believe her, too," Sam says. "She hates us, but she hates Ragnor and Eve more."

"She was Ragnor's fated mate," Kole says darkly. "Will she be able to overcome that bond when the moment arises?"

"Maybe not," Sam says. "But she doesn't have to kill him herself. We've asked her to go after Eve—she's who we need to take down, so we can get into The Hollow and tackle Ragnor."

Luther is strangely quiet. His jaw twitches as he looks up at the sky. "Like fire," he mutters. "It looks like fire."

I follow his gaze. He's right; the orange coloring in the sky slashes across it in thin strips that look like flames. *Perhaps it's a sign.* The thought sends a wave of warmth through my muscles, but I try not to go any further down the rabbit hole. We cannot let ourselves believe it's a sign. If we believe Nova's return is imminent, we will let our guard down and mistakes could be made.

"Focus," I say gruffly. "How long since she left?"

Kole looks at his watch. "Two minutes."

"We'll wait ten, then follow," I tell him.

So, for ten long minutes, we stand staring at one another. Something in the air is different. Snow can sense it and is breathing heavily. It is thick with magick.

"Why does it have to be tonight?" Sam asks quietly. "Did we ever find out?"

I rub my beard with my thumb and forefinger. It's too long. It needs to be trimmed, but somehow the unruliness seems fitting.

"The moon," Luther replies. "There's a different energy on a full moon." He frowns at Sam. "You should know that. You're a were."

"I was locked in an underground club for ten years, Luther. We didn't see much of the night sky."

"But you should feel it," Luther says.

Sam flexes his head from side to side. "Who said I didn't?"

"It's not just the moon," I interrupt. "I wasn't sure whether to keep this to myself or not."

The others turn to stare at me. Kole looks perplexed, but Tanner, Sam, and Luther look pissed that I was thinking of hiding something from them.

I sigh and push my fingers through my hair. My gray sweats aren't nearly warm enough, which is odd because usually Snow and I can tolerate pretty much any drop in temperature better than most. "I'm not sure it helps. But the reason it has to happen tonight—it's to do with the alignment of the planets. They haven't been like this since before The Shadow King was banished. Thousands of years ago."

"How do you know this, Mack?" Kole asks darkly.

"I went to Rev's," I tell him. "While you were at the cabin with Luther, and Sam and Tanner were tracking Kayla, I went to see Rev."

Kole's eyes widen.

"Why didn't you tell us?" Luther asks gruffly.

"Because I knew you'd think me going into town was a bad idea."

No one argues. They know they would have tried to stop me.

"Are they okay?" Sam asks. "Is Sarah okay?"

I smile at him and put my hand on his shoulder. "She was when she learned you're alive," I reply, watching him blink back tears.

Sam clears his throat and nods, ducking out of my grip. "Good," he says. "I hope you told her I'll see her soon, and that I'm sorry I didn't come sooner."

"I explained everything," I tell him. "They're both fine. Town is much as it was before—unruly, but not too dangerous yet. Rev says many have already left. Mostly mages and witches who can feel the power balance shifting." I fold my arms and notice that all five of us are feeling the cold now. "She also leant me one of her grandmother's books. Ivy was a powerful astrologist. She wrote several volumes on the link between magick and planetary alignment."

"And she wrote about tonight?"

"She didn't know when it would come, but she predicted the alignment we'll see tonight would bring a great surge in magick."

"Giving Eve the power to bring The Shadow King back to earth," Kole mutters.

"And Nova the power to rise?" Sam asks the question burning on everyone's lips. I close my eyes and breathe deeply.

"Maybe." A smile twitches on my lips. "I hope so, but we don't know that. So, we stick to what we agreed. Kayla takes out Eve. We take out Ragnor. The ritual never happens." I look around the group of men I've grown to love like brothers. "Agreed?"

They nod in unison. For the first time in days, glistening kernels of hope flicker in their eyes.

15

EVE

Kayla looks like she hasn't eaten properly in days. Her eyes are gray, and the skin beneath them even grayer. She has dirt beneath her fingernails, and grease in her hair, but she has the same steel in her eyes as she says, "Where is Ragnor?"

We are on the lawn. She passed through the barrier with ease. My fault. It didn't occur to me to remove her imprint from the spell.

"Inside, preparing for the ritual." I wriggle my toes into the lush green grass beneath my feet. Pops of electricity scratch my soles. I close my eyes and hum as The Hollow's power trickles up through me.

"It's tonight?" Kayla asks, looking at the sky.

"Can't you tell?" I stretch out my arms and feel the glorious pull of my muscles as they loosen and flex. "It's going to be a *beautiful* night."

Kayla looks down at her feet. "I..." She pauses and licks her lower lip. I almost feel sorry for her; the stench of humiliation is tangible. "I want to come back. I want to be a part of this, Eve. I deserve to be." She meets my eyes and I notice her fingers twitch as she shoves them into her pockets.

"I think that's a decision for Ragnor," I tell her.

"Then take me to him and let me ask him myself."

I tilt my head. My temples throb with the movement. With F.H.B. surging in my veins, I am finding it hard to focus. Sounds and smells and light pummel my senses. I hear the birds in the trees; I hear the wolves sleeping inside; I hear my babies prowling the perimeter, waiting for their master's ascent. "Very well." I turn and lead her past the fountain, up the steps, and through the professor's old kitchen.

Kayla takes in the blood on the walls. She sniffs the air but doesn't break her stride.

I lead her through the belly of the house to the study. "It's Elena's favorite room," I say as we stop outside. "She likes the fire and the view."

Kayla presses her lips together.

"He hasn't told her that you killed her son." I pinch Kayla's elbow. She doesn't look at me. "She would be very upset, but I don't think Ragnor minds. So, you might be lucky. He might let you come back into the fold, Kayla."

I tap my knuckles on the door and we wait.

When Ragnor appears, his face is etched with anger and frustration. "What the fuck do you want, Eve? Haven't you caused enough damage for one day?"

I let my eyes dart toward Kayla.

Ragnor follows my gaze, but his expression doesn't change when he notices her. "You," he growls.

Kayla straightens her shoulders and pushes her chin up. I lean on the wall and press my back to the cool paintwork. I slide this way and that, like the pendulum of a grandfather clock. "Tick tock," I whisper. "Tick tock."

Ragnor shoots me a disgruntled stare, but I ignore him.

"Tick tock, Ragnor. The ritual begins at sundown." I tap my wrist. I wear an invisible watch. It is not very useful.

"What do you want?" Ragnor steps into the corridor, pulling the door shut behind him.

"I want to come back," Kayla says firmly. "I deserve to be a part of this, Ragnor. After everything, I deserve to be here when The King returns."

Ragnor's eyes narrow. He sucks in his cheeks and strides forward, closing the gap between him and his rejected mate. "What about your *son?*" he asks, his eyes twitching.

"*Our* son is gone," she replies. "But I'm still alive, and if the world is about to go to hell, I want to be on the winning side." She takes her hand from her pocket and points a long, thin finger at Ragnor's face. "You owe me this, Ragnor. You owe me a place in the new order. After everything you've done to me, this is the least you can offer." She clenches her fist and lowers it to her side. "Plus, you're surrounded by morons. You need someone who has their head screwed on straight."

A bubble of laughter tickles my throat. I giggle and wrap my arms around myself. "She has a point, Ragnor. Those wolves of yours are next to useless."

Ragnor and Kayla both ignore me. They are staring at one another, and the surge of emotion between them is intoxicating. They want each other, but they abhor each other. They need each other, but they despise one another's presence.

I clap my hands and dance into the middle of the corridor. "It starts soon. When you've made your decision, gather everyone outside." I open my arms and trail my fingers down the blood-crusted walls as I skip back outside.

I'm at the top of the steps when I hear Ragnor bellow, "Fine! But stay out of my way, she-wolf. I don't want to see you sniffing around me all day and all night."

I can't hear Kayla's reply, but I wish I'd seen her face.

Watching the two of them is like waiting for a hand-grenade to go off; you never know if they're going to fuck or fight.

Andre appears behind me. His hair is crumpled—like he just emerged from a long sleep. "Is Kayla back?" he asks.

"She is."

"Is it going to happen tonight?" His voice drips with nerves.

I look at him over my shoulder. "It's happening now."

16

TANNER

We gather as close to the barrier as we can. From just inside the tree line, we can see The Hollow, the lawn, and the fountain.

I look at Kole. He's breathing slowly and deeply, his hands clenched in front of him. He's the only one of us not wearing a hoodie—and I can see his flesh dimpling beneath his tattoos. Waves of sorrow surge around him; the last time he was here, he watched Nova take her last breath.

I reach for the ring I'm wearing around my neck. As if we're all thinking the same thing, the others do too.

If she's going to return, tonight is the night. Especially after what Mack said, it *has* to be the night. So, even as we brace ourselves for what Kayla's about to do, I'm praying we won't have to follow through with the rest of our plan. I'm praying this is the moment our phoenix is reborn, and that she puts an end to The King before he can set one creepy demon foot on Earth.

"There," Mack mutters, pointing at the steps.

Eve has emerged at the top of them. A wolf, in his human form, appears behind her. They talk for a moment before she grins and trots down to the lawn. This time, there are no skulls or candles. There is no altar, no books, no knives.

Eve stops at the fountain and braces her hands on its rim. She peers into it—although it's completely empty—and closes her eyes. Then her hand goes to her throat. She pulls a pendant from her dress. It hangs from her neck on a long chain. She holds it up to the slowly descending sun and the light catches it.

I glance at Kole. He breathes out heavily and grips the nearest tree branch. "That's Nova's blood," he says, the words barely making it out of his throat. His eyes darken and his lips twitch. "That's what they took from her."

Luther places a firm hand on Kole's shoulder. Usually, I'd expect him to push Luther away, but he doesn't. He lets his hand remain there while Eve turns and sits on the rim of the basin.

Swinging her legs like a child, she watches as werewolves emerge from the house. They gather on the lawn—not as many as before—and stand silently.

A mixture of nerves and excitement swirls in the air above them. Some are high, others are hungover, all are unsure whether they believe in what's about to happen or not. Kayla is among them. She weaves her way to the front of the crowd and stands directly in Eve's eyeline.

Finally, Ragnor shows himself. He stands at the top of the steps. He's about to speak when a woman appears next to him. She tugs his sleeve, and he turns to stroke her face. He presses his forehead to hers, whispers something, then points back at the kitchen.

She nods, glances at the pack of wolves in front of her, then turns and goes back inside.

Next to me, Sam takes a large step forward. He's perilously close to the barrier, so I try to tug him back, but he's transfixed on the space where—a few seconds ago—his mother stood. In the flesh. Looking just the way she did twenty-five years ago.

Sam's entire body starts to tremble. "Sam," I warn quietly. "Come back. We mustn't be seen."

He refuses to budge.

I'm about to try again when Mack steps in front of him, puts his hands on Sam's upper arms and meets his eyes. "We'll get her out, Sam. But we need Kayla to succeed first."

Sam tries to look away, but Mack ducks to keep his gaze. After a long quivering moment, Sam's body untenses and he allows Mack to usher him back into the shadows.

Ragnor is making a speech. The usual League vitriol: humans are inferior, supers should rule the world. Yada, yada, yada. No one seems willing to point out that, right now, as he speaks, his *human* wife sits inside waiting for him.

When he finishes, and the crowd roars, my attention moves to Kayla. Except she's gone. I can't see her.

Panic surges in my chest. I scan the crowd, then see a flash of pale fur. It moves quickly between the others then, with snarling and gnashing of teeth, Kayla throws herself at Eve.

It happens so quickly the other wolves don't have time to react, but I see it in slow motion. Kayla's jaws are open wide. She is leaping through the air, aiming for Eve's throat. Any second now, her teeth will puncture the large vein on the side of Eve's neck, and the evil witch will bleed out on the floor.

There's a stifled yelp.

Kayla's eyes flash.

Eve flicks her wrist. There's a loud crunching sound, and Kayla drops to the ground.

The crowd steps back, silently staring. Kayla is not a wolf anymore. She is a woman, crumpled like a rag doll, lying on the ground with her neck clearly broken. I wait for an onslaught of grief, or pain, or even an inkling that someone feels sad for her. Nothing comes; she's dead, and no one cares.

* * *

DREAD TRICKLES DOWN MY SPINE. As if Kayla's murder was a mere inconvenience, Eve carries on where Ragnor left off. The sun is descending more quickly now. A few minutes, and it will be below the horizon. Darkness will come.

Silence descends. Eve takes the chain from around her neck and holds the vial up in front of her. She waves her hand over it, muttering some kind of incantation we can't hear.

I look at the others. We are paralyzed. We can't do anything. We can't stop it; we can't even get close enough to *try*.

As Eve murmurs and chants, a darkness creeps over me. It is cold and heavy as it clings to my skin. I know this feeling. I sensed it before. The last time The Shadow King showed himself to us.

"He's coming," I whisper.

Kole looks at me, his pupils wide. "The Hunger." He grips his chest. "The darkness."

He drops to his knees and Luther crouches in front of him.

"He's coming," I whisper again as pain ricochets through my skull.

I look at Sam. His skin is so pale it is almost translucent.

He drops to the floor too. I sink down and wrap my arm around him. "I feel him," he whispers. "I feel him, Tanner. He's coming."

Mack is the only one still standing. He stretches his arms and braces his hands on two trees as if he simply refuses to bow to the *evil* that thickens the air.

I try to breathe out, but the air feels like it has congealed in my lungs. "We should run." The words leave my mouth before I can stop them, a plume of white air puffing out with them. I look up at Mack, ashamed, but desperate.

"We are not leaving. Not without Nova." He fixes his gaze on the vial in Eve's hand. With a flourish, she removes the cap.

Kole growls and doubles over, clutching his stomach. "I smell her," he mutters, almost a whine or a howl. "I feel her."

When he looks up, dark veins snake out from the corners of his eyes. He licks his teeth. Luther sits behind him and wraps his arms firmly around Kole's chest. I want to help, but I can't. I can barely see straight. Fear, wonder, terror, darkness, and victory merge in a sickening whirlpool that scrapes the inside of my brain.

Sam is shaking. I hold onto him, but I'm not sure if it's to help him or to anchor myself.

A vicious wind starts to blow. The trees tremble. Leaves fall. The sky becomes ink-black, the stars and moon already visible even though the sun has only just set and it should be impossible.

Eve turns to face the fountain. She tilts the vial. A drop of Nova's blood falls into the basin. Then another, and another.

Kole lurches forward and digs his fingernails into the earth. Roots wind up and bind themselves around his wrists, holding him still, stopping him from running head-first into the barrier and begging for a taste.

When the vial is empty, Eve throws it into the basin. It

shatters. A cloud of thick, black smoke swirls up, and Eve moves her hands through it as if she is weaving it into something beautiful. There is a shudder. The earth groans and The Hollow creaks.

Thick red liquid spills over the sides of the fountain. It is full and overflowing. Its central column splutters to life. Water, laced with Nova's blood, pummels down into the basin. The wind blows harder, and the moon glows brighter.

I feel something on my face. Something wet. There are no clouds, but it is raining.

I hold out my palm. A drop falls into it, cold and vicious. But it is not rain. It is blood.

"Let it rain with the blood of The Phoenix! Let her power break the earth open!" Eve has climbed into the fountain. She is standing in it, blood-red water staining her white dress, pulling it tight against her spindly calves.

The wolves look up at the sky. Red rain batters their faces. Several start to run, but Eve sings out, "Those who run from his power will be devoured by it!"

So, they stay.

A cacophony of howling and barking shakes the air, but it's not the wolves; it's the Hellhounds. They emerge from behind the mansion in a pack and race toward Eve.

When they reach her, they put their front paws up on the fountain and lap at the liquid inside it. Eve bends down, allowing the front of her dress to become thick with blood, and strokes their heads.

"It is time!" She hollers at the sky.

There is another rumble, so violent it brings even Mack to his knees.

Eve jumps down, opening her arms and pushing the crowd of werewolves back too.

At the same moment she screams, the fountain cracks down the middle. It splits in half, the blood and the water flood free. They swell around the wolves' feet and soak the earth.

The two concrete halves of the fountain fall. They smash into rubble and litter the earth.

Where the fountain stood, a hole has appeared. At first, it is pure black, but then it starts to glow. Like someone has lit a fire beneath it.

"Are they flames?" I breathe, crawling forward on my hands and knees.

"Nova," Mack whispers. "She's coming."

We stagger to our feet, clutching one another, staring, praying. The hole grows wider. Then it becomes a crack. There is a sound—like the entire world is breaking—and the hole becomes a crater. The earth splits open. The gash widens and spreads. It is moving toward us. Sam and I leap to one side as Mack, Luther, and Kole leap to the other.

It continues through the woods. Trees fall. Roots heave and split. Fire burns beneath it. The ground becomes hot beneath my feet. When I pull Sam away, a rumble fills the air. Like thunder laced with ash.

"Nova," I whisper.

"Not Nova," Sam looks at me. A tear rolls down his cheek. "*Him.*"

17

THREE WEEKS LATER
SAM

"I'm going to look for him again." I take one last sip of Rev's rancid tea and wrinkle my nose.

Sarah shakes her head at me. "Sam, no. It's not safe."

"Nowhere is safe." I pull my dark hoodie on and head for the window. Luther has to move his legs, stretched out in front of him while he sits in Rev's armchair, so I can get past. On the couch, Tanner is sleeping. His face is cast in an eerie red glow. Red from the sky outside, which still looks like it is stained with blood.

"There are three hours until sunset. Most of them will be in hiding."

"Most, not all." Luther stands up and takes a lighter from his pocket. He flicks it open and stares at the flame, making it swell and darken.

"Luther, I said no flames." In the doorway of the bedroom, Rev folds her arms. Her injured hand is now bandage-free, but the scar is deep and ugly. "Sam? Where are you going?" She notices I've got my shoes on, and her tone hardens.

"I have to look for him. I can't just leave him out there."

"Mack will come back when he wants to come back," she sighs.

"*If* he wants to come back," Luther adds.

"When Layla took her own life, he went missing for weeks. He came back eventually." Rev moves into the living room, her jewelry unsettlingly bright and yellow against the scarlet hue of the walls.

"Yeah, well," Luther snaps, "Phoenix Falls wasn't the living, breathing definition of hell on Earth back then."

Outside, the street is deserted. Before the S.D.B. and the Army sealed us off, anyone with an ounce of sense fled. Those who remain are either quivering in their homes or trying to ingratiate themselves with the demons who are running riot.

"It'll never leave me," I say, glancing at Luther. "The sounds they made when they crawled out of the earth."

Luther swallows hard. "It's his face," he says. "I see it when I close my eyes."

"I see nothing." Tanner mumbles as he sits up. His legs are splayed and he leans forward onto his knees. "Just darkness."

"Well, I see a bunch of guys who've lost hope." Rev strides into the middle of the room and puts her hands on her hips. "What the fuck happened to you all?"

"What happened?" The front door clatters open. Kole has been on the roof again, but now he's standing there filling the doorframe. His eyes are ebony black. The smalls veins that appeared in the corners of his eyes when Eve spilled Nova's blood are still there. They haven't grown, but they haven't disappeared either.

"We failed her." He crosses Rev's small apartment and squares up to her. "*I* failed her."

"Stand down, Kole." Luther is at his side, but Rev shakes her head at him.

She doesn't look afraid or angry. "You did not fail her." She moves as if she's going to squeeze his arm but, instead, allows her palm to hover above his skin. "It's not the end yet, Kole. We don't know—"

"Yes, we do!" He turns and sweeps a collection of mugs and ornaments from the coffee table. "It happened. The King returned, and where is she?" His voice is a growl now. A loud, roaring, painful growl. Tanner and Luther grab his arms and wrestle him to the floor. Rev runs to the kitchen and fetches a small bottle of bright blue liquid.

When I reach the door, they are squeezing droplets onto Kole's tongue as he howls in anguish.

Sarah follows me into the hall and down the stairs. At the bottom, in the empty stairwell, she pulls me into a firm embrace. "Please, be careful," she whispers. "If you must go, be careful."

I kiss her forehead. "I will."

Outside, the cold hits me like a sheet of ice. It burns my skin. Funny; I always expected hell to be hot. Turns out, it's the opposite. It scalds in a different way. The way the wind does when it's below freezing.

I shift and stalk down the narrow alleyway between the buildings. The streets reek of sulfur and death. In human form, I can take it. As a wolf, it makes me want to vomit.

When I reach Main Street, I look in The Hollow's direction. The sky there is darker, and redder, and lightning crackles above it even though there is no storm.

Every night, new beasts come. New hellish creatures that I never even dreamed existed. Their energy, and their darkness pulsates beneath the earth telling us there are still more to come.

What happened to Eve and Ragnor, we have no idea.

When *he* came, we ran. We ran as the ground broke, and the sky fell, and evil surged. We ran for the falls, but the split earth stopped us in our tracks.

Rev eventually found us. Everywhere, people were screaming, running, diving into their cars, and getting the fuck out of town. We ran for her place, and it was only when we got there, we realized Mack wasn't with us.

I found his tracks a few days later and I've smelled him on the breeze since then. He's still here in Phoenix Falls. He just doesn't want to be with us.

But we need him.

We need him because none of us knows what the fuck to do next.

* * *

I'm in the woods near the tunnels that lead to Redrock. There was a time when that was the last place in the world I wanted to be. Right now, though, it seems like heaven. An untouchable paradise. Tantalizingly close, but out of reach.

They look enticing, the tunnels—dark, empty. Like it would be so easy to walk through and out the other side and be free.

But on the other side, men with guns, and S.D.B. agents with who-knows-what spells are waiting to take down anyone who dares try to pass the shield. To lock down a whole town, and seal us in, must have taken a truckload of magick. If only they'd listened to Mack and used that magick to help us instead of sitting back and letting us fight this whole fight alone.

I've caught Snow's scent here several times before but, today, there is something else. I move deeper into the undergrowth. By the time I recognize the smell, it's too late.

A Hellhound is in front of me.

Its red eyes blink slowly. Its head is dipped, its teeth showing even though its jaws are closed. I snarl loudly, scratching the ground, waiting for it to come for me.

But it doesn't. It tilts its head and moves a little closer. It sniffs the air. It releases a low grumble in the back of its throat.

Brother...

The word floats through my head. The beast meets my eyes. Then it turns and runs.

18

MACK

Our paws smell of dried blood. For a long time, we forgot how it felt to kill like this. We didn't mean to end up like this but, somehow, stalking the woods to find demons at night has become something of a vocation in the past three weeks.

Perhaps because neither of us knows what else to do. Perhaps because this is the only thing we *can* do that feels like something instead of nothing.

When the ground opened up and hell bled into our dimension, Snow's instinct was to run. Mine was too, but even if the S.D.B. and the Army didn't have the town surrounded, I don't think I could bring myself to leave Nova.

Whatever remains of her, it is here. The same way Layla is here, and my past is here.

I can't leave the memory of Nova because, even though everything is different now, even though the worst happened and our darkest fears came true, this place still carries whispers of her.

We catch them on the breeze when we walk too close to the cabin or in our mind when we're sleeping. We catch them when we veer toward the lake and hear the rush of the falls—not muted, despite what has happened to the town.

We catch them when we remember the caves and the cabin and everything else that happened. But we need to be alone; we learned this after Layla died. The only way we could cope was to be as far away from other people's emotions as possible.

When we think of Nova, the heavy thud of our grief merges with what we felt when Layla left us. We remember our parents wailing and sobbing, and the heartbreak that seeped from their pores for so many years after.

We cannot bear to be around the boys like that. We cannot bear to see Kole so tormented by his craving for blood that he can barely think straight. We cannot bear to see Luther drinking himself into a stupor every night. We cannot bear to see Tanner sleeping all day because being awake is too painful. We also cannot bear to see the glimmer of hope that still flickers in Sam's eyes.

We know this is what's been happening because Rev told us. She found us where she found us the last time, but she promised she wouldn't give us away. She promised, as long as we took care of ourselves and swore we would come back eventually, she would do her best to stop them looking for us.

So far, she has succeeded. Occasionally, we catch Sam's scent, but he's not yet strayed too close to the tunnels. He's sticking to town, to the cabin, and to the lake because he thinks that's where we will go. He thinks we want to be where Nova was. In fact, it's the opposite.

It is easier out here on the edge of town. The only

memory we have of this section of woods is the time we charged through the tunnel on the way to Redrock—when we realized where she was being held and went to rescue her from Ragnor.

Back then, we succeeded. Sadly, when it really counted, we did not.

The demons we have killed have been slow and clumsy—almost like zombies, if zombies existed. Half creatures with broken minds that crave human flesh. But now that the town has been sealed off, they're being driven crazy by their lust for it. They're turning on supers too. The ones that are left, at least.

No doubt The King is hatching a plan. It surprises me that he hasn't already broken the barrier; I believe if he really wanted to, he would have. After all, he is the Devil, and nothing can stop the Devil when he is on Earth.

Last night, we caught a Hellhound. It was easier to kill than we imagined it would be. Having gone several days with no real food—because its brothers and its demon cousins have almost stripped the woods of prey—it was weak and slow. We broke its neck. We might have been tempted to eat it ourselves, because we were ravenously hungry too, but it tasted of acid, ash, and rotting flesh, so we did not.

Something catches our nostrils, the same smell. For a moment, we think we're imagining it, but it grows stronger; another hell beast is in the forest.

We stand slowly and move through the trees. After several weeks alone out here in bear form instead of human form, our white fur is dirty and we are more easily disguised.

We creep up on the hound. It is standing alone in a small clearing, shaking from head to toe. Its head is close to the ground, and it is staring into the bushes ahead as if something is approaching it. Perhaps it is trying to hide itself from its prey—a deer or a rabbit.

Before it has a chance to pounce, we pounce first.

We pin it to the ground with a mighty paw. Our jaws are about to clamp down on its neck when we hear, "Snow, stop. Don't."

We look up. Sam is standing in front of us. He is disheveled, his hair and clothes crumpled, and he's staring at the hellhound with wide eyes.

"It's not a beast," Sam stutters.

We unclench our jaws and sit back. The creature does not move, just presses its belly to the ground.

Sam meets Snow's eyes. "I think it's Nico."

19

EVE

"Ragnor's human pet must be turned." The King's voice slides through me like burned butter. Dark, and smooth, and bitter.

"He won't like it." I look up at the ceiling. It swirls with a dark red cloud. Only I'm not sure if what I'm seeing really is the ceiling or if the roof is no longer there and I'm looking at the sky.

"Do you think I care what Ragnor likes?" The King turns his inky eyes on me. His skin undulates as if an army of a thousand ants live beneath it.

I dip my head as a tingle of excitement runs down my spine. "No, Master." With my chin still pressed to my chest, I ask, "What will she become?"

"It matters not. What matters is that she cannot remain human." He rises from his chair—a throne with beautiful black feathers decorating its back.

As he paces the room, his body catches the muted light

from the window. His skin becomes almost translucent. I can see his veins, his heart, his organs. I can see all of him.

The thud, thud, thud of his heartbeat fills my ears and makes me moisten my lips.

"Bring him to me. Ragnor. He must be told. We have little time."

My eyes widen. I skip to him and bounce on the balls of my feet. I want to touch him. I want to put my hands on his skin *just* so I know what he feels like. "Why, Master? What are you planning?"

Slowly, my king extends a long, gnarled finger and tweaks it beneath my chin. It is razor sharp and draws blood from my neck. It trickles down my throat. He watches it, then licks his lips with a thick, gray tongue. He lowers his head and draws his tongue from my chest up to my chin.

I sigh and rock into his touch.

When he stops, stars are sparkling in my eyes.

"Did you think we would stay in this wretched town forever?" he snarls. "Eve, you and I are going to rule the world. Not just Phoenix Falls. *The World.*"

"But the S.D.B.—"

The King opens his mouth and laughs. A swarm of black flies spring from it and surge up toward the swirling ceiling. He continues to laugh. Thunder rumbles through the sky and rocks the mansion. Lightning crackles. Darkness, and death, and evil vibrate inside me.

"They are children," he says. "Their defenses cannot stop me."

I frown, and he catches it.

Grabbing me hard this time, squeezing my throat so my head becomes fuzzy and my breath shallow. "When the beasts are hungry enough. When my demon kin are so desperate for human blood they are ready to turn on one another; that's when we will break free." He stares into my soul, filling it with daggers of ice. "Not long now, Eve. Not long now."

20

TANNER

Kole is sleeping. The only thing that seems to settle the ache inside him is sleep. Thankfully, Rev and I mixed up a serum that knocks him out pretty fast.

He's in the bedroom, Rev's bedroom, but we left the door ajar.

"You don't trust him?" Luther asks, handing me a mug of coffee. I look at his hand. He's holding a coffee cup too, but his is laced with whiskey.

"When he's like this, I don't think he can trust himself." I look toward the darkening window. Sam has been gone for hours. He snuck out when we were restraining Kole. "It'll be dark soon," I say, turning to glance at Rev.

She nods and moves to the window, pulling down the blinds then dimming the lights. She checks her watch. "We'll give Sam until sunset, but then I'm locking the door," she says.

Ironically, while demons can walk straight through our shields and barriers, they find doors a little trickier.

"If Mack were here, he might know what's different about the S.D.B.'s spell," I say as I wrap my hands around my mug. "The demons can't cross it. They can't get out of town."

Rev looks at Luther, but he shrugs and takes a long sip of his drink. "Don't ask me," he says. "I've been through every spell in my arsenal. Licensed and unlicensed. None of them work. We saw that last night." He rubs his arm. It's still angry and red from where a Farquuze demon tried to claw its way into the building. If Sarah hadn't remembered they hate salt, we'd have all been demon food before the night was out. Sadly for Luther, in order to prevent the wound becoming infected, we had to enact the literal definition of *rubbing salt in the wound*.

"Could Mack have any spells you don't? He was higher up in the Bureau, and he was sheriff," Rev points out.

Luther shoots her a disgruntled stare. "Doubt it," he snaps. "In fact, it wouldn't surprise me if the S.D.B. hadn't turned to their *darker* contacts to create this particular shield."

"You think they're using dark magick?" Sarah asks. She's sitting at the kitchen table, hands knitted together, brow furrowed. Every now and then, she casts a furtive glance at the door in case Sam is about to walk back in.

"I can't see how else they'd be keeping the demons in Phoenix Falls." Luther rubs his palm over his closely shaved head. We're all a little more disheveled than we were a few weeks ago. Not much time for a grooming routine when your town's going to hell in a hand cart.

"Do you think any escaped?" I ask, sitting down opposite Sarah and leaning onto my elbows.

"Oh, I'd say that's a given," Luther replies. "Took the S.D.B. almost twelve hours to get here after The Slice opened. Who knows how many demons escaped in that time."

The Slice is what we've not-so-affectionately named the giant hell-mouth that now splits Phoenix Falls in half. Part gaping crater, part portal to a hell dimension; it burns, blows smoke, groans, and gurgles during the day. And at night, the creatures climb forth.

"We should start keeping a record," Rev suggests. "Of the ones we encounter. Their characteristics. Their weaknesses. Sarah recognized the Farquuze demon, but I've seen ones that are totally alien. If it becomes a case of tracking them down after this—"

Luther cuts Rev off with a loud vicious laugh. "You think there's going to be an *after*?" he says, looking at us over his coffee cup. "The demons are already turning. They might have started off wanting human blood, but they're so hungry now they'll eat anything. So, either we're eaten by demons, or the S.D.B. and the U.S. Army annihilate this place. Bomb us to hell—pardon the pun—and save the rest of the world."

"They wouldn't do that," Sarah says, shaking her head. "Would they?"

Luther shrugs. "Not sure I give a fuck either way." He downs the last of his alcohol-laced coffee then stalks toward the bedroom. "I need to sleep. I'll share with the Viking."

"If he needs to be sedated again—" Rev says, raising her eyebrows.

"I'll give you a call." Luther waves a dismissive hand at her and disappears into the bedroom, closing the door tight behind him.

"Jerk," Rev mutters. "Has he always been so…?"

"Spiky?" I shake my head then push my hair back from my face. "Yep. For a few glorious weeks, when he finally admitted his feelings for Nova, he was different. Happy, almost. Without her…" I trail off. I've been trying to shut out my own feelings and everyone else's. During the day, it's easier. But when night falls, and The Slice purges itself of another enclave of demons, and evil quivers in the air—well, then it becomes impossible. *Then* I feel like I'll go mad. Thoughts that aren't my own haunt me. Fear solidifies in my belly and turns to rust in my veins. Terror scrapes my insides.

Rev is opening the fridge, looking for something—anything—edible when there's a clattering sound in the stairwell.

We rush to the door. I put my arm out and tell Rev and Sarah to stay back. Sarah is holding her wand. Rev's good hand is poised, but her bad hand hangs limp at her side.

"Rev? Tanner?" Feet ascend the stairs. Fists pummel the door. "It's me, it's Sam."

Slowly, I pull back the door. Sam is alone. His face is flushed, and his hands are shaking. Sweat decorates his brow, and his hoodie is stained with it too. "We need your help."

"We?" Rev asks, crossing the room to stand at my side.

"I found Mack," Sam pants. "But I found something else, too."

He beckons for us to follow him. Leaving Sarah in the flat, Rev and I pound down the stairs after Sam. He heaves open the heavy door that leads to the street.

We blink into the hazy red light. Snow is standing in front of us, and he has a Hellhound in his jaws.

* * *

"WHAT THE FUCK?" I breathe as Snow drops the beast to the floor. Instead of running or trying to lash out, it simply lays there like a submissive puppy, breathing heavily.

"Tanner..." Sam grabs my arm. "I think it's Nico. Can you find him? Can you see if he's in there?"

The sun is dipping lower in the sky. I look up and down the street. "Not out here. Bring it into the building."

"Not my apartment," Rev says, shaking her head.

"Just the stairwell," I promise her.

Snow nudges the beast. It staggers to its feet and follows Sam inside. As we watch the scene unfold, Rev meets my eyes. What the hell is happening?

The door closes with a thud. Rev stands on the second step, staring down at the Hellhound. It is sitting on its haunches, its bright red eyes following Sam as he moves. He beckons me over, and I kneel in front of it.

Behind it, Snow takes up almost all the space there is. His fur is dirty, and matted, and there are blood stains on his paws. "Good to see you, buddy," I tell him.

He huffs at me in reply.

The hound reeks. Its smell fills my nostrils and makes me gag. "If it is Nico," I mutter, "he needs a fucking bath."

"Tanner—" Sam's voice brims with desperation.

"Okay," I tell him, squaring up to the beast. Looking into its eyes, I open my mind. A flash of darkness pummels the back of my brain. I see a series of images. None of them makes any sense. I feel pain, and then I hear it. *Sam. Brother. Sam. Saved Sam. Saved brother. Brother lived. Nico died. Brother left. Nico stayed. Brother lived. Nico died.*

The words circle round and round in my head. I grip my temples and fall back onto my heels. Then I reach for the banister and pull myself to my feet. I meet Sam's eyes. He searches my face, his features practically pleading with me for an answer.

"You're right," I whisper. "It's Nico. He's in there."

21

KOLE

I wake groggy. Luther is snoring in the bed next to me, his big sockless feet up near my head.

Fuck knows why he thinks we need to top and tail when we've seen each other naked more times than I can count, and done plenty more than sleep.

He's drunk. He only ever snores when he's consumed enough alcohol to knock him out cold.

For a moment, I'm so distracted by the fact he's drooling onto the quilt that I forget why we're both here in Rev's bedroom instead of back at the cabin, or at the mansion, with Nova.

As her name drops like acid into my head, I groan and sit up. I agreed to Rev's potion. I needed it. I needed not to have to fight The Hunger as well as everything else that's churning inside me.

I don't know if my grief is what's magnifying it or if it's the evil, congealed air around us, or the fact that the sky is laced with Nova's blood.

Whatever is doing it, The Hunger is stronger than it has ever been. Stronger than when I was at the height of my addiction. Stronger than my darkest days in England. The only thing stopping me from losing myself completely is that there are no humans—or dealers—nearby.

I lean onto my knees and breathe heavily. When I stand up and catch my dark reflection in the mirror opposite the bed, I stop and peer at it.

The veins are back. They haven't faded. In fact, they might have grown darker. I pull my hair back and fasten it at the back of my neck, then pull one of Rev's spare guy-sized hoodies over my black tee.

When I emerge in the living room, Sarah is the only one here. I blink into the dim light. She turns and shakes her head. She's holding her wand.

"What's going on?" I ask, clocking the discarded mugs of coffee on the table.

"Sam came back. He said he'd found Mack and that he needed Tanner and Rev to help him." She glances at the clock. "That was a few minutes ago. I heard them in the stairwell, but they haven't come back yet."

"I'll find them." I stride toward the door but, before I reach it, I hear voices.

The door swings open, and Mack strides in. Butt-naked and filthy as fuck.

His beard and hair are longer than I've ever seen them. His skin is carrying a thick layer of dirt. "Professor?" I pull him in for a hug and slap his bare back. "Where the hell have you been, Rhone?"

Hearing his name on my lips, Mack blinks up at me. "We'll discuss it later," he says, pulling out of my embrace. "Right now, we have a bigger problem."

He steps aside to reveal Sam and Tanner. They're backing

into the apartment, waving their arms like they're trying to beckon a frightened cat inside with them.

I step around Mack, and almost fall into the wall when I realize it's not a cat they're trying to coax inside.

I open my mouth to yell but Mack grabs my arm and squeezes it tight. "It's Nico," he says without meeting my eyes "Sam and Tanner believe it's Nico."

Finally, the beast is inside.

Rev follows, skirting toward me, pressed to the wall.

At the table, Sarah slowly stands up and backs away. When she and Rev are standing either side of me, Tanner closes the door.

The huge, salivating, ugly beast stands in Rev's kitchen quivering. It's looking at us like we're the vets on a fucking animal hospital TV show.

Tanner gestures to its foot. "He's hurt."

"I'll fetch some warm water and bandages," Rev murmurs.

"Are you serious?" I boom, and the beast flinches. I try to lower my voice and clear my throat. "Tanner, we can't have that thing here. What are you thinking?"

"It's not a *thing*," Sam says, putting his hand on the Hellhound's flat bony head. "It's Nico."

"I looked into its mind," Tanner says, walking over to me. "I don't know how, but I think Sam's right. I think he made it out when the portal opened."

"And it turned him into one of *those*?" I ask, bracing my hands behind my head and letting my elbows jut out sideways.

"Or The King turned him before the ascension," Mack says, holding out his hand as Rev returns to the room holding both bandages and clothes.

After he's pulled on a customary pair of gray sweats—the ones Rev keeps in stock because he goes through so helldamned many of them—he looks a little more like himself.

He moves to the couch and sits down. I follow him, glancing at where Rev is helping Sam and Tanner bandage the beast's foot.

"You really think that's Nico?" I ask.

Mack looks at me, takes in the veins on my face, and purses his lips. "If Tanner says so," he replies.

"Can he shift? Like a were?"

"I don't know, Kole." Mack rubs his palm over his face. "I found it in the woods. I was going to kill it but Sam told me not to." He glances at the door. "I should go."

"No." I put my hand on his thigh. "You're here now, Baloo. You should stay."

"I don't know if I can, Kole."

"You have to." I swallow hard, then say quietly, "Rhone, we need you. *I* need you. I'm—"

"I know. You're all kinds of fucked up right now, Kole, but so am I. And I don't think I can carry the four of you as well as myself."

"He's seizing!" Tanner yells.

Mack and I jump to our feet. By the time we've crossed the room, the Hellhound is gone.

In its place is the unmistakable body of Nico Varlac.

* * *

NICO DOESN'T SPEAK. The first person he looks at is Rev. She's the one holding a warm cloth and a bandage. He looks at his hand. An angry red gash slices across the center of his palm.

"Nico?" Sam dips his head to meet his brother's eyes. "It's me, Sam."

"Sam returned. Nico stayed." Nico's eyes dart around the room then return to Rev. "Beautiful. Beautiful angel," he mutters.

Rev's forehead twitches, but she doesn't frown at him. She tilts her head, then gently takes his hand, and says, "Can I help you? Is it okay if I help you?"

Nico nods and shudders. He lets Rev lead him to the table and guide him into one of the chairs. His clothes are rags, hanging off him in strips.

Quietly, as she places his hand palm-up on the table and begins to dab the wound, she says, "One of you, go to the bedroom. There are spare clothes in the closet. Take them to the bathroom for him. He'll want a shower and to get freshened up." She looks over her shoulder. "You might, too, Rhone."

Mack doesn't reply. He's studying Nico intently.

"Nico?" Sam tries again, sliding into a seat next to his brother and putting a firm hand on his shoulder. "Do you remember? We were together. You saved me."

"Nico stayed. Sam returned. Nico turned. Sam remained."

Sam looks at Tanner. "He's not making any sense. What's wrong with him?"

"Shock, trauma, maybe more than that," Tanner says softly. "But he remembers you. He found you. Give him a chance to—"

Mid-sentence, Tanner is cut off by a loud clattering sound. Sarah has dropped her wand. She fumbles to pick it up.

When I look back at Nico, he is no longer on his chair; he is cowering beneath the table. Tears stream down his cheeks and he rocks back and forth, hugging his knees. Gently, Rev crouches in front of him. She reaches out her injured hand and shows it to him. "I got hurt, too," she says. "Tanner helped me. Now, you need to let me help you." She meets his eyes. Nico nods, and crawls toward her.

When he's on his feet again, Rev guides him in the direction of the bathroom. "Give us some space for a moment," she says.

"Rev? Are you sure that's a good idea? We don't know what he's capable of." Mack moves in her direction, but she puts up a hand to stop him.

"He's scared. Like the rest of us. He won't hurt me." And then she disappears into the bathroom and closes the door.

Tanner breathes out hard and shakes his arms at his sides. "Well," he says, "looks like the gang is back together." He smiles at Mack, but the professor simply stalks back to the couch and sits down. There's a clinking sound and, instinctively, he pulls one of Luther's hidden whiskey bottles from the floor beneath him. He holds it up, unscrews the cap, and takes a long swig.

"There is no *gang* anymore, Tanner," he says, cradling the bottle. "Nova was the glue that held us together. She's gone. Come morning, I will be too."

22

LUTHER

I feel like I got run over by a freight train. Thinking of trains reminds me of Nova, and then the sensation doubles. I sit up and look at the empty space in the bed next to me. Last night, when I passed out, Kole's Viking-sized body filled it. Now, he is gone.

I toss the sheet to the floor—it's freezing cold no matter how many sheets or blankets we use—and stumble to the window.

No new signs of carnage down below. The bar is in view. Its sign—The Solar Cross—now hangs lopsided, and the windows are boarded up. But Rev is pretty sure she's seen demons going in there.

Wouldn't surprise me if Pete had decided alcohol was his ticket to a demon-friendly existence.

I need to shower. I think the last time I bothered was three or four days ago; getting near the bathroom when you're sharing it with five other people is a rarity. I also need a drink. I'm aware it's getting out of control, but—honestly—I don't care enough to stop.

Why *not* drink myself into oblivion? That's where we're all headed anyway; might as well feel not quite so crappy while we're travelling there.

In the living room, I find Tanner in his customary spot on the couch. Rev and Sarah are, presumably, in her room and... "Mack?" In the armchair, the professor is staring out of the window. He looks over when he hears my voice and rises slowly. "Thank the stars." I pace over and pull him into a firm hug. I slap his back, but he stands stiffly in my arms until I let go.

"Luther," he says.

"You're back? When did this happen?"

"You were sleeping," he says. "Must have passed out pretty hard to have missed all the commotion."

"Commotion?"

Before Mack can answer me, the bathroom door opens. Sam steps out, but he's looking behind him. "Feel better?" he asks.

Who's he talking to? Kole?

I step sideways so I can see, then breathe, "Holy shit," because Nico Fucking Varlac is standing in Rev's bathroom, wrapped in a towel, and looking confused as all heck.

"Turns out, Nico returned from hell just like Sam," Mack says.

"Except, unlike Sam," Tanner has opened his eyes and is slowly sitting up on the couch, "Nico came back as a were-hound."

"A were-what?"

"He doesn't shift into a wolf anymore," Sam says, guiding Nico to the kitchen table like he's a lost child. He glances at me, then adds quietly, "He shifts into a Hellhound."

I lean on the doorframe. The bathroom door is open, and steam billows softly out into the room. It smells of Tanner's over-scented shower gel. I open my mouth, then close it; just when I thought things couldn't get any more screwed up, the one person I had absolutely no desire to see again pops up like a bad penny. A bad penny who can now turn into a frigging hell beast in his spare time.

Abandoning the bathroom idea, I stalk to the kitchen, giving Nico as wide a berth as I can, and slam the kettle onto the stove. "Well, great," I mutter. "No, seriously, this is great."

Sam pats Nico's shoulder and walks over to me. His eyes flash like Mack's do when he's pissed, and he stands with his chest close to mine. "He's my brother, Luther. When it counted, he came through for us. He sacrificed himself for me."

"And that's all very admirable, but you're telling me he's now half-demon and if that's true—"

"It's true. We saw it with our own eyes," Mack says, still not moving from his chair.

"Then, surely, you can see we're playing with fire here?"

"Is that a pun?" Sam asks, looking pointedly at my hands, which have started to smoke as frustration builds inside me.

"No," I tell him. "It's not—"

"Where's Kole?" Tanner's voice makes me look round. He emerges from the bedroom Kole and I shared, and stares at me. "Luther? Where is he?"

"How the hell should I know? He was gone when I woke up."

Tanner pushes the door back to expose the empty bed. "Okay, well, unless he's bunked up with Rev and Sarah, we've got a problem."

"Why a problem?" Finally, Mack gets up.

Tanner shoots him a frustrated stare. "Because since The

Split opened, he's been so hungry for F.H.B. we've been sedating him."

"Sedating him?" Mack looks from Tanner to me.

I nod solemnly. "When it gets too bad and we can't control him, yes. He asked us to."

The kettle starts to whistle, so I pull it from the stove and deposit it in the metal sink. "We should go look for him," I tell Tanner.

Tanner is already pulling his sneakers from beneath the couch. "Mack?" he asks, sitting down to put them on. "You coming?"

There's a long moment of tension, in which Mack simply rubs his overgrown beard. Finally, he says, "Yes, I'm coming."

* * *

OUTSIDE, the air is thick, humid, and metallic. "I didn't realize it was so bad," Mack says as we cross the street.

"You haven't been here," I reply, "why would you?"

He bites the inside of his cheek. "Luther, I couldn't—"

"We'll talk about it another time. Right now, we need to focus on Kole. If he gets his hands on some F.H.B., I'm not sure we'll bring him back this time."

"Not sure he'd want to come back, you mean?" Tanner asks, a grayness filling his usually bright features.

I pull my hood up over my head. No hair means no spending money on shampoo, but it also means being cold as a penguin's ass when the temperature drops.

"Where would a mage who needs an F.H.B. kick go in a town full of demons to get his fix?" I ask, looking up and down the street.

Over the years, Mack and I successfully cleared most dealers out of town, but there are still some less salubrious areas where he could get lucky. "The houses around Mortis

Street are where we busted that gang of French vamps last year," I say to Mack.

He pushes his fingers through his hair. It's crazy long. He looks like a homeless Santa. "Have there been many demons about during the day?"

"Not that we've encountered, although they're getting hungrier. They might start venturing out." I flex my fingers and bring fire into my palm. "We should be ready, just in case."

"Guys, before we go all the way across town," Tanner says, his nose wrinkling as he thinks, "there's somewhere a little closer we should try."

He turns and points up at the wonky Solar Cross signage. "Wouldn't you say Pete is the kind of vamp who'd know where to get F.H.B.?"

"And be willing to supply it," Mack adds.

I nod at them both. "You two go round back, I'll take the front."

As Tanner and Mack move out of view into the parking lot where they can access the rear entrance of the building, I try the front door.

Unsurprisingly, it's not locked. It swings open gently, without a creak, and allows me to pad quietly inside. Pressing myself against the wall just inside the entrance, I strain my ears. There's a clattering sound in the kitchen. Voices are being raised.

Kole. That's Kole.

As I watch from my hiding place, the doors to the kitchen swing violently open and Pete stumbles through them. With force, his back meets the edge of the bar, and he yelps.

Kole is towering in front of him. He grabs a chunk of Pete's hair in his fist, and stares down into his pale, terrified face. "You drugged me, you handed me over to the League, and then you stole my bar right from under me," he hollers. "The least you can do is share your supply."

Pete is wincing. He scratches at Kole's fingers, trying to pry them away from his scalp.

I glance at the door that leads to the hallway past Kole's office. A shadow moves across it. Tanner and Mack are watching too.

"All right," Pete croaks. "All right, I'll share."

Kole releases his grip and stands back. He's breathing heavily and his pupils are twitching strangely. The veins on the side of his neck pulse. He extends his hand and flexes his fingers.

Pete turns and begins to fumble beneath the bar. He pulls out a small wooden box. When he opens it, he takes out a vial. "I found this in your office. It's all I have left. The demons cleared me out of the rest."

"You're selling to demons?" Kole spits, his eyes transfixed on the bottle.

Shrugging, Pete says, "A vamp's got to do what a vamp's got to do."

Kole unscrews the top of the vial.

Pete's tongue darts out to moisten his lips. "Want to share?" he asks. "For old time's sake?"

Kole ignores him. He's about to raise the vial to his mouth when a gust of wind blasts through the bar, knocking it to the floor.

The glass breaks, and the blood spills out.

Kole roars, but Pete has already dropped to the floor and is licking it from the sticky, dirt encrusted floorboards. Kole grabs him by the neck and hurls him across the room.

Mack throws another blast of air at him. It knocks him onto his ass and, before he can get up, Tanner has hurled himself at Kole's chest and is dropping Rev's potion into his mouth.

Kole throws Tanner off, sending him smashing into the side of the bar. By the time Tanner rights himself, Kole is staggering to his feet. Like a drunk giant, he falls into a nearby chair and hangs his head in his hands. "What the fuck am I doing?" he mutters. When he looks up, his eyes are black pools filled with thick, inky tears. "How do I make it stop?"

23

MACK

We leave Pete unconscious in the bar and help Kole back to Rev's. Getting him up the stairs to the apartment is a feat in itself. Six-foot-seven, and floppy from Rev's drugs, it's like moving a tree or a mountain.

When we stumble in the door, Sam and the others are waiting for us. We deposit Kole on the couch and give him coffee to counteract the potion. Tanner opens the freezer, takes out a bag of peas, and holds it to the bruise which is forming on the side of his head.

Standing at the stove, refilling the kettle, Rev's shoulders are shaking. I put my hand on her back and she turns to me with watery eyes. "I hate seeing you all like this," she whispers. "So broken. So sad." She squeezes my arm and looks deep into my face. "You need to let go of Nova. You need to say goodbye to her, properly, or you'll never survive this, Mack."

"We—"

Rev cuts me off, walking to the middle of the room and looking at each of us in turn. "I know you're praying Nova will come back. I know you still want to hope Kole was right, and that she'll walk back into your lives and make all this go away." She waves at the window and the hazy red sky it frames. "I want that too, but you can't live in limbo. You can't exist like this, and she wouldn't want you to." Rev folds her arms and hugs her own waist. "So, please, the five of you, do something. Hold a ceremony. Honor your love for her. *Talk* about her. Then let her go."

Silence descends. Nico looks confused, like he has no clue who Nova is or what we're talking about. Sarah sniffs and wipes her cheeks.

"She's right." Kole is the first to speak. His eyes still strangely wide, he manages to stand and leans on the arm of the couch. "We're broken, and Nova wouldn't want that for us." He sighs a sigh so deep it makes me shudder, and unfastens his hair from its tie. "I don't know if I got it wrong. I want to believe that if we hang on *just* a little longer, she'll come back. But what if it's longer? What if it's a year? Five years? Twenty years? What if, when she does return, there's nothing for her to return to because we've destroyed ourselves." He swallows hard and smooths his hand over his long dark beard. "She survived so much, and she never broke. So, we need to survive this for her."

It's probably the most Kole has ever said, and the effort of it makes him sit down again. He picks up his coffee mug and stares into it but doesn't drink. "We should go to the falls today," he says. "We should honor her like we did when we gave her our rings and pledged our lives to her."

Tanner sits down next to him and puts his arm around Kole's shoulders. He looks up at me and raises his eyebrows. Luther and Sam are looking at me too. Snow growls. Not a growl of anger, but a growl of pain and anguish.

"I agree." I touch the bottom of my throat, the spot where Nova's ring rests against my skin, still hanging on the same pendant I've worn since she disappeared. "I'm not sure I can do what Rev said. I'm not sure I can let go of her. But I can honor her. She deserves that. She doesn't deserve to melt away and leave nothing but pain in her wake. She deserves to be remembered; celebrated."

* * *

WE ARRIVE at the falls just before midday. Sam wasn't sure about leaving Nico with Rev but having him here with us—for this—was not an option.

With the sky so red and sullen, I expected the lake to be the same but, somehow, it remains blue. As if it's reflecting itself, not the sky.

Tanner walks over to it and trails his fingers in the water. "She's warm," he whispers. "Everything else is so cold, but the water is warm."

Luther throws a bundle of fire onto the sand, and we watch it ignite into a large bonfire. He frowns at it, then glances at me. "So's this," he says. "At Rev's, my heat was useless. Here, it feels the way it should." He extends his palms, closing his eyes as the warmth lights his face.

"How are we going to do this?" Sam asks.

Tanner steps forward. He looks at the ring he's holding in his palm. "We could put them in the fire. Scatter the ashes—"

"No," Kole cuts him off. "No fire. I can't sift through her ashes for a second time."

"Water then." Tanner turns and looks out at the lake. "We had nothing but happy times in that lake. We whisper what we want her to know, then throw them into the water. They can rest there together until she returns. If she does—"

"*When* she does," corrects Sam.

"Then I can retrieve them for her. They'll be resting, but not gone."

Snow purrs a little. He likes that. Resting but not gone. "It's a good idea, Tanner," I say.

The others nod.

"Okay then." Tanner pads gently toward the water's edge. We line up beside him, each clutching Nova's rings. One for each mate. One for each finger.

"Not out loud," Luther says gruffly. "Think your thoughts privately. We've shared a lot, but this should be private." He taps his head. "When you're ready, hold out your hand. When we're all ready, we throw them in unison."

The rest of us nod in agreement.

Turning my face to the muted sun, I run my fingers over the smooth wooden circle in my hand. I remember her face when I slipped it onto her finger. I remember how she felt in my arms, how her lips felt against mine, how her body fitted me so perfectly. I remember the first time I saw her, when she was dressed in Kole's sweats. Tired, damp from her shower, but full of a light I'd never seen before.

I will never stop loving you, Little Star.

Snow releases a low-pitched hum.

Neither of us will. We will carry you with us until the end of days.

I keep my eyes closed for a while, breathing slowly, allowing memories of Nova to dance through my head. When I pry them open, I know I'm crying but I don't try to stop. I hold out my hand and wait for the others to do the same.

When we are all ready, Tanner counts for us.

We pull back our arms and throw. The rings arch up into the sky and catch the light. They turn, spinning in the air. I send a gentle breeze to catch them and pull them closer, then Tanner sends a plume of slowly swirling water up to caress them and carry them down to the lake's surface.

They bob for a moment, side-by-side, then they disappear.

* * *

WE STAND for a long time watching the water. Not one of us seems able to turn away. Finally, Tanner looks in the direction of the caves. "Luther? Don't suppose you left some whiskey in there did you?"

"You don't drink, kid," Luther says teasingly.

A calmness has settled over us. Perhaps it's being away from the epicenter of the town. Perhaps it's being close to where we were with Nova. Perhaps Rev was right and all we needed was some kind of ritual to help ease the torment in our souls.

Tanner allows himself to laugh a little. "I don't drink *often*, but we're supposed to be making this a celebration, aren't we? Of Nova's life? Of what she did for us? We can't do that with water."

Luther pats him hard on the shoulder. "Sure, I can rustle something up," he says.

He's part way down the beach, and the rest of us are gathering around the fire, when a small vibration rumbles beneath our feet.

Another joins it, then another.

I turn and look out at the lake. The color of the water has changed. Before, it was surprisingly blue, but now it has become red like the sky.

No, not red... orange.

Not orange... gold.

I run to the water's edge. Luther turns and sprints back

down the beach. Sam is at my side. Kole and Tanner to my left.

The water begins to bubble. Steam rises from the surface up into the cold still air. Then the golden glow at the lake's center starts to swirl. It becomes a whirlpool, moving so fast I can barely keep my eyes on it. Gold seeps from the whirlpool to fill the rest of the lake. It laps our toes but does not stain them.

Silence.

The falls have stopped moving.

There is an almighty rumble beneath our feet. The trees around the lake groan and tremble. Then light blasts out of the water. A beacon so bright we're forced to stagger back, shielding our eyes.

Something hits my chest, hard and flaming hot. When I look down, Nova's ring is back, hanging around my neck as if throwing it into the water was nothing but make-believe. I turn to the others. All four of them are doing the same thing as me—clutching a wooden ring that magickally found its way back to them.

When I look back at the lake, the beacon of light stretches up into the sky. White, and gold, and orange. Then, suddenly, the light dies and the lake becomes still again. Blinking up at the sky, my vision slowly returns.

Something is up there. "A bird," I whisper.

A bird with wings that are bigger and brighter than anything I've ever seen.

"Not just a bird." Sam reaches for my hand. "A phoenix."

24

TANNER

I'm staring at a pair of glowing golden wings—with feathers of fire and an expanse that blots out the sun. Their brightness casts the figure in their midst in shadow but, even so, it does not look like the figure of a bird. To me, it looks like the unmistakable silhouette of a woman.

Our woman.

"Nova," Kole whispers, stumbling forward and dropping to his knees at the water's edge.

Sam is gripping Mack's hand, or Mack is gripping Sam's. Either way, they hold on to each other and stare as the winged creature moves slowly through the air, a tail of fire looping like a firework behind her.

The wings stretch and the phoenix—because it is undoubtedly a phoenix we're staring at—soars higher over the falls. Her glow annihilates the sickening red hue which has tainted the sky since that night at The Hollow.

A small snatch of blue appears. White cloud. Yellow sun. Where a moment ago there was silence, the falls now roar back to life. Hope fills my heart. It's an emotion so strong and so unfamiliar, I don't know whether to laugh or cry. I am on the verge of doing both when the phoenix stops moving. Her wings fold inward. Her light flickers, then she falls.

She plummets into the lake and disappears.

For a long second, I am rooted to the spot. Then I hurtle forward, striding into the water.

I take a deep breath and slice through the surface of the lake. I dive, blinking into her murky depths. Ahead, I see a trail of sparks. I follow them and then I see her, floating but not sinking, and still nothing more than a silhouette in the gloom.

When I reach her, I wrap my arms around her and rocket back to the surface. I daren't look at her. I just loop her arms around my neck, so she's resting on my back, and swim. She holds on. She is warm, and I can feel her breath on my skin.

She's breathing.

I feel like my heart is going to stop. I need to see her face but I'm not sure I'm prepared for what it will do to me to see her again.

I swim faster, desperate to get to the shore. When I reach it, I stop in the shallows and pull her round into my arms. I look down, and there she is.

"Nova..." Her hair is wet and clinging to her face. That face. Her face.

I'm holding her too tightly. I know I am, but she doesn't seem to care. She strokes my jawline and whispers, "Hey, stranger."

The sound of her voice forces a clot of laughter into my throat. Tears spring to my eyes as I press my forehead to hers. "Hey, yourself."

She cups my face in her hands and pulls my lips to hers. Slowly, gently, she runs her tongue along my lower lip then parts my mouth. When she kisses me, she releases a small mewing sound, which is so delightfully quiet it could almost be a sigh instead.

I run my hands down her body. Flickers of electricity meet my palms as they skim her curves.

"You're naked," I tell her when we finally break our kiss, instantly kicking myself because, of all the things I could say right now, I've chosen to be pervy.

Nova doesn't reply. She just scrapes her hands up through my sopping wet hair and smiles at me.

The smile does it. The smile and the fact her boobs are bobbing tantalizingly close to my chest. A pulse of arousal tugs at my balls. I try to ignore it, but flecks of orange flames dance in Nova's eyes and she ducks her hands beneath the water.

"The others..." I can barely speak. Nova is unfastening my jeans.

"Take me to them," she whispers.

25

NOVA

I wake underwater. I can't see or hear. It's dark, and I feel it pressing down on my limbs, but I'm not afraid; I know even the mighty lake cannot pull me under.

I wait, feeling the heartbeat of the falls pulse in my body. Then I feel him—Tanner.

He pulls me into his arms and drags me free. I want to see his face; I *need* to see his face, but he heaves me onto his back and swims like his life depends on it.

On the shore, four stoic figures are watching us. I'd know them anywhere. But they look so broken. Kole is on his knees. Mack and Sam are holding each other up, and Luther is bracing his hands behind his head as if he's watching something he can't bear to look away from.

When we reach the shallows, Tanner stops and pulls me round to face him. If I'd been gone a thousand years, I'd still know every inch of his beautiful face. He stares at me as if he can't believe his eyes.

"Hey, stranger," I whisper, surprised by the sound of my voice.

"Hey, yourself." He is dripping wet, but I know some of the droplets on his cheeks are tears rather than remnants of the lake.

There are so many things I want to say to him; so many things I want to tell him. But words don't seem enough, so I kiss him.

Small, cartwheeling fireworks break out on the surface of my skin the second his lips meet mine. My entire body wakes up. It is alive, and awake, and ready to *feel* again.

"The others," Tanner mutters.

"Take me to them." I meet his eyes.

He smiles a smile that dimples his cheeks, then nods. "Yes, ma'am."

With a flourish, he scoops me into his arms and carries me from the water like a groom carrying his bride over the threshold of their new home.

When we reach the sand, he sets me down gently and stands behind me, hands on my hips as if he can't bear to be physically parted from me.

Kole stumbles to his feet. *Little Star...* his voice fills me up. It surges through me and forces a blissful sigh from my lips.

My Viking.

I take a step toward him, but I don't need to go any further because Kole closes the gap between us in one stride, slams his hands on the sides of my face, and kisses me. The force of his passion almost knocks me off my feet. Our mouths collide. He growls as he kisses me, his hungry hands roaming my body and leaving fire in their wake.

As if he needs my lips more than he needs air to breathe, he nibbles my lower lip then sucks it between his teeth. The sensation makes my knees wobble.

I don't want to stop kissing him, but I need the others too, so I guide Kole's lips away from mine and toward my throat. As he trails torturously slow kisses down my neck, Tanner returns to kiss my shoulders.

Kole clamps his mouth over my nipple. He looks up and meets my eyes, his tongue rolling over my soft pink bud. I nestle my fingers in his hair, which is loose over his shoulders, then realize someone is slowly running their hands up my calves.

I look down to see Mack kneeling at my feet. He lifts my leg, smoothing his palms up and up until his fingers are torturously close to my core.

His fingertips graze the very tops of my inner thighs, then slide back down.

Leaning forward, while Kole continues to suck and nibble and lap at my breasts, Mack kisses the side of my knee. He swirls his tongue over my sensitive skin, then grazes me with his teeth. Tongue, teeth, tongue, teeth. A rhythm that reverberates up through my body and turns into electricity.

Tanner is kneeling too now. He cups my ass, then smooths his hands over my hips. He parts my legs a little, but neither he nor Mack will touch my aching pussy.

I search for Luther and Sam. They are watching, eyes dancing over the scene in front of them like they're desperate to join us but waiting for an invitation.

I open my arms and beckon them to me. I kiss Sam first, then Luther.

Luther dips his head next to Kole's, and the two of them work on my breasts in tandem. They exchange a look that sends a shiver of arousal down my spine; I've never seen them look at each other like that before.

Still on his knees for me, Mack's finger trails between my legs. I rock into it, then turn to Sam and tousle his thick, curly hair.

"I knew you'd come back," he whispers before kissing me

deeply. I'm looping my arms around his neck when I feel a second pair of lips join ours. I open my eyes to see Tanner and Sam pressing their lips together. I add mine to theirs, and the three of us explore each other's mouths and tongues.

"Little Star…" Mack's voice draws my eyes downward.

"Yes, Daddy," I breathe, taking in his too-long hair and too-long beard, and wishing he was wearing a lot fewer clothes.

"I'm going to make you come now. You might want to sit down."

The familiar strength in his voice makes me ache with arousal. My core flutters. Heat pools at the tops of my thighs, sending shocks skittering down my legs and into my toes.

As I sink to the ground, Tanner moves behind me. I kneel in front of Mack and stroke his disheveled beard. "I missed you, Daddy," I whisper.

"First, I'm going to make you see stars," he whispers back. "Then I'm going to spend the rest of my life making you understand how much I love you."

When he catches my eyes and his emotion mixes with his desire, flickering amber and black at the same time, I smile and kiss the bridge of his nose. The ring he gave me hangs on a piece of blue string around his neck. As I look at the others, I realize they are all wearing the same necklace. Kole couldn't rescue me, but he rescued what was left so they could keep me close while I was gone.

Mack sweeps my damp hair from my shoulders then nods at Tanner. "Lay back. Tanner will make you comfortable."

I do as he says. I relax into Tanner's arms, then slide down so my head is resting on his thigh.

As Mack's tongue meets my clit, a cry of pleasure escapes my lips. With my mouth open, Tanner dips his finger into it.

I swirl my tongue around him, aware his erection is growing harder as he finger-fucks my mouth.

"Your mouth looks lonely," I tell him, moving his hands to my breasts.

Tanner's eyes sparkle. He searches for Sam and beckons him closer, barely hesitating before pulling Sam's pants to the ground.

As Sam takes off his hoodie and shirt, Luther and Kole do the same. Pants too. Fully naked, they kneel either side of me. I reach for their cocks. One in each hand.

Sam mutters, "Holy stars," then grabs the back of Tanner's head and thrusts into his mouth.

I lean back, watching them.

Tanner attacks Sam's dick hungrily. He runs his tongue along Sam's shaft, licking the vein that runs from its base to just beneath the head. He takes Sam's entire length in his mouth, then uses one hand to gently tug his balls and the other to pull him closer.

I hum with pleasure as Kole puts his large, firm hand around my neck, making me tear my gaze from Tanner and Sam to look at him instead.

He doesn't squeeze, just rests it there on my throat. The pressure drives me wild. I grind my hips and press into Mack's waiting mouth.

As Mack swirls his tongue in exquisite circles over my clit, I try to keep a rhythm with my hands; Kole in one, Luther in the other, both so different, but equally hard.

While Kole is so thick my fingers barely meet around him, Luther is long and slender and deliciously decorated.

The cool metal of his piercings meets my fiery palm. I've felt them inside me, but it was too long ago. I need him again.

"Luther, fuck me." I meet his eyes and slide my hand up

his torso. I pinch his nipple between my thumb and forefinger, and his eyes roll with pleasure.

He looks at Mack, who is already changing position so that Luther can take his place between my legs.

I bend my knees and hook them around Luther's waist. He reaches down and gathers some of my wetness on his fingers, then rubs it over his shaft until it is glistening and ready to be inside me.

He moves his thumb slowly over the piercing at the top of his dick, then he holds the base and guides his tip to my waiting cunt.

Never breaking his gaze from mine, Luther eases into me. He adjusts my hips and his until my eyes widen. Then he smiles, knowing he's found the spot he was looking for.

While Luther looks down at me, biting his lower lip as if he's already struggling to contain his arousal, there's a guttural cry from somewhere behind me. I look up and see Sam gripping the back of Tanner's head. His orgasm looks almost painful, causing him to jerk and shudder as he shoots ropes of cum into Tanner's mouth.

Tanner is about to let it dribble out of his mouth onto his chin when Kole says, "Stop."

Tanner frowns at him, his lips almost comically pressed shut. Kole pulls free from my grasp and stands up.

"She needs to be filled completely," he growls, looking down at me. "Like we promised she would be."

I groan as Luther changes his rhythm and clasp my thighs tighter around him.

"Flip her over," he says to Luther.

Mack raises an eyebrow. His jaw twitches as he watches Luther slow down, panting.

Without nodding or asking why, Luther does as Kole says. I moan as his cock leaves me, but barely have time to think about how empty I feel because Mack is helping me to my feet—like he's helping a princess into a carriage—and Luther is lying down on his back in the sand.

Holding my hand, Mack helps me lower myself back onto Luther's cock. I sigh and rock as it fills me up once again.

"Lean forward," Mack says, "give Luther your nipples."

I follow his instructions and lean all the way forward. Luther lifts his head, then cups my breast and brings it to his mouth. Mack kneels beside us.

"Did you miss us, Little Star?" he whispers, stroking my hair from my face.

I can barely speak. Waves of pleasure are building deep in my core. I nod breathlessly as I move up and down on Luther's throbbing erection.

"Do you want us to fill you up?" Mack meets my eyes.

I feel Kole's hands on my ass. He is stroking my cheeks, stretching them... a shudder of anticipation trickles down my spine. I manage to say, "Yes, please," and then I feel something...

I look over my shoulder to see Tanner dribbling Sam's cum into the groove of my ass. Wiping his mouth, he grins. Holy stars, he's going to use Sam's cum to...

Kole spreads my cheeks. Tanner's finger traces my tight hole with gentle strokes.

"Have you ever...?" Luther asks, stroking my face as he rocks up into my pussy.

I shake my head, both terrified and desperate to be filled —truly filled—by two of my boyfriends at the same time.

"Tanner will be gentle," Mack murmurs, kissing my neck and sliding his hand between me and Luther so he can play with my clit.

The position looks awkward as fuck for his arm, but it feels so good I can't find it in myself to stop him. I press down onto Mack's hand, Luther still deep inside me.

"I'm ready," I breathe, wriggling my ass a little.

"Not quite yet," Tanner replies softly. "I want to make sure you're okay." He dips his head and kisses my shoulder, then slowly pushes one finger into my tight, primed hole.

At first, I tense, but as he eases deeper and Mack increases the pressure on my clit, I feel myself start to relax.

"Good girl," Mack hums. "Ready for another?"

I nod, bracing my hands on the sand either side of Luther's shoulders.

With Kole still parting my cheeks for Tanner, Sam kneels on the other side of me and gently kisses my back.

Tanner pushes a second finger inside me. I mutter, "Fuck," and warmth scrapes my insides. "Fuck me, Tanner." I need to come so badly I feel like I'm going to explode, but I can't. Not until he and Luther are both inside me at the same time.

"Please," I whisper. "Please, Tanner."

As if he's trying to sooth me, Mack strokes my face, but I reach for his pants and pull them down. He's taken his hand from my pussy, but I don't care. Sam's replaces it. As Mack's cock springs free, Sam begins to strum my clit.

Luther stops fucking me. He lies perfectly still, hands braced on my hips.

At the exact moment I take Mack in my mouth and start to suck, Tanner finally does it. He replaces his fingers with his cock, and it feels so different. It's hot, and tight, and like I'm going to break wide open, but then the sensation changes into something else. A fullness I've never felt before. A warmth that makes me giddy.

Slowly and gently, Tanner fucks my ass while Luther thrusts up into my pussy.

They take a moment to find their rhythm but, holy stars, when they do, I can barely see straight.

26

KOLE

Nova is sitting on Luther's cock. Sam is playing with her clit, almost having his hand crushed every time she grinds down onto it, and Mack is thrusting into her waiting mouth. He's doing it slowly, trying to delay his inevitable orgasm. Now and then, he glances down at Sam and another groan escapes his lips.

I position myself behind Tanner. He's kneeling on one leg, his cock buried in Nova's ass. I reach beneath him and tug his balls. It makes him jerk forward, but then he looks back at me and says, "What are you waiting for, Sir?"

It feels like it's been a lifetime since he called me that. After Nova appeared in our lives, it didn't feel like something we needed anymore, but this? This feels right.

Me fucking him while he fucks *her*? I know for a fact we've both dreamed about that.

I don't lube up, just spit on Tanner's ass, and make sure I'm extra gentle as I ease into him.

I match the rhythm he's using to fuck Nova and growl in his ear, "Make her come for me. Make our Little Star come."

Tanner tightens his hold on Nova's hips, his fingers dimpling her perfect ass.

Sparks start to flutter on her skin. The sky is darkening, and the evidence of her arousal drifts up into the grayness like fireflies.

For just a split second, she takes Mack out of her mouth so she can murmur, "Come for me, Daddy." Then she plunges it back onto him.

He grabs her head, gripping it tight. He holds her mouth still and his entire body convulses. Nova hums with pleasure as his cum drips from her mouth. She's about to wipe it from her chin when Sam sits up, hand still between her legs, and licks it from her.

Mack's eyes widen, so do Nova's.

Sam licks every inch of the professor's cum from Nova's lips, then kisses her deeply.

Breathless, she mutters, "Holy hell," and pulls Luther's hands to her nipples. Her skin is flushed. Her entire body is blushing and glowing.

Hunger pulses in my ears, but when I feel Tanner tense around my cock, and realize he's coming in Nova's most private place, the Hunger disappears. It's replaced with something else—a rumbling, thunderous orgasm.

I want to wait for Nova, but I can't. As Tanner slides out of her, I pull him back onto my shaft. I wrap my arms around his torso and hold him tight against me as I come.

My body trembling, unable to move, I hold Tanner against my chest while we watch Sam and Luther finally bring Nova to the precipice of her climax.

She cries out, pulling Luther into a sitting position so she can kiss him.

Sam takes his hand away and watches as Nova wraps her

arms around Luther's neck and her legs around his waist. She clings to him as if she's lost at sea and he's her lifeboat.

Luther comes quietly, holding her tight, then slips his hand between them and teases her orgasm free. He stares at her as she shudders, every inch of her body trembling.

When she goes limp in his arms, he kisses the groove between her shoulder and her neck, then her ear, then her forehead.

Heat comes off the pair of them in waves. It shakes the air around them and warms the sand beneath my knees.

When Nova finally raises her head from Luther's shoulder, she looks around at the rest of us, then starts to laugh. She shakes her head, so her hair cascades down her back, then says, "Well, boys, it looks like I'm finally back."

27

NOVA

Mack pulls me into his arms with such force I'm almost certain he's ready for round two. Instead, he just wraps his arms around me—a literal bear hug—and I hear a familiar animalistic growl as he kisses my neck.

His body relaxes as I curve into it, but he's still holding me tight. "Little Star," he whispers. "You're so warm."

I look down at my body, flushed and peppered with the indentations of fingers and mouths and teeth that tell the story of what the six of us just did together. There was a time when I'd have been embarrassed to be lying here like this; exposed and vulnerable. But now all I feel is pride and contentment.

"Everything is how it was supposed to be," I murmur, slotting my fingers between Mack's. "I missed you, Daddy."

Mack breathes out forcefully. I turn my face up to look at him and toy with his unruly beard. His eyes look watery.

"Are you okay?"

"We missed you too." Sam has pulled on his pants and is crouched next to me with his hand on my knee. "It's been hard."

Kole leans over and offers me his hoodie. I sit up to pull it on, then tuck it under my butt so it comes down to the middle of my thighs.

Assessing their faces, my contentment wavers a little. They are different, somehow. Like sadness is tainting their smiles, breaking through the happiness. Sitting up, I rub my shins.

"How long has it been?" I look from Kole to Luther. Just behind them, Tanner is standing at the water's edge, breathing slowly, and staring out at the middle of the lake. "Kole, how long was I gone?"

Kole's eyes dart almost imperceptibly toward the sky. I follow them and immediately spring to my feet. It is red... blood-red. There is a snatch of blue just above the lake, but the redness is seeping toward it. Large, heavy, blood-swollen clouds moving in to obscure the sun.

"A little over three weeks," Kole replies.

The others are all dressed now. Mack rubs his beard and pats Sam's shoulder. "A lot happened while you were gone, Nova."

"I can see that." I tilt my head and turn in a slow circle. As the lightness and joy of our reunion settles, reality creeps back in and I notice it—darkness, death, oblivion—quivering in the air. I breathe out slowly and shake my head.

Kole takes my hands, stroking the insides of my wrists. *It happened.* As he stares into my eyes, his voice fills my head. *He returned. Without you, we couldn't stop him.*

A sad smile twitches on my lips. "I know." I bring his knuckles to my mouth and kiss them. "I'm sorry I couldn't come back sooner."

"You know?" Luther finally speaks. He's been watching

me as if he can't quite believe I'm real, but now he's frowning.

The familiar grumpy expression on his face makes me laugh at him. "Yes, I know, Luther."

"How? Where were you, Nova?" He takes a step forward then stops and gestures to the sky. "What was that? We saw… wings."

"I'll explain everything," I promise him. "But it won't be long now until the sun sets. We should leave the lake before night fall."

Over by the water, Tanner still hasn't turned to look at me. I let go of Kole's hand and walk to him. Gently, I wrap my hands around his waist and press my cheek to his muscular back. "It's going to be okay," I tell him. "I'm back. Everything will be okay."

Tanner presses his palm to the top of my hands. He lets it rest there for a moment, then finally turns around and cups my face.

"It's all right," I tell him. "You can check."

"Check what?" Luther looks like he's going to try to separate us.

I keep Tanner's gaze as I answer. "Tanner needs to check that I'm *me*. That I didn't bring something back with me like Sam did."

"Of course, it's *her*." Luther tugs Tanner's arm, but he keeps a gentle hold on my face.

"We need to be certain," Tanner says quietly, his eyes swimming with emotion; his, mine, Luther's.

Sensing that Luther's about to try a second time to pull Tanner away from me, I blink, and a circle of flames envelops us. Luther jumps back.

"It's okay," I tell Tanner. "I'll let you in. I won't resist."

He nods at me, then presses his forehead to mine and moves his fingertips to my temples. He presses hard against my skull. He mutters the incantation he used when he did this exact same thing with Sam. As I close my eyes, Tanner's presence trickles into my mind. It's a strange sensation, and it makes me wonder if this is what it's like for Mack to have Snow inside his head with him. Tanner searches every corner of my mind, and I let him.

I show him everything.

When he breaks contact and stumbles back, he's panting. His eyes are wide, but his pupils are tiny, and his irises are twice their normal size. Twice as bright, too. "Nova..." he breathes.

I let the flames die down. The others are gathered around us in a circle.

"Well?" Luther asks, grabbing Tanner's elbow.

For a moment, Tanner is lost for words. I smile at him, trying to show that he can be happy now.

"Tanner?" Luther pulls his arm, forcing Tanner to look at him.

"It's her," Tanner says, still not taking his eyes from me. "It's our Nova."

Luther's body remains tense for less than a second before he lets Tanner go, grabs me by the waist, and spins me around. When he lowers me to the ground and winds his fingers into the hair at the back of my neck, he mutters, "Supernova," then takes a strand of my hair between his fingers. It's damp and peppered with tiny grains of sand from the beach. "Let me dry you off," he says. "Can't have you catching a cold."

With a wave of his hand, my hair is dry. Still carrying too much sand, and hanging in scruffy waves around my shoulders, but dry and warm.

"Your hair," Luther whispers. He looks at the others, then back at me. "It's not silver anymore. It's bright like copper."

I smile at him and tilt my head, then reply, "Of course it is. Whoever heard of a silver phoenix?"

28

SAM

While Luther runs to the cave to fetch the clothes Nova left there, the rest of us stand in awed silence. I have so many questions I don't know which one to ask first. She's the same, but also different. There is something about the way she's speaking and carrying herself, as if she's now the one who knows—without a shadow of doubt—that everything will be okay.

"This is how I remember you," I whisper, kissing the crown of her head. "With your hair like this. When we were kids."

She tucks herself under my chin and rests her head on my chest. "Thank you," she says. When I frown, she adds, "for always believing you'd see me again."

I don't know if she's talking about the years we were separated or what's happened over the last few weeks. I assume it's the first because how could she possibly know what happened while she was gone?

"Here." Luther is carrying the pack Nova brought when

153

we left the cabin for the caves. "There are some pants in there." He hands it to her. "Although, I quite like the no-pants version of you, if I'm honest."

"Probably best if my modesty is covered when we arrive at Rev's, though." She fishes out her jeans and shimmies them over her rounded hips.

"How does she know we've been staying with Rev?" Luther mutters under his breath.

"That's a conversation for when we're safe inside." Nova raises her eyebrows as she slings the pack over her shoulder.

She shouldn't have been able to hear that. Should she?

Luther and I exchange a quizzical look.

"I'm missing shoes." Nova looks at her bare feet. "Never mind." She waves at us, already starting toward the forest. "We should move. I can protect us if I have to, but it's best if *he* doesn't know I'm back. Not yet."

* * *

WE'RE APPROACHING Main Street when Nova stops. She holds out her arms, causing Kole and Mack to bump into them. Tucking her hair behind her left ear, she says, "Did you hear that?"

Both men look at each other. I sniff the air. I can't smell anything. Mack is doing the same.

Slowly, Nova pivots on her heel and scans the alleyway. We're in the cut through between the grocery store and Elements Cafe. A few doors down from Rev's and opposite The Solar Cross.

Nova beckons for us to follow her and moves quietly toward the end of the alley. The red sky is growing darker. For three weeks, there have been no stars, only blackness when night falls.

Nova stops, pressing herself against the wall, then glances each way down the street.

"It's deserted," Mack says. "There's no one here."

But Nova is frowning. I follow her gaze to The Cross. "Someone needs our help," she mutters. Then, so quickly I barely see her move, she's gone. She's in the middle of the street, then on the sidewalk on the other side.

The five of us follow her, but we're slower than she is. By the time we've reached The Cross, Nova has gone inside.

The bar is empty. Nova is standing in the middle of the room, her eyes flicking quickly over its corners and crevices.

"Nova?" Luther puts a firm hand on her shoulder. "There's no one here."

She walks away from him without speaking.

She's heading for a red curtain on the opposite side of the bar. Kole follows her while the rest of us wait. As Nova tucks her hand inside the curtain and moves it aside, I catch something in the air. Mack does too. "Demon," we mutter in unison.

At the same time, we both run for Nova, but she's already pulling back the curtain and standing aside to let Kole unlock the door. With a wave of his hand—clearly, Pete was too dumb to get the locks changed—the door clunks open. Kole heaves it back.

At first, I'm not sure what I'm seeing. It doesn't make sense inside my head. But when Nova screams, "Leave her alone!" I realize I'm watching a demon *feeding* on a human.

The girl, who can't be much older than eighteen, is lying motionless in a wooden chair. Her arms hang limp at her sides. Blood drips from her throat, and large flaps of skin expose the muscle and bone beneath them.

Nausea springs to my throat.

The demon, who has horns—fucking *horns*—and the same stretched gray skin as the Hellhounds, licks its lips. It lifts a curled fingernail and picks a sliver of flesh from its teeth, then says something I don't understand.

Next to Nova, Kole is shaking. Black veins are visible on his hands and his neck. Luther and Mack pull him back while Tanner yells, "Nova, run."

Without looking at him, Nova flicks her fingers in the direction of the door and all four of us skid toward it like we're moving through butter. When I try to run back into the room, an invisible barrier at the door stops me. We are stuck outside, and Nova is inside. With a flesh-eating demon.

29

NOVA

I stand with my legs hip-width apart and flex my fingers at my sides. My mates' energy comes in protective waves from behind me, but I push it back.

They need to see this, but they do *not* need to be part of it.

"Is she dead?" I ask. The tongue I'm using is not from the human realm. It is something else, something long buried. I don't know how I possess it, only that I *do* possess it.

The demon assesses me. It thrusts out its pelvis and squares its broad but jagged shoulders in a gesture of attempted dominance. "I paid for one hour with a human," it says, tilting its head. "But I think I'd like an hour with you instead." It steps closer. In the chair, the girl's eyes flicker open. She is conscious, but only just. "What are you?" the demon barks. "You smell... not human, not witch, not vampire." It licks its salivating lips. "What are you?"

"I'm the one who's going to kill you." This time, I speak English. The demon cocks its head the other way, trying to interpret what I've said. Its right foot leaves the ground, just by a few millimeters.

Before it has even taken one full step, I have it in my grasp. My magick lifts it into the air like it's suspended in ice.

It cannot move. The elements will not let it.

I leave it there while I walk over to the girl, lift her out of the chair, then pass her through the barrier to Tanner. Holding her in his arms, he looks at Kole. Mack and Luther are restraining him, but I know he won't hurt her. *You don't need her, my Viking. You have me.*

Kole's eyes soften and the black veins subside as my voice fills him up. When I turn around, the demon is still hovering above the floor. "I almost forgot." I click my fingers. At the same moment his body drops, it explodes from the inside out.

Chunks of demon flesh splatter the walls and the floor. Blood, cords of sinew, and broken bones congeal in a heap. I release a loud sigh as the reverberation of my magick hums beneath my skin. Then I turn to the girl.

"She's breathing, but only just," Tanner says. He meets my eyes. "We won't make it to the hospital before nightfall."

I shake my head and hold out my arms, taking her from him. "You won't, but I will."

Then I run.

* * *

TRAVELING like this is a little like flying. My feet barely touch the ground. I move through the air as if its laws don't apply to me anymore, as if I can manipulate it to do as I please. It parts with ease, allowing me to cover the distance between the bar and the hospital in less than a few short minutes.

I don't stop, just leave her at the door then turn back to town.

The boys are outside the door of Rev's apartment when I appear in front of them. I'm covered in the girl's blood, so take off Kole's hoodie and burn it. It disintegrates in my hand in an instant. I pull a t-shirt from my pack and jerk it over my head.

The others are watching me as if they can't trust what they're seeing. I've freaked them out, shown them too much too soon.

"Little Star, what are you?" Mack tucks my hair behind my ear. "What *are* you?"

"Oh, come on, Professor. You know the answer to that already." I stroke his beard, then reach up on my toes to kiss his cheek. "But we should discuss it inside. Now they know I'm back, they'll be coming for me."

"Ragnor and Eve?" Mack's eyes haven't left mine.

"All of them," I say quietly. In the distance, I hear them. The rumblings, and the groanings, and the teeth, and the claws. "Quickly. Inside. I'll put up a barrier."

"It won't work." Luther takes my elbow as the others hurry inside. "I tried every spell I knew plus a few extra."

A smile curves my lips. Luther notices and frowns at me. "What's so funny?"

"You haven't got it yet, have you?"

He moves toward the door as I turn to face the street. "Got what?"

"I'm don't play by the same rules as you anymore, Luther." I slip my hand into his and give it a quick squeeze, then nudge him into the doorway of Rev's apartment. Magick hums in my veins as I raise my eyes skyward. The earth hums beneath my feet, too. The vibrations travel up through my limbs and pool in my belly.

A strong breeze blows down the street, taking leaves and

litter with it. My hair flies across my face as splinters of lightning crackle down from the starless sky to meet my fingertips.

I catch the lightning in my palm, then use it to trace an arch on the ground in front of the building. It glows bright as fire. A wall of light rises from it, forming a pale glittering shield.

I step inside the building and close the door behind me. In the gloomy stairwell, my boyfriends are staring at me. "It should be enough to repel the demons. They're still weak."

"Nova..." Sam looks at Mack, then at me. "How do you know all this?"

"I'll explain, I promise. But first, I'm starving. Anyone fancy making me pancakes?"

30

MACK

S he's back. Snow can barely contain the urge to be near her. His energy throbs inside my head; growling, protective, but also desperate for her attention—like a puppy whose owner abandoned it for a summer vacation and now needs extra levels of attention from them.

She's back, and she's Nova, but she's different. She looks the same, apart from her hair, and she sounds the same. She *feels* the same—every inch of her—but there's a power inside her now that wasn't there before. A light. A magick. A strength.

Upstairs, Nova taps on Rev's door and grins when Rev yelps and grabs her for a fierce hug. Pulling her inside, she strokes Nova's arms and her hair, unable to stop staring at her. I wonder if we looked like that when she appeared on the beach, Tanner carrying her out of the water like a mage lifeguard in a smutty movie.

I wonder if we looked as in awe of her as Rev does or if

our lust took over and we just looked like a bunch of super-aroused men whose girlfriend rose naked from the beyond.

Awe is the word.

I am in awe of her.

She is so beautiful; I swear she's making the air around her shiver.

"Where did you come from?" Rev asks, sitting down hard in a chair at the kitchen table. Sarah is nowhere to be seen. Catching me scanning the room, Rev says quickly, "Sarah's sleeping. I gave her a tincture. She's been having nightmares."

I nod in response, then move to the stove and put the kettle on to boil. I'm functioning on autopilot. Nothing seems like the appropriate thing to be doing because the only thing I *want* to be doing is taking Nova to the bedroom and peeling her clothes off.

Despite everything that happened on the beach, I'm not satiated. I need her to know how broken I was when she was gone. I need to show her the dark places I went to when I thought I'd lost her forever. Because if it happens again, I can't be left with regrets. I can't be left wondering why I didn't tell her, every second I was with her, how much she meant to me.

Nova doesn't sit down. She stands in the middle of the room and holds court with us gathered around her.

When Sam came back from The Shadow King's dimension, he was wide-eyed and traumatized. Nico, too, has been a quivering wreck. But Nova looks like she's been on vacation to paradise island; she's practically glowing. In fact, as Rev closes the curtains on the outside world and dims the lights, I realize Nova *is* glowing. Her skin glimmers and glistens when she moves.

The five of us watch her, transfixed.

"We have a lot to do, and not much time to do it in," she says, her smile stiffening into a more serious line.

The kettle boils, and Tanner removes it to stop the persistent whistle.

"Doesn't sound normal for us at all," Luther grumbles sarcastically.

Nova smiles at him, wrapping her arms around her middle. She rocks on the balls of her feet. "I know you have a lot of questions, and I'll answer them, but first there are things that must be set in motion."

Sam opens his mouth to speak but Nova gives him a small shake of the head and he stops, waiting for her to continue.

"The King is planning to break free from the S.D.B.'s shield. You probably guessed that already; if he wanted to leave Phoenix Falls, he would have."

Instead of asking how she knows this, I ask, "Why wait?"

"The demons..." Rev is still by the window, twitching the curtain to look down at the street below. "They're getting hungrier."

Nova nods slowly. "My guess is they ran out of humans a week ago, maybe longer. They'll start turning on supers, but it's not enough. They need human blood. Feeding on their own kind doesn't satisfy them." She glances at Kole. A shadow of guilt falls over his face. He has often referred to The Hunger as a demon living inside him. Perhaps that was a more accurate description that he realized.

"So, The King's waiting until they're good and hungry, then he's going to set them free," Luther says, sitting down hard in a chair at the kitchen table.

Nova slides into his lap and presses her palm to his chest, as if she's trying to feel his heart beating. His eyes soften, and he sweeps her hair from her neck to kiss her just below her ear.

"We need to warn the S.D.B." Nova meets my eyes. "They need to be prepared in case we fail. Can you reach Annalise?"

"I can try, but—"

"They won't send help," she says quickly. "They're too afraid. They'll try to reinforce the barrier, maybe gather some more soldiers with bigger weapons and darker spells. But at least we'll have warned them."

"What's the point if they're not going to help us?" Tanner is making coffee. Like the rest of us, he can hardly keep his eyes off Nova and curses as he spills boiling water on his hand.

Leaving Luther's lap, Nova walks over to him and kisses his scalded flesh. Then she blows on it; a cool mist settles on his skin and the pinkness disappears. Tanner rubs his hand, staring at it with total confusion on his face.

"First thing tomorrow, Mack, reach out to Annalise." I accept a cup of coffee from Tanner and nod in agreement; Annalise leaked Nova's blood tests for us, she'll at least listen to what I have to say.

"While Mack's doing that, the rest of us need to gather the town." Nova looks around the room. "Who has a phone?"

Luther takes his from his pocket, and she nods.

"Good. Open your profile and start a live recording. Tell everyone in Phoenix Falls to meet at sunrise in the square."

"Nova…"

"How many supers live in this town?" Her forehead twitches as she waits for him to answer her.

"Two thousand, give or take, but a lot left when The Split opened. Before the S.D.B. locked us down."

"Even if there are only five hundred left, it's a start."

"A start of what?" Sam asks. He's standing just behind me, sounding more tense and uneasy than he did *before* Nova returned. Perhaps it's because it's all happening too quickly. Perhaps, like the rest of us, he's freaked out because she can move at the speed of light, heal wounds, and explode demons with a flick of her wrist.

Nova's lips twitch into a smile. "It's the start of our army, Sam. It's the start of us *winning* this fight."

31

NOVA

Instead of arguing with me, my beautiful men do as I've asked. Luther records his message, being sure to remind everyone that he was once the deputy of the town. Probably because he looks less than respectable right now with his overgrown facial hair, Mack doesn't make an appearance.

When it's done, Rev asks if I'm hungry and starts rustling in her fridge for something she can turn into a meal.

"Starving," I tell her. "And I've been craving pancakes.

Rev frowns at me, but doesn't ask why, just takes eggs and milk from the fridge and sets them on the counter.

As she starts to cook, I turn to Sam. "Where's Nico?"

His mouth drops open a little. "Nico?"

"I can sense him." I take a sip of coffee, but the taste is bitter on my tongue, so I put the cup down. "Is he resting?"

Rev is the one who answers. "He's asleep. He's still very shaken."

"Nova, how do you…?" Kole's deep, wonderful voice soaks into my skin like summer rain in a thunderstorm.

Moving to the couch, I gesture for him to sit down so I can tuck myself into his arms. On his lap, I lean into his chest and sigh as his heartbeat fills my ears. "I don't know where I was." I speak quietly, but they're all listening. "All I know is I wasn't *me* anymore." I look up at Kole and stroke his face. His beard is longer but the ink that swirls beneath it, down his throat to his chest, is the same. I know it by heart. "I remember you waiting for me. I knew you were there. Even when the pain blinded me, I knew you were with me."

Kole closes his eyes and presses his forehead to mine.

"It's hard to explain, but I never *wasn't* there. I didn't see what was happening, but I knew what was happening. I had no physical form, but I was still me. Time moved slowly but so quickly at the same time, and everything was warm. Warm and bright and safe.

I sit up a little and look at the others. "I might have stayed if I hadn't felt your pain. All of you." I press my hand to my heart and bite back the knot of tears forming in my throat. "I felt your sadness, and your longing, and your anguish, and it made the warmth colder. I tried to return to you, but I didn't know how, and then when you gathered at the lake, something happened." I frown and pinch the bridge of my nose, trying to recall the sensations and images that filled my head. "I saw it all, and I knew it was time to come back."

There is a quivering silence. Rev is standing stock-still, the fridge door wide open. It beeps at her. She slams it shut and sucks in a shaky breath. "Holy stars, Nova. You died. You died and came back."

I inhale deeply then grin at her and wriggle my fingers and toes. "I sure did, and I know how to free us. I know how to end this, once and for all. So, can we stop being so melancholy now and celebrate?" I kiss Kole playfully on the lips and, despite his instinct to remain stoic and sullen, he allows himself to smile.

"What about the demons? You said they know you're here." Mack points to the window. "Will they come?"

"They will. They'll have sensed my magick." I twitch my nose from side to side. "I probably shouldn't have Johnny'd that guy from the bar, but he really did piss me off." I climb free from Kole's lap and brace my hands in the small of my back. "They won't get past the barrier I made. Not tonight."

"And The Shadow King?" Kole stands up and folds his arms. It makes his biceps look deliciously big and strong. "Will he have sensed you?"

"Undoubtedly. He might have even seen the video Luther posted. But he thinks he's more powerful than me." I shrug a little. "To be fair, he's right. Alone, I couldn't fight him. One of me against a demon king who's thousands of years old?" I shake my head. "Even I can do that math."

"Then how exactly do we win?" Luther asks, trying to be gentle but letting his abrasiveness creep into his voice. "Even with every mage and witch in town on our side, Nova, I still don't think that's enough."

"No," I reply. "But what if there were six of me instead of just one?"

* * *

INSTEAD OF ANSWERING THE BOYS' endless questions, I insist we eat first. Honestly, a little part of me is enjoying being the one with the answers for once. Not Mack, not Kole... me.

"I'm starving. I haven't eaten since I came back, and I've already used way too much energy." I look pointedly at them and they collectively grumble their apologies, even though I don't mind one bit.

"Nova—" Mack uses his deliciously stern Daddy-

Professor voice, and it sends a shiver down my spine. I love Rev, but right now I wish she was someplace else so I could rip Mack's clothes off and make him bend me over the kitchen table.

Seems like being dead and reborn full of powerful magick really turbo-charges your sex drive. Especially when your boyfriends look so handsome and forlorn and, frankly, like sex on legs.

"Food first." I shake my finger at Mack. "Don't make me gag you," I warn playfully.

There's a moment of silence, and then Tanner laughs his loud, familiar laugh and slaps Mack on the shoulder. "Not sure that's a threat, Little Star," he says, winking at me.

At the stove, dropping batter into the pan, Rev rolls her eyes. "Do I really have to listen to this?"

I walk casually over to Mack and tweak his unruly beard. "I like your hair a little longer, but with this beard you look a bit like a homeless Santa Claus."

Mack's eyes flash amber and the familiar rumble of Snow's growl fills his throat.

"That is *exactly* what I said," Luther laughs, looping his arms around my waist. A little more seriously, he adds, "Baloo was pretty lost without you." He clears his throat and squeezes me tighter. "Too sad for his grooming routine."

Slipping my hand around his neck and turning so my hips are pressed against his, I kiss him softly on the lips. As Mack tells Luther to fuck off, I laugh and tell them, "I'm sorry. I'm going to spend a lot of time making it up to you all."

Rev coughs loudly. "Too much information, Nova."

"*After* we've eaten," I add, hopping up onto the kitchen table to sit with my legs hanging down over the side.

"And after you've left my apartment for a soundproof dungeon somewhere," Rev quips.

"Dungeon?" Tanner reaches over Rev to steal a piece of green pepper from her frying pan. He wriggles his eyes. "Now you're talking."

A familiar contentedness settles in the room. I let it wash over me as I watch them—laughing, cooking, teasing each other. Everything feels so *normal* that, after all that happened, it's almost *abnormal*.

Then my eyes catch on Sam. He's leaning against the wall near the fridge, watching the others. Unlike them, he is not smiling or making jokes. My gut twists, and my smile falters; he can't know already. There's no way he can know what I know.

But maybe he senses it.

Maybe something inside him has started to wonder…

32

TANNER

I wake with my arm draped across Nova's stomach. The six of us fell asleep sometime after midnight on the blow-up mattress Rev set up in the living room. With Nico in one room, and her and Sarah in the other, there was little other choice unless we wanted to try and fit four mages, a werewolf, and a phoenix on Rev's small couch.

The coffee table is pushed up against the wall beneath the window. The radiator is on, warm air making the bottom of the curtains sway a little.

All night, the sound of snarling, salivating demons filled the air outside the apartment. Now, finally, everything is still. I let the quiet settle into my skin and my head.

After what Nova went through, I'd expected her to be exhausted but she wasn't. All evening, even as the howling and barking and screaming started outside, she was wide awake. Full of an infectious kind of energy that gradually took away the ache we've been feeling for the past four weeks.

As the others' darkness began to lift, my own did too. Only Sam was strangely quiet, melancholy still hovering around him. Looking at him now, asleep with his arms curled around Nova's legs, I can't figure out why; he was the one who believed. He was the one who knew without doubt that Nova would return. Why would he not be as buoyant as the rest of us?

As if he can feel me watching him, Sam opens his eyes. He catches my gaze and smiles, then slowly sits up and pushes his curly hair from his face. Glancing at the ceiling, he points at it with his index finger then mouths, *"Roof?"*

I nod, unfurl my arm from Nova, and grab my sweater on the way to the door.

We don't speak until we're on the roof. It's almost sunrise, so the flying Karakal demons—huge bastards that look like giant eagles with horns and no feathers—will be flying back to their nests on the roof of The Hollow.

"She's back," Sam says, leaning on the wall and looking out at the horizon.

"She's back," I repeat, positioning myself next to him. "But you don't seem as happy as I expected you to be."

Sam doesn't look at me, just slots his fingers together and moistens his lip.

I nudge him with my elbow. "I thought you'd be floating on air, building castles in the sky, doing cartwheels, but you're lost in your own thoughts." I tap his head with my knuckles. "What's going on in there?"

"Can't you tell?" Sam straightens up and turns away from the view, resting his back on the low wall.

"I can tell you're confused, worried, sad."

"Aren't you?" Sam says quickly. "After everything she said?"

"Confused and worried, yes. Sad?" I laugh and shake my head. "I'm not sad. I'm fucking *ecstatic* to have her back. All the demons and the *hell being unleashed*? They don't seem to matter as much today as they did yesterday." I shrug and rub the back of my neck. "But you don't feel that way, and I can't figure out why. She's still our girl. She's still Nova. Just with a few added powers." I frown and try to meet Sam's eyes. "Was it seeing her unalive the demon in the bar? Because personally, I thought that was smoking hot."

"No," Sam laughs darkly, "it wasn't that."

"Then...?"

He sighs. It's a heavy sigh that makes his shoulders droop. He opens his mouth to speak but, before he can, whatever he's about to say is lost because the door to the stairs flies open and Nova appears.

Holding her hands to her chest, she looks at us as if we've just given her the fright of her life. "I didn't know where you were," she says, hurrying over and wrapping an arm around each of our waists. "Why are you up here?"

"Needed some fresh air." Sam kisses her forehead. "I better go check on Nico. Have you seen him?"

At the mention of Nico's name, something surges from Nova's aura. Like a splinter of panic, it's so strong it makes me wince. But nothing shows on her face. Not a single thing. "Not yet," she replies.

"Do you know what he is?" Sam asks, meeting Nova's gaze.

She tilts her head to the side. Her heart is racing, yet it *still* doesn't show. "I do."

"Are you okay with him being here?" Sam takes Nova's hand.

"I'm okay with it." She squeezes his fingers, then lets go as he nods and moves toward the door. Before he enters the stairwell, he glances at the sky. "Almost sunrise."

"We won't be long." Nova smiles until the door closes, then exhales loudly and folds herself into my arms.

"What's going on?" I look down at her, trying not to get lost in the fact she's here and she's mine. "Sam's got the wiggins and you nearly had a panic attack at the mention of Nico's name."

"Sam's wigging out?" She pulls back but keeps her arms around me. "Why? What did he say?"

"Nothing. He was about to tell me something when you got here."

Nova steps away from me and pinches the bridge of her nose. Then she leans on the wall, just like Sam did, and looks out at Phoenix Falls.

"Is it something to do with Nico?" I'm trying not to look at her ass. I'm trying to be serious for a hell-damned minute but all she's wearing is a t-shirt and the flash of creamy skin peeking out from beneath it is practically making me salivate.

As if she can tell, she wriggles her hips slightly and looks at me over her shoulder.

"Don't try to distract me, woman," I tell her, sliding my hands up her body and over her soft stomach, then leaning in to nuzzle her neck. "I want answers."

"I can't give them to you, not yet. Not until I've spoken to Sam." She smiles wickedly at me and presses back against my crotch. "I can give you something else, though."

"Shouldn't we be…?" I suck in a heavy breath. Who am I kidding? Like I'm going to say no.

"We'll be fast." Nova spins around at a freakish speed then back to face the wall. When I look down, I realize my pants and boxers are around my ankles and my cock is danger-ously close to her behind.

"Fast? I can do fast," I whisper, arching my body over hers, knowing it'll take barely a minute for me to climax if I truly let go. Slipping one hand up beneath her t-shirt, I tease my thumb over her already-hard nipple. Nova sighs and sways her hips.

With my other hand, I guide myself inside her.

We fuck quickly and hungrily. She slams back onto me, grips the wall, scratching it with her fingernails, and shouts my name while she plays with her clit; her super-quick fingers bringing her to a fast, shuddering climax. Sparks flutter up into the brightening sky. As we come, I tug her hair, so she jerks backward, then hold her against me. Her body tenses, every muscle vibrating with pleasure, while mine does the opposite. Coming inside her, I turn into a ball of mush; the sensations so intense that I'm barely able to stand up, barely able to keep hold of her.

We collapse into a heap, our bodies half slumped over the wall, breathing in jagged gasps.

Nova spins beneath me and hooks her arms around my neck. "Hi," she says, smiling.

"Hey." I kiss her nose.

"I love you." She pushes my untidy hair from my face.

"I love you too, Little Star." I'm focusing on her face, about to tell her I almost broke without her by my side, but something moves in my peripheral vision. I shift my gaze to the street below. "Nova… look."

Untucking herself from beneath me, Nova turns to look down. "They saw the video," she whispers, reaching for my hand. "They saw it. I knew they would."

On the sidewalk beneath us, the supers of Phoenix Falls are emerging from the shadows. They are answering Nova's call.

33

LUTHER

Nova and Tanner hurtle into the apartment. Their cheeks are flushed and, even though I've never been jealous of the others and their time with Nova, something inside me somersaults uncomfortably at the thought I just missed out on being with her again.

"It worked." She runs over to me, grabs my hand, and pulls me to the window. Tearing open the curtains, she points excitedly down at the sidewalks of Main Street. "They're gathering in the square."

Mack emerges from the bathroom, sees Nova, and heads straight for her. Before he can speak, he clocks the movement below us and scrapes his fingers through his hair. He's wearing nothing but a towel, chest dimpled with water droplets, suave as fuck.

Nova glances at him, then does a double take. Her eyes flicker with heat, and she runs her hand up his arm. "You kept your hair longer," she says approvingly. "But I'm glad you tamed the beard."

"Snow too," Mack replies, tweaking his index finger under her chin and planting a deep, searching kiss on her lips. "It was itchy."

"Did you call Annalise?"

"I called. She said she'll do her best but—" Mack doesn't bother finishing his sentence; we all knew Annalise wouldn't be able to make anyone take action.

Nova kisses Mack's cheek. "We need to get to the square. Hurry, everyone."

We're in the midst of locating our clothes and shoes when the bedroom door opens. Nico stops in the doorway. I haven't seen him since Rev ushered him into the bathroom yesterday, not long before Nova came flying down from outer space. He's cleaner than he was, and a little less vacant in his expression. When he spots Nova, his face visibly pales.

He searches for Sam, who crosses the room quickly and takes his brother's hand. "It's Nova." Sam looks at our girl, smiling. "She came back, Nico. Like you did. Like I did."

Nico presses his lips together. "Sam returned, Nico stayed."

Sam's jaw twitches. "No, Nico. You came back too."

Interjecting, from the kitchen Rev says, "He's still getting acclimatized. I'll stay here with him." She looks past us at the brightening sky beyond the window. "But you should go. All of you. Whatever you need to do, people are waiting."

"Sarah?" Sam asks, glancing at the other bedroom door.

"Sam, she's having a hard time with..." Rev trails off, purposefully *not* looking in Nico's direction.

"With what I am," Nico whispers. "She doesn't like what I am."

"Unelementals are terrified of demons, Nico. They have very few defenses against them." Rev squeezes his arm. "It's not your fault. She'll come around."

"I'm sorry," Nova interjects. She hasn't acknowledged

Nico properly but is almost at the door already. "We have to go. We'll be back soon." She pauses just outside and looks back at Rev. "Keep him safe while we're gone."

Rev nods but before she can ask *from what,* Nova is disappearing down the stairs.

* * *

WE FOLLOW Nova to the town square. Just past the fountain, there is a large, paved space which is used for summer festivals, street parties, and to display Phoenix Falls' traditionally huge Christmas tree.

Jake and Tanya—who are still running the Sheriff's Office in Mack's absence—spot us almost immediately. I'm surprised they haven't left town; neither struck me as the type who'd put themselves at risk to stay and herd cattle in a situation like this. Yet here they are. Tanya tries to wave and mouth something at Mack and I through the crowd, but we push on, following Nova.

There is no stage for her to stand on and we have no idea what she's planning, so the five of us just gather at the front of the gathering and wait.

The air is tight and cold. An icy breeze whips around the corner of the town hall—located at the back of the square—and swipes at our faces. Instinctively, the supers who have come are staring at it; probably waiting for their sheriff , Mack—even though he was robbed of his position—to speak up.

Nova straightens her shoulders. At her sides, her fingers twitch, and sparks flutter to the ground. Without looking back at us, she strides forward and ascends the town hall's steps. When she reaches the top, she turns.

There is a moment of dull chatter before people realize she is there. Then a hush falls over the crowd. Nova scans their faces slowly. Up there alone, she looks completely vulnerable. Small, wide-eyed, young.

Everything in my body is telling me to go up there with her. My skin begins to warm. Heat rushes to my palms. Next to me, Mack is breathing deeply. Snow's protective purr rumbles in his throat.

"It's her," someone shouts. "The witch who killed the human!"

"The sheriff's witch!"

"She was at the mansion with the sheriff. He was protecting her."

"Did you do this?! Did you bring evil to our town?"

"Is this because of you?"

The shouts grow louder. Kole's eyes darken. Head and shoulders above the rest of the crowd, his muscles tense. "Quiet!" he roars.

The voices die down to a nervous murmuring.

"Let her speak," Tanner adds, his fists clenched.

"Yes!" Nova's voice sings out above the rest. "I'm the witch. The one who killed her human boyfriend." She draws her shoulders back and casts her voice so it floats on the wind. "I have a lot to explain to you, and not much time, so please listen."

Something in her tone has made the muttering around us stop. Everyone is watching her now. Everyone is listening.

"I was born a human to human parents. You all saw my blood tests on the news. They proved that is no longer the case." She draws in a deep breath. As she moves her arms, flames spring to life, trickling from her wrists up to her elbows then to her shoulders, tracing the contours of her hands and fingers. "Many years ago, Mack—your sheriff—Luther, and Kole came upon a prophecy called The Phoenix Prophecy." Her voice is growing louder, and bigger, and so are the flames. Her hair is redder, too. Glowing. Moving like liquid fire.

The murmuring starts again, but this time it is laced with a mixture of awe and fear.

Nova casts her gaze in our direction. Kole steps forward and recites the words we now know by heart. Tanner joins in, then Mack. I add my voice to the chorus. Finally, Sam and Nova do too.

When above turns to darkness
And below breaks free
A witch born to humans
Salvation shall bring
Fated to five who are not what they seem
The Phoenix will rise and become Earth's Queen
Into the embers
Devoured by Flame
The Phoenix is She

As we speak, the sky crackles. Clouds race and the red sky brightens. When I look back at Nova, she is floating. Her feet are no longer on the ground.

Kicking off her shoes, she rises higher. She stretches out her arms and, just like when she appeared above the lake, wings of fire bloom from her back. As if she is suspended in water, her hair swirls around her face. The wind blows harder. Trees groan and creak. The water in the fountain bubbles like it is boiling. The ground shakes.

"I am The Phoenix," Nova cries, her voice travelling through me like a series of electric shocks. Without thinking, I drop to the floor. To my knee. The way I did when I told Nova I would be hers forever. In the blink of an eye, the others follow suit. We kneel in a line in front of the steps while Nova hovers above us, suspended, heat and sparks raining down on us.

Her eyes flash orange. Flames dance in her pupils. Slowly, she floats back down to the ground. She smiles and reaches out her hand, telling us to stand.

As I rise to my feet, there is a swell of movement behind me, and I realize we were not the only ones kneeling for her; they all were. The entire town.

Pacing, Nova speaks more quickly now. "I need you to know that if we work together—all of us—we can defeat The Shadow King. We can prevent him from destroying our town and, bigger than that, we can stop him from destroying the world."

"How?!" someone shouts.

Nova tilts her head. Her eyes flicker in the direction of the woods that surround The Hollow. "It will happen soon. Watch the skies. Watch for a sign. You'll know it when you see it." She races back to the top of the steps and peers over the sea of faces at something I can't see. "When you see my signal, come to The Hollow. That is where our final battle must be."

"She's talking in riddles," a woman next to me mutters.

"She often does," I reply, even though the prune-like woman wasn't talking to me. "That doesn't mean she's wrong, though."

"Something's happening." Tanner grabs my elbow. "Do you feel that? Something is..." He trails off, looking down at his feet. The ground is trembling.

In front of us, Nova raises her arms and throws them out sideways. Her wings are gone, but a pulse of air flies from her hands and splits the crowd down its middle, sending her spectators sliding to either side of the square, falling into one another and losing their balance.

Now, opening her palms, she repeats the movements she

made last night. Two walls of fire appear, hemming in the people of Phoenix Falls. Then a dome-like barrier appears above them.

"What is she doing?" Mack asks. "People are panicking."

"Eve..." Kole points into the distance. "Eve is coming for her. She's protecting them." Without hesitation, Kole races to the top of the steps. Nova glances at him, then widens her stance, bracing herself.

Tanner and I take the steps two at a time. By the time we reach Nova, Mack and Sam are no longer human. Sam snarls and gnashes his teeth. Snow opens his mouth and releases a gut-rumbling growl.

Then she appears.

The witch who sends shivers through all of us.

"Eve," Nova calls. "I'm so glad you could join us."

34

EVE

I felt her, but I thought I was imagining it. Yesterday, when that ghastly window of blue appeared in the sky, and the air became thinner and cleaner, and the beautiful darkness lifted, I *knew* the Fire Bird had returned.

I should have gone to her then. I should have ripped off her wings and torn out her song before she had the chance to fornicate, and rejuvenate, and plot, and scheme.

But I was lazy. I was lacking. I was naïve to my own senses.

It wasn't until I felt the ground move, and the elements bend, and the earth grow warm beneath my feet that I knew I was right.

"Eve!" My master's voice shakes the walls of The Hollow.

He doesn't need to say any more. I know what I must do. "She will not live to see the sun at midday, Master," I whisper, kissing his knuckles.

"Go!" He bellows, snatching his hand away from me. He wants to join me. He wants to destroy her himself, but he is still clawing back his strength after his long, long journey. So, I will do it for him.

I run to my babies in their stable and I wake them from their slumber. They are angry at being woken, but that is a good thing; I need them at their most bloodthirsty.

With the hounds baying at my heels, we move like shadows—weightless, dark, unbound by the laws of nature—to the town square.

When I see her, glowing and glittering and bright, a funny idea wriggles itself into my head. She and I are not so unalike. We are darkness and light, yin and yang, two halves that make a whole.

We are the same; our powers are evenly matched, our loyalty to our masters unwavering, except the Fire Bird's master is fate and my master is going to be so much more than that. He is going to rule the world and *every* dimension that surrounds it.

"Eve," she calls my name, "I'm so glad you can join us."

In front of me, she has cast a barrier spell over the pathetic, power-lacking supers of Phoenix Falls. The ones who remain in town were too stupid to get out when they had the chance. I throw a ball of dark magick to try and break it, but it holds.

"You've grown, Fire Bird," I sing, sweeping down the aisle she made for me. I tick my head to the side and examine her. "Do you have scars? From where we drained your pretty little body of its blood, I wonder?" I lick my lips. Oh, how I wish I'd tasted her blood.

A flutter of movement. The seer is lunging for me.

I catch him in mid-air, tighten my invisible grip around his thick neck, and squeeze. "I thought you'd have learned your lesson the last time we sparred, Ink Heart," I spit.

He flexes his fingers, trying to pull roots from the ground

or branches from the trees, but he fails, and I throw him loose, sending him hurtling into the fountain.

"Go back to your *devil*," the Fire Bird says, striding forward.

Even with my babies salivating for her flesh, she does not falter.

"Go back and tell him his end is near."

I study her for a moment. She is very brave, but very stupid. Although, I have to confess to being impressed that she is so *whole* after still being so *dead* a few days ago. "Oh, poor little Fire Bird—" My voice catches in my throat before I can finish my insult. My breath is trapped too. My lungs feel hot—like there is acid inside them, bubbling, swirling, pushing on my insides.

I try to laugh, but the feeling grows stronger, and the laugh turns to a whimper.

My babies know I'm in trouble. They begin to bark and howl.

The Fire Bird raises her hand, twists it, and slams my airways shut. I grab my throat, eyes wide, half terrified, half transfixed by her sudden burst of power.

The hounds won't let her take me. They surge forward, barreling toward her but—keeping me in her intangible grasp —she turns her eyes on them. Fire blooms in her face. A wave of heat rumbles through the cobbled path. It undulates, like waves of fire are surging beneath it, and knocks my hounds from their feet. They roll away from me, crying and howling.

The Fire Bird lifts me into the air with nothing more than a flick of her wrist. Then she stares up at me and calmly says, "Do you remember what to tell him?"

This time, when I try to speak, my voice returns but it is reedy and weak. "His end is... near," I stutter, acrid hate swirling in my belly. She will regret this. When he breaks her in two and drinks her blood from her splayed veins, her last thought will be that she should not have been so arrogant. She should not have underestimated him.

The Fire Bird studies my face, then nods and throws me to the ground. I tumble over myself and land in a heap. My body still burns on the inside. It makes me want to scratch my arms and pull my clothes off and yank out my hair.

"Go," she sings, her voice like metal, piercing my skin.

I stumble to my feet. Her mates gather behind her. Three mages, a polar bear, and a werewolf. Even rolled into one, they would not be powerful enough to protect her from what is to come.

I tip my head back and laugh. It fills the surrounding air, but before it can echo off the walls of the town hall, I have turned on my heels and I am fleeing back to my King.

35

NOVA

When Eve disappears from view, I release the crowd from their bubble and tell them to go home. They seem reluctant—lingering and staring at me as if they want to remain here where I can protect them.

"It is not enough," I tell them. "Eve is just a witch. She's powerful, but her magick can be broken. The Shadow King is much more, and there are things I must do now. Watch for my signal. When you see it, come to The Hollow."

As they shout questions and plead for answers, I push through them with my mates at my heels. Before we reach Rev's, I veer away from Main Street and head for the woods behind The Cross.

"Nova?" Tanner catches my arm. Despite everything, he looks at me in exactly the same way he always has; with deep, sparkling eyes that are full of love and lust.

"We need to go back to the lake." I look past him at the

others. "It's time for me to show you how we're going to win."

Snow releases a low grumble. I walk over to him and wind my fingers into his thick, surprisingly soft fur. I kiss the top of his snout and he rubs his forehead against my chest. Then he dips his head and shoulders so I can climb onto his back. I don't need to; I could make it to the lake a hundred times faster than him if I wanted to. But somehow it feels right to approach it like this. All of us. Side by side.

* * *

When we reach the falls, Snow turns back into Mack. Luther hands him clothes from a backpack he was carrying and, when he pulls them on, Mack says, "Nova, what happened back there—" He sucks in a deep breath. "Your power. I've never seen anything like it."

"Coming from you, Professor, that's a true compliment." I smile cheekily at him, but he returns it with only a stoic expression.

"You were right." I look at each of them before settling on Kole. "You were right all along—I died, then I came back. I'm more powerful than before."

"More powerful than Eve," Kole replies. "Which means more powerful than any witch I've ever encountered."

I cast a fire on the sand and gesture for them to join me around it. I sit down, crossing my legs and resting my palms on my thighs. "But it won't be enough. Taking Eve down a peg or two, exploding demons, and running super-fast isn't the same as destroying The Shadow King." I straighten my shoulders. "Because that is what we must do—we must *destroy* him, so he can never return."

"All right, so how do we do that?" Luther asks. "You said it's time to share, Supernova." He raises his eyebrows. His tone is like it was before—in the days when I still thought he hated me—but now I know what lies beneath it, his grumpiness is even more delicious.

"My blood." I meet Luther's eyes. "We will do it with my blood."

There is a long moment of silence. Kole's pupils have grown wider and darker. His jaw is twitching, but the black veins that show The Hunger is taking control of him are gone.

"Kole has drunk from me before and we saw what it did to his powers. Tanner too. But that was before I came back." I wiggle my fingers, watching vines of fire loop around them like rings.

"You want us to drink from you?" Sam says slowly. "That's what you meant when you said what if there were six of you?"

I look quickly from him to Mack, who I can tell is already railing against the idea. "You are strong, all of you, but with my blood inside you... *that's* how we'll win."

"Nova, are you sure?" Luther slides his hand onto mine. My fire loops around his fingers too, tying us together in a tangle of heat.

I draw in a deep breath. "This isn't going to be easy. It's not just a case of you getting a super-boost of your powers. It could be dangerous. There could be side-effects, but it all fits. All of it makes sense, don't you think? From the beginning, we've known my blood was special. Kole was drawn to it, but it didn't behave the way human blood did. My blood brought Sam back. My blood opened the portal, and my blood will seal it."

"We'll do it," Tanner says quickly. "Of course, we'll do it."

Kole and Luther hesitate for a moment, then nod. Frowning a little, Sam says, "Me too."

I look at Mack. He rubs his beard. His eyes flash amber, and Snow's familiar grumble fills his throat.

"You don't like it, Professor?" I stand up and move behind him, hands on his shoulders. He reaches up to smooth his hands over mine, then climbs to his feet and pulls me close.

"I will do whatever you ask, Little Star." He brushes my hair from my face. "No question."

I tilt my head to the side, exposing my neck and running my index finger down the shadow of a vein that Kole has tasted more than once.

"Now?" Luther stands. They all do.

They were okay with it when it was something that would happen in the future, but *now*? Clearly, it's too much too soon because they all look terrified. All except Kole.

Letting go of Mack, I walk to my Viking and run my hands up his broad chest. *You have to show them the way*, I whisper using the voice only he can hear.

He tilts my chin up toward him, balancing it on the knuckle of his thick index finger. *Are you certain, Little Star?*

I don't reply, just stare into his eyes and pull his hair loose so it falls over his shoulders. His lips curl, exposing a flash of his slightly pointed teeth. He runs his tongue over them, and I raise my wrist to his mouth. *Tanner first*, I tell him.

Kole keeps his eyes on mine but brings the soft skin on the inside of my wrist to his lips.

"Kole—" Luther tries to interject but it's too late; Kole has already pierced my skin.

As blood trickles slowly from my veins, I turn and find Tanner. I pull him toward me and lift the wound to his mouth. At first, he licks it, slowly sweeping his tongue over the puncture wounds Kole made. Then he takes hold of my arm and starts to suck. He closes his eyes and groans as my blood coats his lips, and chin, and teeth.

Sparks of pleasure start to flutter inside me. I grip the

back of his head, then push my fingers through his hair and pry his mouth away from me.

Tanner stands up, breathless, wiping his lips with the back of his hand. His eyes roll back in his head, and he stumbles as if he's drunk. Then he lets out a loud exhilarated cry and punches the air. "Fuck!" He grabs Luther and pushes him toward me.

I lift my other wrist to Kole's waiting mouth, and he opens it for me. Luther stares at the pooling red liquid on my skin. "I don't know if I can…"

"You can," I tell him, licking my own wrist and holding the blood on my tongue. "Here…"

Luther lets me guide his lips to mine, then welcomes my tongue as I roll blood into his mouth. He releases a guttural grunting sound, and his whole body stiffens. But when I replace my mouth with my wrist, he seals his lips over it and drinks.

Seeing Luther, Tanner returns and grabs my other wrist. He takes another drink, sucking congealed blood from my fingers, licking my palm, hungrily trailing kisses up my arm toward my throat.

When he reaches my shoulder, he grabs the hem of my shirt and pulls it up over my head. He throws it to the ground, then tugs my bra strap down so he can graze his teeth over my collarbone.

I reach for Sam. He flinches as he drinks from me; despite being a wolf and accustomed to the metallic taste in his mouth.

While Sam drinks, Luther stops. He turns and blasts a wave of fire at the flames on the beach. They billow upward into the sky. Smoke is coming off him in waves. Returning to me, he grabs my face and kisses me hard. Then—holy stars— he kisses Kole.

Kole's eyes widen for a split second before he tastes my

blood on Luther's lips and sinks into the kiss. Hungrily, they devour each other's mouths and then Kole lunges for my neck. He pierces me with his teeth and starts to suck.

The pressure of his mouth, drawing life from my body, makes me fall to my knees and whimper with pleasure.

While Kole drinks from my throat, Luther laps at the blood that is now trickling down between my breasts and Tanner removes my bra.

I search for Mack and meet his eyes. Slowly, he walks toward me. Sinking to his knees, he positions himself in front of me. I offer him my wrist, and he licks it gently. Just one stroke of his tongue against my flesh.

I sigh and lean back onto Kole's chest as Mack lowers his head and peppers my stomach with electric kisses. When he reaches my chest, he dips his finger into the blood seeping from my throat and uses it to moisten my nipples. Then he swirls his tongue over them, groaning as my taste fills him up.

By the time he reaches my neck, his eyes are bright, and his beard is stained red. He cups my face in his hands, then closes his eyes, releases a deep throaty sigh, and seals his mouth around the holes in my throat.

When Mack sits back on his heels, eyes still dancing, body trembling, I rise to my feet and stand in front of them. I close my eyes and send waves of fire through my body. When I look down, the wounds are sealing shut. My skin is healing itself, putting itself back how it was before, but the blood remains. As my flesh warms, the blood dries, and leaves me painted with large red stains.

I meet Kole's eyes. My Viking looks hungry. Ravenous. But not for blood... for me. A smile twitches on his lips and he runs for me. I bolt for the trees, adrenaline coursing through me. I am about to reach the shadows when he catches me. Except it's not him... it's a vine. A long, thick, creeping vine. Springing from the ground, it winds around my ankle. Then another grabs my wrists.

Both hands and both feet are yanked back by four curling green ropes, sending my slamming into the trunk of a sweet-smelling pine.

Kole appears in front of me, fists clenched, body vibrating with lust.

He reaches for my pants and rips them from my body, then tears my underwear off too. When I'm completely naked, unable to move, the others appear behind him. Luther, Mack, and Tanner.

Like a horny teenager who can't control himself, Tanner whips off his own clothes, drops to the ground, and slides his hands up the inside of my thighs. Immediately, he nestles his tongue between my folds and uses it to massage urgent circles around my clit. My knees wobble, but another vine loops around my waist and hugs me tight against the tree.

Arousal floods my core. I strain against the vines, desperate to get closer to my mates, but I can't move.

I want one of them to come to me and seal their mouth over my nipples. I want them to break me free and fuck me on the forest floor. Instead, they strip off their clothes and watch while Tanner brings me to a violent, shuddering orgasm.

It lights up my skin, sending smoke and sparks into the trees.

Mack steps forward. To my right, Kole is fisting his dick hard and fast. To my left, Luther is doing the same. As he kneels, Mack teases my breasts with a brief, tantalizing lick of his tongue. Then he nudges Tanner out of the way and settles between my legs.

His tongue is different to Tanner's; larger and rougher. I shudder as he laps my sensitive core, applying just the right of pressure before sliding two fingers inside me while he sucks.

I want to grab his hair, hook my leg around his neck, thrust my pelvis into his face. But I can't. I am stuck.

Another fiery orgasm takes over, causing me to scrape my back on the tree trunk behind me as I writhe and yell.

"Untie me." I pull on the vines. I could break them if I wanted to, but that's not the deal. They have to *allow* me to do it.

Kole shakes his head at me, his hair—which is crusted with my blood—hanging loose over his shoulders. "I don't think so, Little Star."

Before I can speak, he has taken Mack's place, but instead of using his tongue to make me climax, he thrusts his throbbing length deep inside me. He fucks me harder than he's ever fucked me. His hips do things I've never even dreamed of, then his hand reaches down between us.

"I can't come again, I can't," I pant, my clit pulsing as he strums it hard and fast.

"I think you can," he growls. "Spark for me, Nova."

I whimper and throw my head back. Finally, Luther is there licking my nipples, sucking as if he wants to savor every last taste of blood that remains on my skin. I look down to see Kole's hand around Luther's erection. The sight of Kole's thick, tattooed knuckles moving up and down Luther's pierced shaft makes me yell.

I can't take it anymore. I rip my legs free from their ties.

Kole growls at me, but I don't care. I wrap my legs around his middle; the vines around my arms and waist still holding me in place while he shudders and climaxes inside me.

As Kole grunts and slams into me once last time, Luther comes too. I look down to see him painting Kole's fingers white.

Kole kisses my neck, grazing me with his teeth as if he

can't help thinking about biting me again. But then Tanner pushes him out of the way, pulls me free from my restraints, and into his arms. His dick is still hard. It twitches against my stomach. I sink to my knees and take him in my mouth. With just three deep thrusts, he comes at the back of my throat. I swallow it, then turn to Mack. Instead of using my mouth, though, Mack sits with his back against the tree and gestures for me to climb on top of him.

I slide down his shaft easily, my pussy slick with Kole's seed, and brace my hands on the tree trunk as the professor settles his large hands on my full hips. I move slowly, easing up and down, teasing his lips with my nipples. Mack runs his hands up my back, digging his nails into my skin as I ride him faster and harder. When he comes, I am staring into his amber eyes, but I don't just see pleasure…

I see pain.

36

TANNER

"Something's wrong with him…" Nova stumbles to her feet. Luther grabs her hand and pulls her toward him.

"Is he having a heart attack?" Kole asks, squatting next to the professor.

"I'm not that fucking old," Mack growls, but he is gripping his chest. "I just don't feel…" He yells and lurches forward. His back is moving. *Literally* moving. Like tectonic plates are shifting beneath it.

He yells again, but this time it's more like a growl. His fingers dig into the ground. His elbows bend. They snap, moving the wrong way, and Nova yelps. She rushes forward, but Luther loops his arms around her waist and drags her back.

Mack's jaw stretches, cracks, widens. There's a shudder of movement. The ground vibrates. He screams at the top of his lungs, and then… Snow is there. The giant bear peels itself from Mack's body like a spirit being sucked from a vessel. At first Snow is air and mist and particles, then he is real.

He's real, and he's standing *next to* Mack.

Nova slams her hands over her mouth and whispers, "Oh my stars, Snow?"

"Professor..." I crouch in front of Mack and put my hand on his shoulder. His body is his again, not moving or breaking open, just still. Panting, he looks into my eyes.

"What the fuck was that?"

I move my gaze to his right, and Mack follows. When he sees Snow, he looks like he might pass out.

I help him to his feet.

Snow's eyes lock onto Mack's and the polar bear releases a sound that's half-yawn, half-growl.

Mack walks slowly forward like he's trapped in a dream. He reaches for Snow's fur and gently presses his palm onto the polar bear's shoulder. "Snow? Buddy? Is that you?"

Snow huffs and shoves his snout into Mack's chest.

"Yeah, I know I'm naked, but that's not really the issue right now, is it?"

As Mack and Snow start to communicate—Mack speaking, Snow offering a series of huffs and snuffs and growls—my brain almost can't compute what's happening.

"Holy hell," Luther mutters. "Was that supposed to happen?" He looks at Nova.

She's deathly pale, and I'm not sure if it's because we drained her blood then gave her four orgasms or if it's because she just watched Mack separate from his shifter self.

"This has never happened before." Kole sweeps his hair back and ties it at the back of his neck. "Has it?" He looks at me and I shrug, shaking my head. "Has this ever happened to a shifter before?"

"Not that I've ever seen or heard of." I look for Sam, because he saw all sorts of freaky shit in *Spine* and he's the only other shifter among us, then realize he's not actually here. "Guys, where's Sam?"

Nova looks back at the beach. She frowns. "He wasn't..." Her cheeks flush as she replays the things we just did. "He drank from me but then...?" She trails off, clearly torn between running to find her foster brother and staying with Mack.

"I'll go," I tell her.

But she shakes her head at me. "No, I will. You're a nurse. Mack might need you."

She turns and runs to the beach, her ass swaying from side to side like she's a freaking goddess. Grabbing her clothes, she puts them back on then looks at the sand, spots some wolf prints, and heads after them.

While Kole gathers the rest of our clothes, I try to assess Mack. My head is buzzing. I feel like I've had twenty energy drinks in a row; wired, twitchy, like everything is louder. Everyone's emotions are louder, but they're also easier to shut down. With a shake of my head, they're gone. I blink and they're back. Suddenly, for the first time in my life, I have a gate that seems easy to close.

"Mack?" I put my hand on his shoulder. He's smiling, shaking his head as he walks a circle around Snow. "Professor, are you alright?"

Mack turns to me and slaps my upper arm. "It's Snow!" he says, laughing. "He's here. He's right here."

"We know, buddy," Luther says. "We watched him... I don't even know what the word is... *separate* from you?"

"What did it look like?" Mack asks, his hand on Snow's thick furry neck.

"Gross," I tell him. "Really gross."

Mack looks down at his hands. He frowns then trails a finger through the air, bringing with it a gust of wind so strong I can barely stay standing. "This is it," he says. "Nova's blood... it separated us so we can both help her. Before, I had to choose. Either my elemental powers or Snow's strength. Now, we have both."

"Has it been done before?" Kole asks, swotting away some tree roots that are slithering along the ground toward him; drawn to his supercharged earth affinity like moths to a flame.

"Never." Mack is still staring at Snow with awe and wonder in his eyes. Snow nudges him out of the way and heads for the water. Without looking back at Mack, he wades in then starts to swim.

"Looks like he's pleased to be free of you," Luther chuckles.

"Looks like it." Mack scratches his beard, which is still laced with Nova's blood.

"Can you hear him?" I ask, tapping my head. "Feel him?"

Mack nods. "He's still in there. I'm still inside him. But now we're separate, too." He pushes his fingers through his hair. "It's—"

"A head fuck?" Luther finishes.

Mack nods. "Yeah, you could say that."

Watching Snow lounge lazily in the water, I glance at Kole. "So, she was right. It worked."

"It worked," Kole repeats, following the trail of Nova's and Sam's footprints. "Except..."

I lower my voice. "Except what?"

"Fated mates. With Mack and Snow separate, doesn't that make six?"

37

NOVA

"Sam?" just before the caves, his footprints turn from wolf back to human then disappear. I can't tell if he went inside or climbed the rocks to the top of the falls, but my instinct says the latter. Instead of climbing, I unfurl my fiery wings—it's still a freaking *buzz* feeling them unleash—and soar upward.

Sam is close to the edge, sitting with his knees tucked under his chin. When I land in front of him, he barely looks up.

I sit down quietly, putting the wings away. "Mack and Snow got separated." When I eventually speak, Sam frowns and turns to look at me.

"How?"

"My blood, I guess." I gesture to the stains on my wrist; shadows of where the others fed from me.

"I threw up." Sam turns back toward the lake and pushes his fingers through his hair. "I couldn't do it, Nova. The taste in my mouth... it was like acid. I puked, and watching you with the others? Normally, that stuff would be hot as hell but..." He trails off, a shadow crossing his face. "I couldn't even watch. I had to get away from there."

I reach for his hand and slot my fingers between his; a hand I thought for so many years I'd never hold again.

"It's not me, is it?" Sam's voice is small but deep.

It brings a knot of emotion to my throat and forces me to screw my eyes closed. When I feel him watching me, I open them and wipe a tear from my cheek.

"I'm not one of the five." Sam meets my gaze, staring deep into my soul, not just my eyes.

I can barely breathe. From the second I got back, I knew —and I knew I had to tell him—but now the moment is here, I feel like I'll break if I have to say the words. I reach for his face and hold it tightly between my hands. "Sam, it doesn't matter. I still love you."

Sam looks down and releases a sorrowful sigh that turns into an ironic laugh. "Of course, it matters."

I duck to meet his eyes. "It doesn't." I press his hand to my chest then kiss him, trying desperately to make all the love I feel flow from my lips to his. "I love you. I'm yours. I always will be. It doesn't matter what the prophecy says."

"Who is it?" Sam takes my fingers between his and squeezes. "Mack and Snow? They're two, not one, so there's no room for me?"

I breathe in deeply and bite my lower lip. "No, not them. They're still one, even if they look like two."

"Then who...?" Sam frowns for a moment, then his eyes widen. As realization settles in his face, the heavy weight of the knowledge he now carries claws at my stomach. "Don't say it." He stands up and paces away from me. "You don't need to say it. There's only one other person it could possibly be."

I put my hand on his back and try to make him turn to

face me. When he doesn't, I flit so I'm standing in front of him, sparks fluttering from my skin. "I choose you." I reach for his neck and grab the ring he has been wearing all this time. Close to his heart. I loop the string over his head, then take the ring and slot it onto my finger. "I still choose you. Fate can tell me how to save the world, but she cannot tell me who to love."

"It's not the same, though, is it?" He smooths his finger over mine, caressing the ring he gave me when he swore he'd love me forever.

"Yes, it is. I still need you, Sam. You have to believe me." I'm crying now, but don't bother to wipe the tears away. As my emotions swirl and flicker, a cold wind blows across the top of the falls. Sam studies me for a long moment, then folds me into his arms.

He kisses the top of my head. "I believe you, Nova. I'm just sorry I'm not enough."

* * *

SAM REFUSES to leave the cliffs. He tells me he needs some time and asks me to break the news to the others so he doesn't have to hear it again. On the beach, they have cleaned themselves up and are waiting for me. Snow is lying on the sand, licking his large paws. Mack is next to him, but stands up when he sees me.

"Are you alright?" I can't stop looking at him next to Snow. In a strange way, their mannerisms are the same; the way their heads move, and their eyes follow me.

"I'm fine, Little Star. What about Sam?" Mack hands me a mug of coffee. On the ground next to the fire sits the remains of our camping equipment from the caves.

I take it and move to stand with my bare feet in the shallows of the lake. The cold lapping against my toes is comforting.

"He couldn't drink my blood. It made him sick." Before the others can speak, I hold up my palm to show I'm not done talking. "Sam figured it out before I could tell him, and he asked me to tell you all."

"Figured what out? Tell us what?" Tanner and Mack exchange a worried glance.

"Sam..." My voice falters, but I shake my head when Luther attempts to comfort me. Turning to Kole, I say, "Do you remember what the voice told us? When it said we should find the werewolf and I was convinced it meant Sam?"

Kole nods, his fingers twitching at his sides. "I remember."

"Well, it seems we got the wrong werewolf." I try to smile, but it doesn't work. The smile falters and I force out a heavy breath, trying not to cry again. "Sam isn't one of my fated mates. My blood couldn't help him—couldn't make him stronger or more equipped to fight." I shake my hands at my sides to try and release the burning tension in my muscles. "Sam isn't the werewolf I was supposed to find."

"Then who the hell is?" Luther asks darkly.

I close my eyes and force out the name I've been holding back since I returned. "Nico."

38

KOLE

Nova wants us to wait for Sam but Mack volunteers to stay. "Rev and Sarah will be waiting for news," he says. "I'll be okay with Snow. We'll make sure Sam gets back safely."

Knotting her fingers together in front of her stomach, Nova looks genuinely torn. "I don't want him to think..." She bites her lower lip as her words catch in her throat.

"He won't. He just needs some time to get used to the idea. It's a lot to take in for all of us."

Trying to make light of the situation, Tanner punches Mack lightly on the arm and says, "You just want time alone so you can play with your new air bending skills."

Mack and Snow, at the same time, shoot him a withering stare. Snow even releases a low grumble from the back of his throat, which makes Luther laugh. "Ha, there's two of them to gang up on you now, Tanner."

Usually when we're like this—gently cajoling each other, teasing, and laughing—Nova smiles. She loves to see us behaving like brothers, making fun of each other, punching each other on the arm, occasionally hugging. But right now, she just looks sad and confused.

It'll be okay, Little Star. I send my voice to slither through her, hoping it brings comfort. *Sam will be okay. No one can tell you not to love him, even if he isn't—*

"I know," she says out loud, making the others all turn and look at her. "Sorry," she breathes. "I didn't mean to snap. I told him I still love him, but it didn't seem to help. Even if he's not one of the five, who says I can't have six or seven mates if I want them?"

I catch Tanner raising his eyebrows; clearly, he's okay with Nova being in a relationship with the five of us, but not quite okay with her adding another three or four mages to the mix.

"I just don't know if Sam gets it." She turns to Mack and folds herself in his arms, tucking her head under his chin. "Rhone, please try to make him see that this isn't the end of everything. Just because he didn't drink my blood, it doesn't mean there isn't a bond between us, and it *doesn't* mean I love Nico. Because I don't. He might be part of this, but he's not part of my heart." She looks up at Mack again and says, "Promise me you'll make Sam understand?"

Mack kisses her forehead. "I'll do my best, Little Star." Then he strides off up the beach with Snow ambling behind him.

Seeing the two of them like that will never stop being weird; in all the years I've known Mack, I don't think it ever properly sank in that he and Snow were one being—that Snow was living inside there somewhere.

Even after all the times I saw him shift from Mack to Snow then from Snow to Mack, there's something about seeing them next to each other—the way they move and the way they look at each other, and the way they talk as if they genuinely understand what the other is saying—that brings their relationship into sharp relief.

They really are one, a part of each other's psyche, two halves of a whole.

"They're all right, aren't they?" Nova says as we strive towards the trees.

"They're fine," I tell her, moving a branch out of her way, even though she doesn't need me to. "Stop worrying, Nova. They're okay. We all are."

For a while, we walk in silence. The energy of the forest swirls around me, presses down on my limbs, and makes my muscles twitch. Usually, I have to tune myself into it but since I drank Nova's blood, it's like the earth's energy is a part of me and I'm a part of it.

I can move it without really thinking; I didn't mean to make those vines twirl around Nova's wrists and ankles. They just did it, like they knew that was what I wanted without me having to even say anything.

I glance at Tanner, wondering if he's struggling with an onslaught of emotion. As if he can tell what I'm thinking, he says, "I can switch it off—thoughts, emotions, stuff I usually have to try really hell-damned hard to get out of my head. It's like I can shut it off now. I can just flip a switch and boom, I'm alone in my own head. It's fucking crazy." He smiles and scrapes his fingers through his floppy hair.

His face is lighter, as if a literal weight has been lifted from him.

"Then when I do open it up, it's more intense than ever." He breathes out hard, looking ahead to where Nova and Luther walk side-by-side. "I think she was right. I think this is what we had to do but—"

I raise my eyebrows waiting for him to continue.

"What does it mean for Nico? He has to drink from her too? And then what? I mean he's not just Nico anymore—

he's a fucking Hellhound. What's Nova's blood going to do to him?"

"Maybe it will get rid of the hound, maybe it'll turn him back into himself," I reply.

"But what would be the point in that? If she needs a werewolf, she already has Sam."

"Tanner," I sigh, my jaw twitching, "I know I'm supposed to have the answers, but I don't know. Nova's the one now—the one with all the visions, and all the plans. I did my part and now I'm just doing what she tells me to."

Tanner wrinkles his nose and makes a gesture with his mouth that's not quite a smile. "Must feel like shit," he says, "not being the all-knowing one anymore."

I nudge him with my elbow and tell him to fuck off, which makes Luther turn around from up ahead and hush at us to be quiet because we're approaching the town.

Under my breath, I say, "Actually, it feels pretty nice."

* * *

BACK AT THE APARTMENT, Rev, Sarah, and Nico are waiting in the kitchen.

"Where the fuck have you been?" Rev shouts, striding towards us as if she's going to wag her finger and give us all a detention. "I was watching from the window. I saw what happened, and then you all just left! You walked off. You didn't think to come back here and let us know that you were all right."

"If you were watching, you knew we were all right." Luther smirks, heading for the fridge. He takes out a bottle of water for himself, then throws one to Tanner while Nova reaches around him and grabs a carton of orange juice.

"Well?" Rev says, putting her hands on her hips. "What

happened?" She narrows her eyes. "Nova is that blood in your hair?"

Nova takes a strand of hair between her thumb and fore-finger. A slow smile twitches her lips, but she shakes it away and says, "Long story, Rev."

In the corner of the room, Sarah says nothing just fiddles with the hem of her cardigan and keeps looking furtively at Nico, as if she's worried he's going to rip her head off at any second. She watches the door, but when it doesn't open again, she says, "Where is Sam? Why isn't he with you? And Mack?"

"There's a lot we need to explain," Nova says, sitting down at the table. For the first time since she returned, she seems tired. But she rallies and straightens her shoulders as she says, "I'm going to move quickly, so pay attention." She looks from Sarah to Rev then, just as she promised, rapidly reels off what happened by the lake.

She tells them we drank her blood, and that we are now supercharged mages capable of pretty much anything. She tells them that Mack and Snow split into two separate creatures, and then she pauses. She squeezes the carton and it crumples beneath her fingers. It's empty, so she throws it into the trash and starts to pace.

I want to do something to help. I want to do something to make her feel better, but I can't think of anything. The others can't either.

Finally, she stops and says, "Kole and I were wrong about Sam."

A quivering silence hangs in the air.

Sarah looks as nervous as usual, and Nico? Well, I still can't tell what Nico is thinking. "Sam?" he says. "Is he okay?"

Nova turns to look at him. He is the same as he always was; lanky, unassuming, with a placid face and irritating hair.

"Are you feeling better?" she asks, not answering his question.

"I feel more like myself." He looks past Nova at Rev, then continues, "Rev's been helping me. The voices are gone now."

"There were voices?" Luther asks roughly. "Nova, are you sure we need *this* guy?"

Nova shoots Luther a frustrated stare.

From her corner, Sarah says, "What are you talking about?" She has taken her wand from her pocket. I don't think she intends to use it, but she is moving it from one hand the other. "Please Nova, where is Sam?"

Nova inhales slowly. Looking at Nico instead of Sarah, she says, "Sam is not one of my fated mates."

My stomach lurches. Just to say those words must be killing her. The blood bond we share, stronger now than ever and surging in my veins, tells me to go to her. Make her feel better. Soothe her. Take away the ache in her heart.

"We thought he was because we have such a strong bond." She inhales sharply, like she's in physical pain. "When the voice told us to look for a werewolf, we assumed it was talking about Sam because I *wanted* it to be him. When Kole's mother showed us a vision of the Original Six, we assumed it was Sam because he looked..." She hesitates then makes herself say it. "Because he looked so much like you."

Nico's face remains completely still. Even his eyes barely move. I try to focus on him and Nova instead of the pounding dread in my ears when I think of the voice and my mother's part in it. I should tell Nova, but not now. She has more important things to worry about right now.

"Nico? Can you hear me?" Nova asks.

Nico dips his head almost imperceptibly. "I hear you. I just don't understand."

Nova bites back a sigh and swallows hard. "When Sam tasted my blood, it made him sick. He couldn't swallow it. He couldn't even watch the others—" She stops, her cheeks flushing a little. "He knew it before I even said anything, and I knew it as soon as I came back." She steadies herself with the back of one of the kitchen chairs. "It's not Sam I need for the final fight. I love him and I always will, and I don't love you, Nico, not even a little bit—" Her voice hardens and pride swells in my belly as I watch her square up to the man who once hurt her so much. "But I do need you."

"What do you need me to do?" Nico asks, drawing back his shoulders. This time, he isn't scared like he was before—when he was pathetic and terrified of putting himself in danger—just utterly clueless about how he could be of any help.

Nova glances at the door and taps her foot nervously. "I wanted to do this when we were all together, but I don't know when Mack and Sam are coming back, and we have a timeline to stick to." She pulls out the chair and sits down.

As if she can tell Nova needs either some caffeine or some sugar, Rev presses a mug of coffee into her hands. Nova sighs and stares into it for a moment, then looks up.

"Nico is our way in into The Hollow. He's a Hellhound shifter now not a werewolf, which means he can get through the barrier."

"Can't you do that?" Luther asks her.

"No, Luther. I'm powerful but even *I* can't break Eve's protection spell on the mansion. It's reinforced with The Shadow King's dark magick. But if Nico gets inside, he can do what you were trying to do before the ritual." She looks at me and my stomach turns.

She knew what we were doing. Even though she wasn't here, she knew, which means she knew we had failed her.

Turning back to Nico, Nova steeples her fingers together and says, "Nico, you're the only one who can do this. Trust me, I wouldn't be asking unless I had to."

Nico hangs his head, but Nova stands and dips hers to meet his eyes. "You put Sam's life before your own when you jumped in front of your father's blade, so I'm hoping you have the guts to do that for the rest of humanity, too. Because you are genuinely the only one who can get into that mansion."

"What do I do when I get inside?" Nico asks quietly.

Nova glances at Luther, Tanner, and me, then stares right into Nico's eyes and says, "You rip out Eve's throat, so the barrier comes down, and we do the rest."

39

NOVA

"**D**oes it really need to be tonight?" Tanner asks as I lift a knife from the kitchen drawer. Taking in the shining blade, he gulps and slips his hand around my wrist. His eyes shift. A moment ago, they were dazzlingly bright but now they are darker. Searching. He's opening his mind, sifting through my feelings to make sure I'm not hiding a knot of fear or apprehension.

I let him look. I meet his eyes and show him I'm feeling both. As he inhales sharply with the force of my emotion, I stroke his face and whisper, "Just because I'm afraid, doesn't mean we should wait."

"Why tonight?" Luther is holding a bottle of whiskey but has yet to pour himself a glass. The three of us, and Kole, are alone. Shortly after I told him I wanted him to kill Eve, Nico freaked out and ran to the bathroom. Rev went after him, and Sarah took the opportunity to shut herself back in her room, telling us to make sure we let her know the second Sam returns.

"Nico has to get into The Hollow tonight because tomorrow morning, he must kill Eve and tomorrow *night*, we must end this."

"Nova, you got back less than twenty-four hours ago. We've barely had a chance to absorb it all or to talk about what happened while you were gone." Luther puts the whiskey bottle down, his fingers moving to the ring hanging around his neck.

"It has to be fast because this time *we're* taking control," I tell him. "We are doing this on our timeline—not *his*." I smile and put the knife down on the kitchen worktop, then slot one hand into his and one into Tanner's.

"But tonight…" Luther grips my fingers.

"I want it to be over." I look past him at Kole, who's been watching me carefully. "I want all of this to be over, so the six of us can be normal."

Tanner stares at me for a moment, then chuckles. "You realize that's an oxymoron, right? Six people in a relationship isn't what most people would call normal."

"It's *our* normal," I say gently, opening my arm so that Kole joins us for a three-way hug.

We're nuzzling into each other, and I'm starting to think about taking the three of them into the shower and having them help me wash the remnants of dried blood from my skin, when we hear thundering footsteps in the stairwell.

Kole hurries to open the door and welcomes in Mack, then Sam, then Snow—who pushes the kitchen table out of the way so he can fit into the room.

Rev emerges from the bathroom just in time to see one of her favorite vases go flying, but Mack swiftly catches it with a plume of air. Unimpressed, Rev plucks it from mid-air and sets it down near the TV. "Well, shit," she says. "Snow, it's good to see you. But I'm not sure there's room for a two-ton bear in my apartment."

"He doesn't weigh—" Mack starts to correct her but, catching her raised eyebrow, stops and clears his throat. "I can't be separated from him," he says, a slight tremor in his voice. "If there's not room, we can sleep on the roof."

"No. You can't." Rev folds her arms, taps her foot on the floor, then huffs and says, "We'll make do."

"It won't be for long," I tell her.

She meets my eyes. When she glances back at the bathroom, there's a protectiveness in her stance that I hadn't noticed before. "He's barely himself, Nova. Does it have to be tonight?"

I don't repeat what I said to the others, but nod at her and mirror her pose, crossing my arms over my stomach. "It does." I turn and pick up the knife, then reach into the cupboard above the stove and take out a glass. "If I fill this, will you take it to him?"

Rev inhales slowly, then nods.

"Nova?" Mack looks from me to the knife.

Setting the glass down in the sink, I raise the blade to my palm. All at once, the five of them lurch toward me.

"It's okay." I pause with the metal close to my skin. "I'll heal." I flick back my hair to show them there are no wounds on my neck. "It won't be deep. I'll heal."

As I pierce my palm with the tip of the knife, everyone but Kole looks away from me. When I wince, he steps forward and takes hold of my wrist for me, tilting the stream of blood toward the waiting vessel.

"How much?" he asks softly.

"I'm not sure. How much do you think you drank?"

Kole shakes his head, moistening his lips as if he can still taste me. "This should be enough." He nods at the glass then grabs a dishcloth to stem the flow of blood.

While Tanner winds the cloth around my hand, Kole

hands the glass to Rev. She sucks in her cheeks. Her nose twitches when she looks at it. "I'll see he drinks it."

"Rev, do you need company? We don't know what will happen." Mack moves across the room, but Rev lifts her palm at him and shakes her head.

"I trust him. If I need you, I'll shout."

Mack stops beside Snow, who is sniffing the air.

Quietly, Rev closes the bathroom door. When she's gone, Sam finally crosses the room and wraps his arms around my waist. Burying his face in my neck, he breathes me in and runs his hands up my back. "I'm sorry," he whispers. "I was hurt and angry. I've always wondered what use I was to you when the others are so strong..." He pulls back, his dark curly hair falling over his face.

I brush it free and stroke his stubbled jawline. "You have nothing to be sorry for, but you have to believe me when I say that *you* are still part of this. I don't love Nico. He's not even feeding from me. Just drinking it like a nasty shot in a skanky bar."

Sam chuckles a little and lightly pinches my lower lip, then kisses it, then me. "Tell me what you need from me, Nova. I might not be a super powerful mage or a Hellhound from another dimension, but I'm in this with you. I'll do anything you need."

"I know." I reach down and playfully squeeze his butt. "And I'll let you know what I need later. But first..." I unfurl the cloth from my hand and flex my fingers to show off my undamaged palm. "We need to discuss the exciting part." I spin in Sam's arms and, while he hugs my stomach, look at Tanner. He frowns and tilts his head at me. Grinning, I wriggle my eyebrows. "Want to do something really cool?"

40

TANNER

"How cool?" I ask, nudging a chair out from behind Snow so I can sit down. He huffs at me, then barges through to the living room and lowers himself onto the rug like some overgrown sort of dog.

Nova levers herself onto the countertop and sits swinging her legs. She shivers and glances at the bathroom door. "We'll get Nico into The Hollow's grounds before sunrise. The Hellhounds sleep during the day, so he can bunk up with them."

"Can he control his shifts well enough to do that?" Sam asks, sitting down next to me.

"He's in there drinking Nova's blood," Luther says gruffly. "Pretty sure by the time he's done, he'll be stronger. Physically *and* mentally."

I reach for Sam's shoulder and squeeze it gently. "I think Luther's right. My head is clearer than it has been in a long time. After I jumped to find you…" I tap my skull with my knuckles. "Things up here were hard to control. Now, it's like the fog has lifted. Like I can breathe again. Hopefully, her blood will do the same for Nico."

Sam nods slowly, pressing his lips together. I don't have to search his feelings to know he's finding all of this impossibly hard; the idea that we are all going to have a piece of Nova that he can't have must be almost killing him. And the fact *Nico* is to be a part of this, but he isn't? I move my hand to rub his back. He doesn't pull away, but he doesn't relax either.

"When do I kill the witch?" The bathroom door has opened, and Nico is standing just behind Snow.

Snow sniffs the air, staring in Nico's direction, then heaves himself to his feet and moves so his nose is inches away from Nico's face. Mack watches, but doesn't step in.

To my surprise, Nico doesn't falter or look scared. He stands stock still, staring down at the huge polar bear whose jaws are within easy biting distance of his throat. "It worked," he says, looking past Snow at us. "I can feel it." He shudders and rubs his upper arms. "I'm stronger, and my head is clear. So, when do I kill the witch?"

Grumbling, Snow moves just enough to let Nico past. When Rev appears, he lets her stroke his head and returns to the rug.

Something about Nico is different. He moves more confidently all of a sudden, like whatever was inside him that made him feel weak and pathetic has been replaced by something stronger.

Nova assesses him carefully. She's gripping the counter but has stopped swinging her legs. "You'll break through the barrier before sunrise, then sleep with the Hellhounds until mid-day."

"The werewolves are usually sleeping then, too. They stay up all night partying and fucking," Mack says darkly.

I frown at him; I had no idea he'd strayed so close to The

Hollow while he was gone. Close enough to know what was going on inside.

"Good. That will give Nico time." Nova watches him as he crosses the room and stops in front of her.

"I'll kill her while the others are sleeping," he says.

Nova nods. "It has to be quiet. No one must know."

Nico rolls his tongue over his top teeth and pushes his jet-black hair from his face. I look from him to Sam. His hair is straight, and Sam's is curly, but they share the same dark features and—now that Nico's demeanor is less *insipid*—they resemble each other more than ever.

"If you look like one of her hounds, she'll trust you," Kole says.

Nico's jaw twitches. "I can do it," he says. "It will be done."

"Are you sure?" Rev is leaning against the wall near the window, looking down at the street. She turns slowly. "Nico, you don't have to do this."

"Yeah, he fucking does," Luther barks. "I'm sorry, Rev, but he *has* to do this."

She meets Nico's eyes. Something has happened between the two of them in the last few days; there's a bond that wasn't there before. And there's a fear in Rev's face that I haven't seen before either.

"I'll be okay," he tells her, but Rev looks quickly away, back at the window, and hugs her arms around her waist.

"You'll need to time it right," Nova says, breaking the silence. "So there's not too big a window for someone to find out she's missing."

"When do we get to the cool part?" I lean forward, arms on my knees. "You promised me something cool, Little Star."

She raises her eyebrows and smiles at me. "Depends if you're up for it."

"When is Tanner *not* up for anything you suggest?" Luther quips, his hand resting on Nova's thigh.

Flashing him a knowing smile, Nova then shimmies her shoulders and hops down from the counter. "Okay, guys, listen up because this is the important part… as soon as Eve's dead, her spells will stop working. Kole, Mack, Luther, and Snow, you'll be in the woods waiting for my signal. Rev, Sarah, Sam, you'll be back here in the town square doing the same."

Sam blinks at her but doesn't object to being told to stay behind.

"And what will you and I be doing?" I ask. "I'd love to think you're going to say something sexy, but I get the feeling it'll be a bit more life-threatening than that."

Nova meets my eyes. "You're right." She walks over and puts her hands on my shoulders. I sit up straight and take hold of her waist. "You and I, Tanner? We're going to raise the dead."

41

NICO
TEN HOURS LATER

I'm almost at the door when I hear footsteps behind me. Rev trots quickly down the stairs. She's wearing pajamas and a bright yellow robe, her hair wrapped in a similarly bright, patterned scarf. I smile and fold my arms. "You look good when you're worried," I tell her.

She taps her foot and shakes her head at me. "I'm not worried," she says. "You'll be fine."

"Then why did you chase me down here when we already did a big group goodbye upstairs?" I raise my eyes toward the apartment, where the others just gave me slaps on the back, brief handshakes, and encouraging words like, *You've got this, Nico,* and, *See you soon, Nico* as if they suddenly care whether I live or die.

Sam was the only one who meant it when he told me to stay safe. The others, even Nova, just see me as a means to an end. And who can blame them? The bad things I've done in my life far outweigh the good. I'm not arrogant enough to believe otherwise.

"Because I wanted to say..." There's a tightness to Rev's voice that makes me smile.

"You don't have to say anything."

"I wanted to say..." She takes the last few steps in two strides and stands in front of me. She's my height, and her lips are suddenly tantalizingly close to mine. "Do *not* die." She stares at me, and the commanding tone of her voice sends a shiver down my spine.

"Yes, Ma'am," I mutter.

Rev's eyes soften. She nods but doesn't hug or touch me. "Good," she says sharply. Then she gestures to the door.

I want to kiss her. Since the moment I entered her apartment and saw her shining face, I wanted to kiss her, but something tells me that will only happen when she gives permission for it. So, I just turn away and step out into the street.

Of course, Sam offered to go with me. But it's not quite sunrise and the streets are too dangerous. For a Hellhound, they're okay. For anything non-demonic they're a death-risk.

Making my way from the apartment toward the woods, the dark, pulsating energy of The Split calls to me. The demon living inside my head scrapes its claws at my insides. It longs to be near others of its kind. Soon, it will be.

I shift before I reach the woods. It's easy this time; Nova's blood saw to that. The second it touched my lips I knew I was about to become part of something so much bigger than myself.

Her essence and her power cleared my vision and turbo charged both parts of me, the human and the demon. The demon is hungrier and more desperate for bloodshed, but the human now has the power to control it.

Whatever happened to me when I was gone, wherever I

was, whatever thoughts tormented me... none of it matters anymore. Her blood has cleansed me, and now I will help her cleanse the world of the evil my parents brought here.

Finally, I'm about to do *something* worthwhile.

"You've already done that. You saved me," Sam whispered when I told him I was ready to make amends for the lies and deceit of my previous life with The League.

I appreciated the sentiment, but he was wrong. I may have started to atone, but I have a long way to go. And the journey starts here. At The Hollow.

The building looms large in front of me. A huge slash splits the grounds in two. The fountain on one side, the trees and the river on the other. The Split groans and bubbles with heat. I picture the demons below, clamoring for their turn—their chance—to rise and enter the human world. But the sun is about to rise, so whatever is left down there will have to wait until the next sunset.

Rev says it's the power of the moon that helps them ascend and that—because they are not yet accustomed to the light—the sun burns their flesh. Even though the sky is tainted with blood-red hues, and the sun is obscured behind swollen red clouds, they must stay in the dark. At least, for now.

There are powerful astrologers, Rev's family, and she knows more about demons than anyone I've ever met. Perhaps that's why she is the easiest to be around; because she doesn't fear me the way the others do.

I walk beside The Split, its energy bleeding up into my paws and making the hunger for blood beat stronger in my ribs. I see Eve ahead of me on the steps. At the same time, I sense *them* approaching.

Hellhounds who look just like me slither out of the darkness and press close to my sides. We walk as a pack toward the steps. They accept me as one of them, not sensing that I am anything other than their kin.

Eve opens her arms and coos, "My children, you are returned. Have you had fun?" She stops and frowns. Her eyes scan the pack in front of her. "There is one more," she says.

The other hounds growl, so I do too.

She stares for another long moment, then claps her hands with glee. "You found your lost brother!" she cries, although she clearly does not know which of us is the new addition to her flock. "Clever babies," she murmurs, trotting down to stroke and pet and kiss us.

When we have finished licking her hands and face, she stands and claps a second time. "Bedtime," she says. "Off to the stables. You need your beauty sleep."

Immediately, the others start running. Jostled along with them, I run too. We run close to the house, across a narrow stretch of ground at the pinched end of The Split. When we reach the stables, the hounds flop down in a large bed of straw and almost instantly fall asleep.

I curl on the outskirts of the group. Their stench catches in my throat and makes me nauseous. They sleep noisily, grunting, gnashing their teeth, scratching their bedding with their large, curled claws. While they sleep, I wait.

42

NOVA

"Little Star, what you're talking about doing..." Mack smooths his firm hands over my shoulders. My skin is still carrying remnants of my blood, as is Mack's beard. We should have showered last night, but there was too much talking. Hours and hours of talking, and they are still not convinced of my plan.

Reaching around me, Mack turns on the shower over the bathtub.

"I like it hot," I tell him, increasing the temperature with a blink that instantly fills the room with steam.

"Nova." Mack's voice is stern. He meets my eyes and tucks my hair behind my ear. "I don't doubt your power. Not for a second. But this is a level of dark magick no one here has ever seen, let alone played with."

"That's where you're wrong." I hook my arms around his neck and wriggle closer. "It's not dark magick. It's the opposite."

"Raising the dead? You think that's—"

Before he can finish speaking, I press my finger to his lips. "I don't want to talk anymore. We've talked all night. I've said all there is to say." I slide my other hand down his front and tease the line of hair that disappears beneath his waistband.

Mack growls and reluctantly takes hold of my waist, the bulge in his pants already straining to be set free.

"I want you to show me how much you missed me, Daddy."

Roughly, he pulls me closer, so my hips press against his. "You know how much I missed you."

Stepping away, I peel off my clothes and drop them to the floor. Mack catches my hand and makes me stand in front of him. His eyes roam my body as if he's trying to memorize every inch, then he takes off his clothes too.

The piece of blue string around his neck looks strange against the salt and pepper hair on his chest. He catches me looking at it and loops it over his head. Removing the ring, he drops to his knees in front of me and slides it back onto my finger.

I smile down at him as his hands roam up over my stomach. When they reach my waist, he spins me around, then stands and spanks my ass so hard the sound makes me yelp. "In the shower," he growls. "Now."

Eagerly, I step into Rev's tub and stand under the stream of hot water. When Mack joins me, I rub his beard to free it of the blood stains, then pull his face to mine and kiss him.

Before I can ease my hand down between us and take hold of him, Mack spins me around to face the cool, tiled wall. With one swift, practiced movement, he's inside me, hooking my leg up to balance my knee on the side of the bath. He holds me still, pressing the weight of his chest into my back, then reaches for the shower head.

For a moment, he simply washes me with it; moves it

over my back, and down my arms, and over my hips, all while his dick remains perfectly still inside my cunt.

Then he jerks my hips back, making room for his hand to move in front of me. He changes the setting on the shower head. The pressure stings my inner thigh. "Where do you want it?" Mack whispers as he finally moves inside me; easing out, pausing, then ramming back in with a force that makes me hum.

"You know where I want it, Daddy."

At the sound of the word *daddy* on my lips, Mack sighs heavily and scrapes his teeth along my bare, wet shoulder. He presses the jet of water to my clit, holding me close, running his spare hand up and down my body while the other moves the shower in tantalizing circles.

I orgasm hard, grab the shower head, and pull it from his hand because the pressure is too much. The water sprays up onto the ceiling, covering the bathroom and our faces with its mist. I reach for the taps, but Mack holds me in place. "You're not going anywhere until you come again," he growls.

His fingers arrive at my clit. The bathroom is soaking wet. Mack puts his hand around my throat and tilts my head up so I'm looking at him.

He thrusts into me as he says, "Did Sam tell you what I did to him in the woods?"

My knees almost buckle. I *knew* something happened between the two of them. "No," I moan, bracing my hands against the wall.

"I wrapped my hand around his cock," Mack says breathlessly. "Held it tight against my own. Both of us, in my hand."

Another moan flutters from my lips as Mack teases my sensitive core with both his dick and his fingers.

"We came at the same time, then Sam licked it from my fingers."

"Holy stars, Mack..." I slam back onto him as a second

orgasm rattles through me. The steam is so thick now I can barely see. Someone bangs on the door.

"Guys, what the hell? You're steaming up the whole fucking apartment." Tanner yells.

The thought of Tanner listening makes me yell louder as the orgasm settles gently on my skin. Like a gentle breeze, it keeps rolling over me as Mack punches the wall.

"Let me watch." I pull away from him, so he's standing with his throbbing dick in his hand. "Show me how nicely you can come for me, Professor."

Mack meets my eyes and, barely a second later, he shoots ropes of hot cum into the bathtub. It paints my toes creamy white but is soon washed away.

With shaking legs, I grab the showerhead as Mack turns it off at the tap.

He trails a line of kisses up my spine, then spins me around and moves to my lips. "I love you," he mutters, nuzzling my neck. "Don't leave me again, Nova." He stands back and meets my eyes. "Whatever's about to happen, don't leave me again."

"Never." I kiss the bridge of his nose, then squeeze his far-too-perfect butt. "Never again, Daddy, I promise."

When we emerge in the living room, clean but flushed, a round of applause breaks out. Luther and Tanner whoop and whistle. Kole thumps the table. Even Sam is laughing. Thankfully, Rev and Sarah are nowhere to be seen, and Snow is snoring loudly enough from the other bedroom that perhaps *they* didn't hear what was going on.

I roll my eyes and saunter to the kitchen to make coffee.

"Shame we only had the soundtrack instead of the live show," Tanner says. Looking over at me, he adds, "Excuse me,

Little Star, I need to…" He looks down, adjusts a bulge in his pants, and disappears into the bathroom, closing the door behind him.

Luther rolls his eyes but looks equally uncomfortable in his seat.

"Shouldn't we get some sleep?" Mack asks gently.

Wrapped in a towel, hair damp on my shoulders, I wait for the kettle to boil and shake my head. "Don't think I could sleep now if I tried. I'm too wired."

Mack looks rather pleased with himself.

"Not just because of that," I tell him.

"I know." He kisses my forehead. His towel is slung delightfully low on his hips. I glance at Sam and catch him studying the outline of Mack's butt from his seat at the kitchen table. Sitting down next to him, I cross one leg over the other and whisper, "I heard about your woodland encounter with the professor."

Sam's eyes widen, and his cheeks flush.

"When do I get the action replay?" I ask, wriggling my eyebrows at him.

"What replay?" Luther asks butting in.

"Never you mind." I gesture to the kettle, and he rolls his eyes but obliges by taking it off the heat and setting out six mugs. When he puts my coffee down in front of me, he kneels and runs his hands up the inside of my legs, stopping just under the hem of my towel. "So, you don't want to sleep. What *do* you want to do while we wait for sunset?"

Leaning forward, giving Luther a view of my cleavage that makes him moisten his lips, I put my hands on his shoulders and whisper, "You know what I'd really like to do?"

A low grumble comes from Luther's throat.

"I'd like to eat some of Kole's pancakes, drink my coffee, then snuggle down and watch a movie with my boyfriends."

Luther smiles ruefully at me. He sighs a little, but then

stands and kisses my forehead. "If that's what you want, Little Star. That's what we'll do."

I hop up from my seat and kiss him firmly on the lips. "Although," I say slowly. "I could be persuaded to come up with something else to pass the time. If you can catch me..."

Luther frowns. Before he fully understands what I'm saying, I race across the room, letting my towel drop. Kole catches me, flinging his arms around my naked waist, but I kick my legs, squeal, and send a heat to my limbs that makes him yell. He lets go, and I wrestle free.

"That's cheating," he growls.

"Then you'll have to punish me, won't you?" I back into the corner, Luther and Kole advancing toward me, shoulders squared, biceps twitching.

I catch Sam watching us and meet his eyes. Slowly, he rises from his chair. Mack pats his shoulder. "I'll make the pancakes," he says. "You go get your girl."

As Sam joins Luther and Kole, penning me in with looks on their faces that make my heart race, Tanner emerges from the bathroom. He clocks what's happening, mutters, "Sweet," and rubs his hands together.

Four of them and one of me? That's a ratio I can get on board with.

43

NICO

Every minute feels like an hour. I watch the light through the stable door but, with its scarlet hue, it's almost impossible to tell the passing of time. Instead of thinking, I count. The seconds, the minutes, the hours.

When it reaches what I'm sure is close to mid-day, I crawl free from the Hellhounds' nest. Outside, The Split is dark. Just a large, cavernous hole that divides the lawn in two then snakes into the woods and through the center of Phoenix Falls.

As a hound, my vision is strange. Like I'm looking at everything through a curved fishbowl. As a wolf, it was never like this. Things splinter and shudder. Sounds are louder. Smells are violent assaults on my nostrils.

I head for the steps and locate Eve's scent. She reeks of death. Like she's rotting from the inside out. Possibly, after all the F.H.B. she's consumed, she is.

In the house, everything is silent. The place is filthy. Excrement and blood and filth fill the rooms.

Like an apocalypse has ripped through the entire place, weeds and vines creep up from the floor to break huge cracks in the walls and windows. Splinters of glass crunch beneath my feet.

The times I spent here with Nova and the others feel like they took place in a different lifetime. To a different person.

I pass Mack's study. It is empty, but Eve was here at some point because I can smell her in it. I smell Ragnor too. His scent grows stronger as I approach the living room; the one with the huge fireplace and the comfortable sofa. I smell something else, too. Sam's mother, Elena; a strange mixture of flowers and death.

In the entrance hall, I stop, staring at the door behind which Ragnor and Sam's mother must be sleeping. A fourth scent twitches in the breeze. It is faint, disguised by something acrid and nauseating.

Mother?

I spin around, searching for her. She's here. I smell her. She's here somewhere. In the house. My heart pummels my ribcage. I want to shift and call her name. Why is she still here? After everything Ragnor did to her and to me? Why would she come back to him?

I sniff the ground, then follow her scent up the walls into the air. I stop. It's above me. She is above me.

Slowly, I raise my eyes. At first, it is too gloomy to see anything. Thick, black, web-like reeds coat the ceiling. Beneath them, something bulges. Pinned like a fly in a spider's trap.

I strain my eyes. The shape solidifies in my vision. I stifle a howl and scoot back, slamming against the wall as I bite down the urge to run.

My mother's face stares down at me. Gray cheeks,

unblinking eyes, head hanging at an unnatural angle while the black web pins the rest of her body to the ceiling.

She is dead.

My mother is dead.

* * *

I STARE at her for too long. I don't know how much time has passed or whether I'm about to be discovered at any moment. Eventually, I tear myself away, vowing with every breath in my body that I will return for her when this is done. Vowing that she will at least have a proper burial despite the path she chose to tread with Ragnor.

I move deeper into the belly of the building. Vines trail along the wooden floorboards, growing thicker and darker the further in I go.

Ahead is the ballroom with its chandelier and its pool table, except something tells me those things are no longer there. Something tells me that is where *he* is. The King.

I find myself drawn toward it. The door undulates and shifts in front of me. His energy bleeds through into my nose, and my skin, and my lungs. The familiar ice-cold darkness that turned every waking second into torture when I was with him in that place returns. I want to run, yet something inside tells me I need him. I need the pain. I need his darkness to fill me, and blind me, and help me see.

I reach the door and rub against it, nuzzling it with my furless skull. A howl bites at my throat, but I swallow it down.

"Baby, are you lost?" Eve's voice brings me back to myself. I whimper as she crouches in front of me. "Are you hurt, my love?"

I lift my paw, then lick it, whining plaintively.

She tilts her head. "Poor darling." She cups my skeletal

snout and kisses it. "Come with Mommy." She drifts off down the hall, patting her hip to tell me I should follow her.

Tearing myself away from the throbbing call of The King's darkness, I pad after the witch. In the entrance hall, I try to keep moving but my feet stop of their own accord. The heavy knowledge that my mother is suspended, lifeless, above my head weighs down on me. I don't want to look at her, but I can't help it.

Ahead, Eve stops. She looks back and smiles. "When she's fermented a little longer, you and your brothers can have her." She tilts her head and rubs her hands. "I'm glad I only broke her neck. If I hadn't kept her whole, I wouldn't be able to watch you tear her apart." She smooths her palms over her hair and sighs wistfully. "And I will take such joy from that." She blinks and returns her gaze to me. "Come, we will feed on the wolf later. Now, come, let me look at your foot."

When we reach the kitchen, Eve moves through the filth toward the sink, taking a cloth and muttering something about cleaning my hurt paw, but I whimper again and stand in the doorway.

Eve tilts her head. "You need to show me something? Did something hurt you?"

I trot down the steps. Now, she is following me. At first, I have no idea where to take her, but then a flash of memory reminds me of the day I left—through the river—to fetch Nova's blood results from the hospital. So, I head for the water.

We use the same narrow place to cross to the other side of the lawn. At the river bank, panting, Eve catches up with me. I stand at the edge, staring down into the water. She kneels beside me. "What is it, my darling? What have you found for Mommy? Is there something here that hurt you? Some nasty water beasts that crept up from beneath?" She puts her thin hand on my shoulder.

I wait, my heart thudding loudly in my ears. Then I let it take over... I let the bloodlust race through my veins. I feel it rip through me, but I don't make a sound. I fix my eyes on the witch's face. Eve frowns. She opens her mouth to speak, then I clamp my jaws around her head and rip it from her shoulders.

44

NOVA

"You're okay with this?" I take Sam's hands and pull him away from the group. "I know we haven't had enough time to talk." I reach up and brush his curly hair from his face. "I'm sorry."

Sam looks down at my fingers, now once again decorated with all five rings. He runs his thumb over the one he gave me. "I'm sorry too." He presses his forehead to mine then kisses me so deeply I'm almost knocked off my feet. "I love you, Nova. I might not be fated to be a part of this, but I still believe I'm fated to be yours." He smiles and strokes my hair from my face.

"From the moment I saw your flash of red hair, standing on the doorstep when I was dropped off at your parents' house, I knew I would love you forever. I just didn't know *how* I'd love you."

A sigh hums inside me. I hold him close, my fingers tracing the shadow of his scars, only just noticeable beneath his black t-shirt. When he pulls away from me, Sam looks at the others. "Take care of her. I'll see you all soon."

There's a moment of hugs and goodbyes between the boys, then Tanner and I stride out ahead with Mack, Snow, Luther, and Kole following.

When I get to The Cross, I turn and look back. I can make out Sam's silhouette in the town square. With Rev and Sarah, he will wait for my sign. Then they will bring the supers of Phoenix Falls to The Hollow for one last fight.

We walk in silence, following The Split all the way to the mansion. As the sun fades in the sky, the hole begins to steam and bubble. Sounds that make me shudder drift up from below us, and the air hums with the threat of darkness.

"Where do they hide during the day? The ones who are already here?" I ask Mack.

He puts his hand on my lower back, the warmth of his palm comforting me. "We believe they've made dens in abandoned buildings throughout town. To start with, some of the townsfolk tried to fight back. A group of vigilante vamps took out at least three demon nests before they were caught."

"What I want to know is what's *he* been doing all this time?" Luther narrows his eyes and looks ahead through the trees. We are almost at The Hollow.

"The King?" Tanner asks.

"I hate that we call him a *king*." I wrap my arms around my waist and hug myself. "He isn't my king."

"What do you prefer?" Tanner asks, trying to make me smile. "Big fat idiot?"

"He doesn't deserve to be named." I look up at the forest canopy and catch snatches of the darkening red sky. "But we know what he's been doing; he's been gathering his strength."

Tanner frowns. "Why didn't he come after you when he learned you were here?"

I allow myself to smile. "Because he's a big fat idiot, and

because he thinks we are weaker than him." I point ahead, bracing myself for what's about to happen. "He's about to learn he was wrong."

The shadowy outline of The Hollow is visible in the distance. The Split now divides the lawn in two, the broken fountain on one side—a tributary of broken ground leading directly from it to The Split itself—and the river on the other.

I take Tanner's hand and point to the pile of rubble where the fountain once stood, bright and beautiful on Mack's lawn. "That's where we must do it."

"There?"

I nod at him. "It was where they burned the witches. It has to be there."

Tanner squeezes my fingers between his, gives the other men a stoic nod, then steps aside so I can say goodbye. This time, there are no tears and no loving whisperings. Instead, I kiss them each on the lips, hug Snow tightly, and simply say, "I'll see you soon. Watch the sky. You'll know when it's time."

Carefully, Tanner and I approach the edge of the wood. He picks up a stone and throws it at the place where the barrier should be. Instead of bouncing back, it skitters onto the lawn. So, we move forward.

"He did it," I whisper as we break into the open. "Nico killed her."

The knowledge that Eve is gone weighs heavy in my gut. After everything she did to us, she is no longer breathing. Under any other circumstances, I'd celebrate but there isn't time.

Ducking behind the fountain so we're out of view of the house, I smooth my hands over the grass. The sun is about to dip behind the tree line at the back of the house. "We only have a few minutes to make this happen, Tanner. We need them to rise before the demons wake. And before *he* realizes Eve is gone."

"I'll do my best, Little Star, but I've never brought a bunch of angry, burned-at-the-stake witches back from the dead before. So, I'm getting a fair bit of performance anxiety right now."

Putting my hands on his shoulders, I stare into his bright hypnotizing eyes. "You can do this. It's just like jumping, only..."

"Only I need to convince them to wake from their thousand-year-old slumber and come help us defeat the biggest, baddest demon of all time?"

I tilt my head and wrinkle my nose. "Easy, right?"

Tanner breathes out hard. He glances at the remains of the fountain as if he's wishing it was full of water so he could use it to ground himself. Purposefully, he takes a long, slow breath then presses his palms to the floor and prepares to bring the Original Six back to Phoenix Falls.

"Focus on Ava. You saw her in the vision. Focus on her. Reach for her first. She'll bring the others." As I speak, Tanner closes his eyes. His eyelids start to twitch as he mutters the same incantation he used when he tried to reach Sam.

At first, his voice is normal but then it changes. It grows louder. I hiss at him to be quiet, but he doesn't hear me. His fingernails dig into the earth, gathering large clumps of it in his hands.

The sun is moving faster now. The light fades and a deep, bloody blackness sinks over us. Through The Hollow, lights illuminate the windows and shadows move across them. The wolves are waking up, which means *he* is too. He will sense us, sense our magick; we must do this quickly.

Tanner stops chanting. He opens his eyes, and they are jet black. He sits back on his heels, his arms flinging out sideways. The ground rumbles. At the same moment, The Split starts to glow. Just as they have every night since my blood brought The King back into our world, creatures appear from beneath.

Salivating, groaning, hollering for blood, they crawl out of the earth. One, two, five, ten. I shake Tanner's shoulders and beg him to hurry, but he is immovable and utterly unreachable.

Instead of waiting for my signal, the others run from their hiding place. A creature with huge, hooked claws and a face with no eyes lunges for Kole. He sends a mound of earth up in front of it, knocking it from its feet. In a flash, Snow bites down on it and rips its head off.

"Tanner, please, what's happening?" I grab his hands, but they're stiff and do not move.

Luther and Mack try to heave him to his feet, but Tanner releases a huge, bellowing roar. His head snaps back so he's staring at the sky. His mouth opens, and a beam of bright blue light soars from somewhere deep inside him.

"No, no, no." I stand up, staring at Mack. "Sam and Rev will think it's time. Everyone in town..." I spin around. The Split is heaving. It looks like its sides might buckle with the weight of what's coming from below it.

I suck air down into my lungs and try to breathe. It's not working. Tanner was supposed to bring back the witches who died at The Hollow. They were supposed to fight with us. I was so sure. It all made sense; our connection to Ava and her men, our history, our bond...

I search for Kole. He and Snow are fighting back as many creatures as they can. Snow wails as one clamps its jaws down on his shoulder. Then from the other side of The Split, I hear the Hellhounds. They charge toward us, but before they can leap over to our side, one of them turns on the others.

Nico...

There is a flurry of snarling, howling, and teeth. Sounds that send ice-cold fear to my soul, filling my ears. I slam my hands over them. My heat flickers and starts to fade. I try to pull my magick to the surface, but I feel *him* coming. I feel his heavy footsteps, and his breath on my neck even though he is still deep inside the house. Dread washes through me, scraping my insides raw. Johnny's face fills my head. I see him staring down at me. I feel his mark on my skin. I feel my flesh burning and hear it sizzle as the red-hot poker scars me forever.

Except... it wasn't forever.

My eyes spring open. I latch onto Kole. The first time we met, I saw him through the rain. As if it knows, the sky rumbles and the clouds open. Water drops divine honey-like clarity onto my skin. With each raindrop, I see more clearly what needs to be done.

I see what he is doing. He is trying to break me.

He will not win.

With a roar, Mack sends a cyclone of air ripping across the grounds, sweeping demons up into it, then slamming their broken bodies into the outer wall of the mansion.

Luther opens his arms and splays out his fingers. He is staring at The Hollow. Wolves appear on the steps. Some race toward the fight, some away from it. Luther hems them in. Walls of fire, as high as the mansion itself, spring from the ground, licking the sky.

Behind us, the trees sway as if they might pull themselves free from the earth and walk beside us. Kole heaves one from the ground and sends it hurtling toward The Split. It rolls in, taking a huddle of demons with it.

I plant my hands on Tanner's face.

I press my fingers to his skull and use every morsel of power inside me to find his magick with my own. I close my eyes. I see my bright orange light reaching out, swirling around his. When I open my eyes again, fire surrounds us. It circles up into the sky and down into the ground.

Tanner's eyes clear. He meets mine and nods at me. Then we chant together. At the final word, a blast of energy hits me. I bend double and press my palms to the ground.

With a scream that makes me feel like I'm going to explode from the inside out, I feel their magick surging through me. The women who died here. The women who were wronged, and accused, and torn from their loved ones. The women who *burned* because of the evil that ravaged men's hearts. Not *his* evil but an evil all the same.

Their pain, their strength, and their love bleeds into my fingertips and rushes through my veins. I clamber to my feet, pulling Tanner up with me. Our hands are shaking. Blue and orange light swirls around our fingers. My entire body starts to convulse. The magnitude of the force I'm holding inside me brings another scream from my lips. Tanner nods at me. I keep his gaze but turn to face the fountain that lies broken behind us.

At the same time, we turn our eyes on the crumbled concrete, and extend our hands. Our light rushes toward it. It gathers up the pieces of the fountain and carries them up into the air. Then it crushes them to dust.

When the dust falls, it settles on the ground like glittering hot snow.

Tanner reaches for me. We hold each other up, legs quaking. Then the dust turns to something else; a fine blue mist that shimmers in the air in front of us. A shape appears in the mist, like the indentation of a person hiding behind a thin, willowy curtain.

I step forward, leaving Tanner, and reach out my hand.

There she is... her name parts my lips with such force I'm almost brought back to my knees. "Ava..."

45

RAGNOR

"My darling, listen to me." I try to stop my voice rising in volume, but she is making it very hard. "You must listen. Many things have changed since you were last here."

Elena frowns at me. Her beautiful face crumples and she shakes her head. "Since I was last *where*? Ragnor, please, I don't understand. I keep telling you, I don't understand. I want Sam. I want the baby. I want to go *home*."

I sigh and grip the mantlepiece. We've been going round in circles for hours, days, weeks. The King wants her to be turned. He doesn't care into what; she just cannot be human when we leave this place.

At first, I objected, but then I thought about it and realized he is right. She deserves to be strong. She deserves to live a long life unhindered by human concerns. She deserves to be at my side when The King takes his place.

Whether or not I believe, like Eve does, that it is his *rightful* place is of no consequence. What matters is that I picked the right side. Everything we planned is coming together. Elena is the final piece. She has always been the final piece.

"Who is the girl Eve talked about?" Elena stands up, worrying the hem of her cardigan with her lithe fingers. "She said *Nova* had returned. You looked upset. Is Nova your girlfriend? Have you been cheating on me, Ragnor? Do you love someone else?"

At the mention of The Phoenix's name, I punch the wall beside the fire. My knuckles are bleeding when I turn to her and stride forward. Grabbing her wrist, I yank her toward me and lower my face to hers. "Don't *ever* accuse me of loving someone else." I wave my hand at the disgusting dark hovel of a room we've been living in. The whole place is infected with The King's evil. It quivers in the walls and seeps from the ceilings. "All this was for you. All of it!"

"Then who is she?" Elena tugs away from me, her eyes flashing. "Why do you care so much about her?"

An ironic laugh shakes my chest. I tug my hair and turn away from her. "She's the fucking phoenix," I mutter. "And she was supposed to be dead. I watched her die."

"Ragnor?" Elena's voice is smaller now. "You killed someone? A girl?"

I breathe in slowly, feeling my shoulders shake. I don't have time for this. Trying to smile, I turn back to my wife and cup her face in my hands. "The Phoenix is an evil, powerful witch, my love. She is here to hurt us. But don't worry, Eve and The Shadow King will make sure she doesn't get anywhere near you. They'll send her back to hell where she belongs."

"King?" Elena blinks up at me.

I grit my teeth and bite the inside of my cheek. I'm about to kiss her, just to stop this incessant line of questioning, when a flash of light fills the window.

Leaving Elena, I stride over to it and peer out at the lawn. The Split is glowing. Just like they do every night, The King's loathsome creatures are slithering free from it. But beyond them, something else is happening.

"The Phoenix…" I press my palms to the glass. She is here, in the grounds of The Hollow, with her mages. How did she break through? How did she take down Eve's barrier?

Three mages are using their magick to manipulate the elements and fight the demons rising from beyond. The bear —huge and white—rips at heads and limbs with its powerful jaws. Another mage sits on the floor. The empath. The one I let slip through my fingers when the seer stole him from The League's grasp.

The empath's head snaps back and a bright blue light billows from his mouth up into the sky. The ground begins to shake. From the inner core of the mansion, The King's voice fills my ears. A scream so high-pitched it almost breaks my skull in half rattles the walls.

He is calling for me, and for Eve, and for the wolves, but I do not heed his cry. I am done. I am not risking my life for this, not anymore. "Come with me." I grab Elena's hand and run for the entrance hall. Throwing open the front door, ignoring Kayla's rotting body that hangs above us, I drag her down the steps.

"Where are we going? Ragnor? What's happening?" Her feet slow. She's staring at the lawn. A small cry escapes her mouth. "What is *happening*?"

I keep hold of her hand and tug. When she doesn't move, I pick her up and throw her over my shoulder and run to the river. "We'll swim across. I'll scale the wall and pull you up with me."

"No, I don't want to." She shakes her head, pummeling my back with her fists.

"Elena, for fuck's sake, be quiet and do as I say!" I throw

her to the ground, towering over her. Her eyes widen, but she isn't looking at me. She's pointing at something behind me. Her finger trembles.

"Ragnor..."

I spin around, ready to shift, teeth flashing. Then I realize what she's seen. Hanging from a branch, which is bowed across the river, is Eve's headless body. I move toward it and my foot catches on something.

When I look down, bile springs to my throat. Eve's head is touching the toe of my shoe. Her eyes are open, her neck torn, her lips black. I kick it away from me, and it lands with a splash in the river. Elena is screaming. I grab her shoulders and shake her. "Stop it. Elena. Stop this, now."

I am yanking her to her feet when she says again, "Ragnor..."

I turn, still holding her wrist. Something steps out of the shadows. A wolf. A familiar wolf. Its voice fills my head as it meets my eyes. *Get your hands off my mother.*

46

SAM

The minutes we wait in the square are like torture. Sarah wraps her arms around me, and I hold her close. "I'm sorry we haven't had much time to talk," I tell her. "Everything has been…"

Sarah steps back and cups my face in her hands. "All I ever wanted for you, Sam, was to be happy. Are you happy?"

I feel my forehead crease as I absorb her question. "When all this is over, I think I will be."

Sarah pats my cheek. It sends a shockwave of memories through my head. I see her younger, smiling, chasing me through the grounds of a large empty house. "What about your mother?" She meets my eyes. I try to pull away, but she doesn't let me.

I suck a deep breath past my teeth and put my hands on Sarah's shoulders. "I'm going to get her out of there."

I expect Sarah to look scared, start fiddling with her sleeve or biting her lower lip. But she doesn't; she just nods. "Yes," she says. "You must. She cannot stay with him." She squeezes my elbow and meets my eyes. "I will help you, Sam. I'll be at your side. I let you down all those years ago. I allowed them to take you away and—" Her breath falters but she draws her chin up and tries to look a little more stoic.

"You did *not* let me down. You tried your best." I look down at her pocket. Her wand is sticking out of it.

Catching me staring, she takes the wand out and holds it in front of her. "I am not as strong as the rest of you. I'm not even as strong as the weakest elemental witch in this town, but I will not take the easy road this time. When you disappeared, I could have fought to find you. Instead, I worked for Ragnor. I betrayed Nova. Because I was too weak to stand up to him." She turns the wand over in her hands, her thumbs tracing the smooth wood. "This is my chance to make it up to you all."

I nod slowly and hug her for a second time. "I won't tell you to stay behind," I whisper. "I know what it's like to feel as if you're a spare part because your powers aren't as kick-ass as everyone else's."

Laughing, wiping her moist eyes, Sarah shakes her head at me. "You can kick ass, Sam. You've always been feisty. Don't underestimate yourself." She turns and looks up at the sky. It is almost sunset now. "You might not have Nova's blood in your veins, but you have her love. And love is a very powerful thing."

I reach for her hand. On my other side, Rev steps up next to me and slots her arm through mine. "Any minute now," she says. "If their plan works, we should see Nova's sign any minute now."

As we stare at the sky, up and down the street, doors begin to open. Despite the fact Nova's sign has yet to appear, witches, shifters, and mages head toward the town square. In quivering silence, they gather behind us and tilt their heads toward the setting sun like they know it must be tonight.

The sun's final descent is fast and, as soon as it has ducked below the horizon, the vamps join us too. The town's collective energy presses down on my back, almost propelling me forward. I glance at Rev, and she smiles softly. "Seems like whatever happens, Phoenix Falls is not going down without a fight."

Murmurs begin to ripple through the crowd. The sky is dark now, but there are no stars, and people are getting twitchy. "They'll be here soon," someone shouts. "Those hell creatures will be waking up. When will it happen? When will we see the sign?"

Someone else yells, "Are you sure it's tonight? She never said it would be tonight."

Another joins the chorus, pointing at me. "That's one of her boyfriends. He wouldn't be out here if it wasn't tonight."

I run up the town hall steps and wave at them for quiet. I'm about to tell them to go back to their homes until we know it's time. But before even a whisper can leave my lips, we see it... a beam of bright blue light shoots up into the sky and breaks apart the blackness.

Everyone turns to look at me. "Can't get much more obvious than that," I shout, taking the steps two at a time to arrive back at Rev's side.

"Time to go," she says darkly.

I look from Rev to Sarah, then nod. "Time to go."

* * *

THE THREE OF us walk ahead, telling the rest of the town to follow behind and remain as quiet as possible. When we reach the woods, the shifters turn. Mostly wolves and panthers, but a couple of tigers, too.

The vamps flit quickly from tree to tree, preferring the air to the ground. At first, there is an air of confidence, a surge of adrenaline as we march toward the fight. But the closer we get to The Hollow, the thicker the air becomes.

Thick with the same creeping, black terror I felt when I was in *his* realm. Sarah takes out her wand and holds it so tight her knuckles whiten. Rev's hands are at her sides, ready to use whatever magick she can muster. The one with the scar on it twitches. She's in pain, but she's not showing it.

I stay human until we reach the tree line in front of The Hollow. I'm about to shift when I realize all is not as it should be. Nova is shaking Tanner, yelling at him. Behind them, The Split is aching, heaving, crawling with demons.

Snow, Kole, and the others are fighting them back, but they keep coming.

"Something's gone wrong." Rev scans the grounds. "I don't see any ghost witches, do you?"

Sarah grabs my arm. "It looks like they're losing."

My eyes roam the scene in front of me. "It doesn't matter what was supposed to happen. They need help." I turn and raise my voice. "This is it. If we give up now, Phoenix Falls is gone and The Shadow King will be released on the world. So, do we run like cowards or fight like supers?"

No one speaks.

Groans, and shrieks, and howls fill the air.

Rev grabs my hand. Staring out into the trees, at the blinking eyes that are watching us, she yells, "I'm not giving up my town without a fight!"

A vamp drops down from a tree and lands in front of us. "Me neither." He flashes his fangs and cracks his knuckles. "I've never tasted demon blood, but there's a first time for everything."

"We're with you." Three young witches, hugging one another's waists, nod at Rev and me.

More voices speak up. The wolves bark, the panthers yowl. Somewhere in the undergrowth, a tiger roars.

I turn back to face The Hollow. We charge forward. I'm about to shift when Sarah grabs my arm. "There, Sam. Is that Ragnor?"

My eyes jolt toward the front of the house. Ragnor is running across the lawn, my mother slung over his shoulder. She is kicking and punching him. Her hair is wild, blowing in the wind.

I shift in an instant and race through the trees. When I reach The Split, I take it in one leap. The vicious heat surging beneath me scalds my belly. I reach the other side, paw slipping on the edge, scramble up, and keep running.

I dart into the shadow of the trees and slow my pace. I approach slowly, creeping through the undergrowth. My mother is on the ground. Ragnor kicks something, which lands with a splash in the river. Then he rounds on her. He towers above her and grabs her wrist.

I jump from the trees, eyes flashing. She sees me. My mother's eyes catch mine. Her mouth hangs open. She stares at me, then my father turns. He is still holding her wrist.

I send my voice to splinter through his skull. *Get your hands off my mother.*

Ragnor drops her hand. She falls to the ground and scrambles back. He lunges but, before he can shift, I leap for his throat.

His flesh is between my teeth when he shifts. Skin becomes fur. I rip at it and tear a chunk free. He is bigger and stronger than me, but I am angrier.

Rolling over one another, claws and teeth clash, fur is yanked from its roots, and the metallic taste of my father's blood fills my mouth. I am on my back, gnashing my teeth, fighting to keep him away from my throat. His teeth pierce my neck. My eyes roll back. Then the pressure is gone.

There's a blast of light and he rolls away from me, howling with pain.

I scramble to my feet as Sarah strides into view. She holds her wand in one hand. Its tip glows silver. With her other, she reaches for my mother and helps her to her feet. "I'll get her to safety," she says, backing away as Ragnor and I square up to one another.

I scrape the ground with my front foot, gathering cold earth beneath my claws. As Sarah moves away, her arm around my mother, Ragnor howls and lunges for them.

I jump at him, aiming for his neck, but there's a flash of gray and something barrels into his side. He falls to the ground, rolling over, bones cracking.

Back on all four feet, I stare at the Hellhound which now stands between me and my father. It backs up slowly, and meets my eyes,

Nico?

Brother, it replies. *We will finish this together.*

Ragnor is human again. He crawls back, feet slipping on the damp mud next to the river bank. His hands reach the edge and give way behind him. He tries to right himself.

At the same time, Nico and I each grab a foot and drag him toward us. "I am your father!" he screams. His voice is sick with fear. "I am your father…." Now it's a whisper.

Nico licks his lips. He glances at me. *Ready?*

I growl deep in my throat, and then we rip the bastard apart. We tear his body in two separate directions and when he is nothing more than two halves of blood, and bone, and muscle, his head barely hanging onto his neck, we roll him into the river and leave him to sink.

47

NOVA

She looks so much like me; I feel as if I'm staring into a mirror. "Ava?"

She extends a shimmering hand. When she touches my cheek, heat surges beneath her palm. "You look like me," she says.

"There isn't much time to explain…"

Ava nods slowly. She looks past me, then up at The Hollow. Her eyes narrow as she takes in the flames. "I know this place." She rubs her arms. "I've *felt* this place before. This is where…" She trails off and turns in a slow circle. "This is not my time," she mutters. "And *those* are not humans."

I take her hand and press my fingers to hers. They are solid but I feel like, if I pressed hard enough, I could pass right through them. "Ava, we need your help. We are your descendants." I gesture to Tanner, then search for the others. They are fighting, desperately trying to look at Ava, but stuck behind the wall of flame I created. "We called you back because—"

"There is a great evil..." Ava raises her eyes to the sky. "I have felt it before. In the men who accused me, who burned me, who took my baby and my life."

I nod, tears filling my eyes. "They call him The Shadow King. He has broken free from his realm, and we are the only ones who can stop him. He is not the one who harmed you. That was the doing of men, but..."

Ava frowns at me.

"I'm sorry, there's so much to say—" A cacophony of screams pierces the air behind us. Supers emerge from the forest.

Ava sweeps my hair from my face. "Shhh. Fear not. We will help you."

"We?" Tanner finally speaks. He is staring at Ava as if he can barely breathe.

She tilts her head and smiles at him. "You remind me of..." Her eyes widen, she blows on the flames I made, and they peter out into nothing but embers. Taking in the others —Mack, Luther, and Kole—she nods. Her eyes sparkle. "We found each other again," she whispers. When she turns to me, she smiles like a mother looking at her child. Then she closes her eyes.

She stretches out her arms and turns her palms to face the ground. She doesn't chant or wave magick beams of light, but her arms start to shake.

The ground moves. Vibrations trickle up into the soles of my feet.

All across the lawn, where the dust from the fountain pieces fell, the same glittering mist appears. The demons stop fighting, swiping at it with their arms, and claws, and teeth.

Figures shimmer to life. Women. Hundreds of women. Some with long hair and aprons, others in nightgowns or creased white robes. Among them, just five men. There is a moment in which no one and nothing moves.

The ghosts of our past move between the demons—who are frozen in time—staring at one another, at the burning Hollow, and the aching split in the earth. A figure, the image of Mack, finds the professor and stands in front of him. I watch, trembling as Tanner, Luther, and Kole are suddenly standing side-by-side with ghosts who look so much like them I can barely tell them apart.

There is only one without a doppelgänger to stand beside; the one who I thought looked like Sam but who—now he's in front of me—I realize looks more like Nico.

Before I can tell him I don't know where the brothers are, time speeds up again. The freeze-frame stops, and the fight intensifies.

The Hollow shakes. A skull-rattling roar bursts from inside it, making Luther's flames tremble and the walls crack. Ava grabs my hand. "Together," she says. But I shake my head. "No, I will go. You must protect them." I gesture to our mages and to the supers of Phoenix Falls. "Protect them for me."

Ava stares into my eyes, then she nods. A smile curls her lips.

As I open my arms and let my wings of fire burst free from my soul, I watch Ava stride into the center of the fight. I leave her with her army of ghosts, and the power of our mages, and follow the acrid stench of evil into the depths of The Hollow.

48

MACK

A ghost who looks like Nova throws a burst of blue light at the demon who's about to take my head off. It hits the ground, rolls away, and falls screaming back into the hellish depths of The Split.

I hear Snow roar, and search for him through the chaos. I feel his heartbeat in my chest. I hear his thoughts in my head. *Snow? Buddy? Where are you?*

I find him fighting side-by-side with a female panther. He hates cats, but this one has some serious claws. As she ducks and yowls, Snow rips the arm of something with no eyes and eel-like tentacles growing from its back. The arm regrows instantly, but the panther goes for its throat.

"You're separate?" The ghost who looks like me yells as he draws back his elbows and extends his palms so that, if I didn't know better, I'd think he was doing Tai Chi.

I copy his movements, and the two of us push a torrent of air toward the pack of filthy League werewolves who are trying to grab hold of three wide-eyed young witches.

"How?" the ghost asks me.

"Long story." I turn and use a gust of wind to bring down a tree full of Karakal demons.

"Can you still shift? Can ghosts do that?"

"We can do it, but right now I'm stronger than he is." A pained smile crosses the ghost's lips. "He doesn't like that very much."

I let out a loud laugh and glance at Snow. "He'd be pissed, too, if he caught me saying that out loud."

We're turning on another group of demons I can't name when pain rips through my upper arm. I stumble and fall forward. The ghost catches me. "Snow," I breathe, straining to stand through the pain. I look up to see him lying on the ground. Blood blooms on his shoulder, slickened by the rain that's still falling, coating his white fur a deep ferocious red. A burst of red light sweeps toward him, hits the same place on his shoulder, and sends him skidding through the wet earth. Next to him, the female panther lies motionless. Her body shivers and she turns back into a human with long black hair. She's not breathing.

I run to Snow as my alter-ego ghost roars and pummels the demons with slashing bursts of wind. They don't even budge. They stand firm, at least ten feet tall, huge feet making indents in the ground.

Kole sees what's happening and brings a tree down at the same moment they charge for us. A howl fills the air. From the other side of The Split, two shadows appear. They leap over it, taking it in one bound, and land in front of me and Snow. A wolf and a Hellhound.

Sam and Nico.

I scramble over to Snow, examining the huge, charred section of flesh on his shoulder. Ripping off my shirt, I press it to the wound—which is both burned and bleeding.

Tanner appears at my shoulder. He pulls a bottle of something from his pocket and sprinkles it on Snow's mutilated skin. Snow's eyes roll back. He roars with pain, and I scream with him.

"He's out of the fight, Mack. Get him to safety in the trees. Nova will fix him later." Tanner makes me look at him, sensing panic is about to take over. "She will fix him, but he should be some place safe."

I look away from Tanner, stroke Snow's head, and stare into his big black eyes. They flash amber, showing me a glimpse of my own face. "Snow, buddy, we've got to move."

He groans and refuses to get up.

"Snow, if you die, I die. 'Cause I sure as *hell* can't live without you. You wanna be responsible for my death?" I grab the scruff of his neck and press my forehead to his. "Move, Snow. You've got to move."

With another loud groan, Snow heaves himself to his feet. I support him with every ounce of strength inside me, but he's heavy as hell. "This is what it was like for the others when we got drunk and smashed stuff up," I mumble as we stagger toward the trees. "We're getting a taste of our own medicine."

Snow huffs. The bleeding has stopped, but the pain hasn't.

"Almost there," I tell him.

When we reach the trees, he collapses and drags himself under the shelter of a low-hanging branch. He growls and sniffs the shadows.

Two pairs of eyes are staring at us. One of them moves closer, then I hear a familiar voice. "Mack? Snow? What happened?"

Sarah pushes free from the undergrowth. Behind her, lingering in the darkness, is Sam's mother.

"Look after him for me? I have to go back." I squeeze Sarah's arm. "Don't let him get up. Keep him here, right?"

"You think I can hold down a polar bear?" Sarah asks.

"Right," I mutter. Turning to look at Snow, I say sternly, "Do not move, that's an order." He huffs at me, but I shake my head. "I don't care. Right now, I'm giving you orders. You stay put. Got it?"

This time, he nudges my hand with his nose; he gets it.

I'm emerging from the trees when I hear Nova scream.

49

NOVA

The Hollow is crumbling. Chunks of stone and brick clatter on the floor around me. Dust falls, and the ceiling creaks. Cracks create deep grooves in the walls. The chandeliers quiver.

Instead of walking up the steps, I flew toward the roof and entered through a window at the top of the house. I pass Tanner's room, then Mack's. Memories swell against the darkness. I pull them deep into my soul and breathe their light instead of *his* thick, black mist which now swirls around my feet.

For each dark, fear-filled memory *he* uses to try and infiltrate my head—Johnny, Kayla, Eve, the A.M.A., my scars, my pain, my parents—I call on a happier one. I allow feelings of love, and light, and power to surge in my belly. I remember how it felt when my flames first set themselves free. I remember how it felt when *I* set myself free. I remember seeing Kole through the rain and waking to Tanner's smiling face. I remember the first time Mack kissed me, and the day Luther finally told me he loved me. I remember Sam ripping off his mask and showing me his face after twenty years apart. I remember it all, and I know *he* cannot take those things away from me.

When I reach the top of the stairs, I find myself eye-level with Kayla. She is hanging from the ceiling in the entrance hall. Her gray, sunken face is the only thing visible beneath a tangle of black weeds.

For a moment, I feel sorry for her, and I hope Nico didn't have to see her like this.

I walk to the bottom of the steps then look up. With a burst of flames, I sever the weeds and she tumbles to the floor. I let her body catch light and watch my fire burn away *his* evil from her skin.

When I put them out, she is still whole. She is not burned or mutilated; she looks peaceful. I descend the stairs and swipe my hand over her face to close her eyes. At least now Nico can bury his mother.

Fire Bird, finally, you have come to join me...

The voice of The Shadow King trickles down through the cracks in the walls. "No," I say loudly, speaking his tongue. The same tongue as the demon from The Cross and all the others who have crept free from his realm. "I have come to finish you."

His words turn into laughter. It shakes the walls and sends the chandelier crashing down from the ceiling. I jump sideways and watch as the glass splinters into a million pieces, narrowly missing Kayla's body.

"Show yourself. Stop hiding." I move past Mack's old living room toward the center of the house. It pulsates as if it is living and breathing. I step on a floorboard, which bends and breaks beneath me, but my wings carry me up and over the gaping hole it creates.

In front of me, the door to the old ballroom is closed and

covered with the same black weeds that bound Kayla. It bows and creaks, like it's trying to swell beneath them, but the weeds hold it shut.

I slice them free with a wave of fire.

They squeal, and squeak, and slither back into the shadows. Then the door slowly opens. Blackness, like ink, fills the air and bleeds toward me. I blink but can't see, so I close my eyes and listen.

I tune out the sounds coming from the grounds—the screams and the hollering and the fighting—and the feel of the crumbling walls. I search for his breath. I find it slithering through the air; raspy, uneven, hollow.

I hear his heart beating fast and urgent in his dark, evil chest.

I *feel* his darkness and, instead of running from it, I follow it.

It makes me scream. It's a scream that threatens to rip my chest open and tear my heart from my ribs. When it stops, the mist clears, and he is there.

He fills the doorway, more than double my height with gray, translucent skin stretched tight over his angular bones. I see his black heart beating and the blood in his veins. He opens his mouth and shows me lines of shark-like teeth. His eyes flash, then he grabs me.

His long, gnarled fingers tighten around my throat, and he squeezes. "You shouldn't have come back, Fire Bird. You should have stayed where it was safe."

As my breath constricts, my wings flicker and die. My fire fades. Its heat is replaced with a cold so violent it brings another scream from my lips.

As pain ricochets through me, I force myself to look into his eyes. A thousand visions batter my brain. Phoenix Falls crumbling, the earth turning to darkness, demons consuming the world, humans in cages, death, sickness, and destruction.

"It's a shame you will miss it," he whispers, a forked tongue sneaking out to moisten his lips. "But it will be worth it to taste your flesh."

I go limp in his grasp. I let the fight fall from my limbs as he lifts me into the air, staring up at me, one hand around my throat and the other snaking up my thigh.

When his dagger-like fingers reach the spot where Johnny once inked his name onto my skin, my eyes fly open. It all surges back. The power, the heat, the flames. They pummel through me, surging to life on my skin and in my eyes.

The Shadow King's hand shakes. It sizzles. Smoke fills the air and surrounds him. He yells and lets me go, then I run. I hurtle through the dying corridors of The Hollow, through the kitchen, down the steps, straight into the belly of the fight.

He surges after me, moving like a shadow, slithering, screaming, searching. When he appears, he roars. The demons flock to his sides, turning to face me as my mages, Ava's ghosts, and the people of Phoenix Falls form an army behind me.

At my side, Ava grabs my hand. I nod at her, and she tightens her grip.

Pushing my feet off from the ground, I rise into the air, taking Ava with me. We hover above the heaving gash in the ground, then reach out our splayed fingers and scream as we pull his darkness toward our light.

The rain falls harder, the wind blows stronger. Our faces sting, and our hair blows, and I feel like my body will collapse under the weight of his resistance.

His demons roar. They reach for him and try to hold him

down, but we have him now. Our fire swirls around him, capturing him in a vicious burning vortex of heat.

We drag him toward us. He is trapped. He tries to speak, but we burn his lips shut. We lock eyes, take a deep shuddering breath, then plough through him with our magick.

Just like I did to Johnny and the wolves and the demon from the bar, I penetrate The King with my magick. Ava's power joins mine and grows and multiplies inside him. It fills every sinew, every fiber of his body. It nestles deep; it wriggles and grinds its way into his bones as he writhes and resists. But his darkness cannot overpower our light. Not this time.

A crack appears in his face, like the jagged rivets that now pepper the walls of The Hollow. His skin becomes liquid, slipping down his skull. He screams a silent scream.

Then our light breaks him open.

Fire burns him from the inside out. It bursts free, filling the air with brightness and heat, and chasing away the darkness. The flames that were holding him fade. He is nothing but ash now, a swirling cyclone of ash.

Ava waves her hand and sends the ash hurtling toward the ground.

The second the ashes disappear inside The Split, the earth heaves, and shudders. The Hollow groans. The walls buckle. The mansion falls.

With a gust of air, Mack and his ghost sweep the demons back toward The Split. They fall one-by-one, screaming and howling as we return them to the realm they came from. The Hellhounds bark and try to hold onto the earth, but it is no use.

When the last creature has been sucked into The Split, Kole stretches out his arms. Muscles shimmering in the moonlight, he roars like the Viking he is and seals the ground shut.

As the earth heals itself, returning to the way it was, Tanner brings a wave of water from the river to wash the ground clean.

Ava and I float back to our feet. Luther rushes to me and pulls me into an embrace so fierce I can barely breathe. Then the others are there—Kole, and Mack, and Tanner, and Sam.

I kiss them all.

When I open my eyes, Ava is standing in the middle of a circle of men who look just like mine. They stroke her face and kiss her forehead and hold her close.

The other witches, shimmering blue visions of the women who died here over so many years, gather in front of us. Behind them, Phoenix Falls' supers watch in awe.

Ava turns to me and smiles. "Our work is done," she says.

"Yes," I tell her. "It is. *Thank you*, Ava."

Turning away from us, Ava walks to the spot where the fountain once stood and raises her arms to the sky. Moonlight catches on her hair. She looks up and whispers, "We can go home now, ladies."

Instead of turning back into dust and ash, and filtering into the ground, Ava and the witches of Phoenix Falls soar like shooting stars up into the sky.

Her fated mates watch her go, then join hands and follow her.

We watch until they are nothing more than twinkling dots on a velvet black canvas. A cheer breaks out in the crowd. Rev stumbles forward. Nico is holding her up, and her side is bleeding, but she is smiling. "You did it, Nova. You did it."

I run forward to hug her, then I look up and raise my voice. "No, *we* did it. Together."

As a stunned hum ripples through everyone, people begin to assess their wounds and hug one another. Sam takes my arm. "Nova," he says, gesturing to the trees. "This is my mother."

A woman with thick, black hair and rose-red lips emerges from the shadows. Sarah is on one side of her, an injured and limping Snow on the other.

Sam runs to them and stands, arms shaking, in front of his mother. She tilts her head, then reaches out to stroke his face. "Sam? Is it really you? How did you get so big?"

Sam pulls her into his arms. He hugs her, but my breath catches in my chest as I watch them because Elena has started to glow. Sam stumbles back and stares at her. She looks at her arms. They are translucent. Her fingers turn to small particles of light that shimmer and drift away on the breeze. Sam tries to catch hold of her, but it's too late. She smiles at him, and then she is gone.

He stands for a while, staring at the spot where he lost her. Then he allows Sarah to hug him. She pats his back but, as I approach them, she guides him into my arms instead.

I hold him tight, feeling him sob against my chest. When he finally stands up, I wipe his cheeks and kiss them. "I'm sorry," I whisper.

"Don't be. I got to hug her goodbye." He shakes his head. "It wasn't right for her to stay."

I nod at him, pride swelling in my chest. Fighting back tears, I turn around and pull the others into a tight group hug. The six of us stand, holding each other for a very long time before Snow nuzzles into our midst and forces me to hug him too.

Stroking his poor, singed fur, I kiss his nose. "I'll get you fixed up," I promise him. "Just as soon as we get home."

Tanner taps my shoulder. A smile dimples his cheek. "I want nothing more than to go home with you, Little Star," he says as Kole steps up behind me and wraps his arms around my waist. Nodding at the crumbled heap that is the remains of The Hollow, Tanner adds, "But where the heck *is* home?"

I laugh and take hold of his hand. "Home? Home is wherever the five of you are."

50

NOVA

TWO MONTHS LATER

"It was nice of them to let us clear up the town before they sent in the reinforcements," Luther mumbles. "I'm going to have serious words with those S.D.B. assholes when I get in front of them. They owe you an apology too…"

"Oh, hush." I nudge him in the ribs and motion for him to fill up the flutes with champagne. "You and Mack have enjoyed every second of being cops again."

"Not every second we've spent away from you," he says smoothly.

"You're going to have to stop being so sweet," I tell him, tucking my thumbs into his waistband. "I only fell for you because you were aloof and grumpy."

"Kole's aloof and grumpy. I'm damaged and mean."

"You're not damaged." I lift up on my tiptoes and kiss him slowly. "But you are mean."

"And you like me that way?" he asks, raising an eyebrow.

I shrug. "What can I say? You're hot when you're angry."

He rolls his eyes, reaching around me to top off the last two glasses with more bubbles. "Fire pun—very witty."

"Are you two bringing the drinks over here, or do we need to leave the room for a moment and give you some time alone?" Tanner calls.

"Patience is a virtue," Luther tells him. "But, yeah, we're coming. You got the cake?"

Tanner flicks his eyes toward the table. He and Sam have strung some balloons above it and Kole is fixing bunting to the ceiling. The sight of them making the cabin all pretty and colorful makes my chest swell with love and happiness.

"You might act like a bunch of big, tough boys, but at the heart you're really just soppy little kittens." I put down the glasses I'm carrying, then tease Sam's hair.

"Did you just liken me to a *cat*?" he asks with a growl in his voice.

I shake my head and bite back a smile. "Never. You're a big bad wolf." I kiss him swiftly, then click my fingers at the knot Kole's trying to tie and finish it for him.

"If you could do that, why didn't you do it sooner?" he says, climbing down the stepladder and folding it away.

I shrug. "Don't like to show off."

He kisses my forehead as he passes to put the steps away under the stairs.

"When's he due back?" I glance at the clock.

"Five-ish. Rev and Nico will be here soon too, but Sarah said she can't make it. She's doing another press call... seems she's become the poster-witch for unelementals all over the country." Luther arranges the champagne glasses in front of the cake, then stands back and folds his arms. He nods proudly and says, "That'll do. Right?"

"Right." I tuck my arm through his and rest my head on his shoulder.

"How old actually *is* the professor?" Sam is sitting on the arm of the couch. Tanner slaps his hand away from the dish of party nibbles on the coffee table.

"As old as time," Tanner quips.

"Fifty-something," Luther says. "He's fifty-something. Right, Kole?"

A growl interrupts us. On his way back from the stairs, Kole opens the door and Snow ambles inside. A fetching piece of metal armor, made for him by the town's grateful blacksmith, covers the burned patch on his shoulder; a drop of my blood healed his wounds, but apparently I can't re-grow hair.

"Still looking like a badass," Kole tells him, patting the giant bear on the back as if he's one of the gang.

"Is it weird that they spend time apart now?" I ask, hooking my arms around Snow's neck for a cuddle. As usual, a deep purr rumbles in his chest as he nuzzles me.

"Nah. You're your own bear. Right, Snow? You're not attached to Mack's apron strings." Tanner sits down on the couch and puts his feet on the coffee table, crossing them at the ankles.

Snow glares at him witheringly, as if he still just doesn't *get* the way he and Mack work.

"Before Mack gets here..." Luther starts to speak but there's a knock on the door. I hop past him to open it and throw my arms around Rev the second she steps inside.

Nico hovers next to her. When she nods at him, he offers me a brief hug too, then takes her jacket.

"Is he here?" Rev scans the cabin.

"Any second now." I point to the clock. "We better get ready."

As we all huddle together behind the couch, Snow tries to join us. He barges into the table, causing Luther to jump up and tell him to mind the drinks. Snow squares up to him and huffs, so I slip between them. "Snow, why don't you wait by the door? Mack will be expecting you anyway."

Snow meets my eyes, grumbles, then does as I say. He is only just in position when we hear feet on the steps outside. The door opens. We wait as the familiar sound of Mack's footsteps fills the room. I expect him to turn on the light but, when he doesn't, I nudge the others. I count to three under my breath, then we spring up and yell, "SURPRISE!"

Luther and I throw balls of light into the room, illuminating the entire cabin.

"What the hell?" Mack is standing in front of us, hands on his hips... butt naked.

"Holy hell, Rhone, where are your clothes?" Rev says, shielding her eyes.

"What is this?" Mack is staring at the balloons. He strides to the wall and flicks on the light, then sends a gust of air to open the curtains.

"A party," I grin. "Surprise!"

"At least he came dressed appropriately," Tanner mutters. "Birthday suit? Get it?"

"We get it, Tanner." Luther strides to the cupboard under the stairs and takes out Mack's customary spare sweats and a t-shirt. Tossing them to him, he says, "Seriously, what's the deal, boss? We know you didn't just shift."

Mack shrugs, his eyes sparkling as he notices me appreciating his unclothed lower half. "Guess I just like being naked," he says. "But seeing as we have guests..." He pulls his pants on then walks over to give Rev a hug. "I'll wait until later to strip off." As he moves away from her, he winks at me.

I take his arm and kiss his cheek. "Happy Birthday, Professor."

Luther hands him a glass of champagne. "Happy Birthday, Sherriff."

Mack puts his arm around me, then gestures to Snow. "It's his birthday, too."

"Ah, we know." Tanner jogs to the kitchen and opens the fridge. Looking at Snow, he says, "You thought we forgot?" Then he heaves out an enormous bucket of fish. Snow opens his mouth and yowls excitedly, but Tanner wrinkles his nose. "You gotta eat them outside, though, buddy. They stink."

As Tanner opens the door and ushers Snow onto the porch, I tuck myself close to Mack's now-clothed upper half and stroke his beard. Kole cuts the cake—an image I never thought I'd see—and Luther fetches another bottle of champagne from the ice bucket in the kitchen.

"To Mack," he says.

But Mack shakes his head. "No…" He raises his glass. "To all of us."

* * *

IT'S dark outside when Rev and Nico head back into town. When the door closes, I dim the lights and Luther sets out some candles.

In the armchair by the window, Mack yawns and stretches. "Anyone want coffee?"

I glance at Tanner. A smile curls his lips. "Actually, Professor, the night's not over yet."

Frowning at him, Mack's about to sit forward when Sam appears behind him and slams his hands onto his shoulders.

Quick as a flash, I kneel at Mack's feet and pull two black scarves from my pockets. He doesn't have a chance to resist as I fix his wrists to his chair.

When he takes in the sight of me on the floor in front of him, his eyes narrow. "What's going on, Nova?"

"Surely, you didn't think we forgot to get you a birthday present?" I ask, leaning in tantalizingly close to his mouth as I stand up.

Mack breathes in sharply and looks around at the others.

Luther is holding a paper bag. He hands it to me, and I lift out the contents. As Mack takes it in, Tanner releases a low whistle. "Is that…?"

"A little something Luther kept from our visit to Spine." I hold it up against myself, so Mack can absorb the shine of the leather.

"You're going to…?" The professor licks his lower lip.

"I'm going to slip into the bathroom and put this on."

Sam moves from Mack's shoulders to stand behind me. He runs his hands down my sides, then nibbles my neck. "I've been teaching our Little Star some dance moves I think you'll like," Sam says, his fingers drifting over my belly.

I turn and kiss him lightly on the lips. "Keep the professor company while I go change."

He nods at me and sinks to his knees in front of Mack.

"You might need a hand getting into this," Luther says, taking the outfit from me.

"It looks complicated." Tanner runs his hand down my arm.

"Very complicated." Kole hooks his hands under the hem of my shirt and lifts it over my head.

As Kole, Luther, and Tanner guide me to the bathroom, I look at Mack. He meets my eyes as he leans back in his chair and lets Sam plant kisses over his stomach. My own stomach twitches with excitement… this is going to be fun.

THE END
(OR IS IT?)

* * *

Want to know what happens next?! A BRAND NEW three-book storyline is about to begin for Nova and the gang. And it'll start riiiiight where we just left them.

THE JOURNEY ISN'T OVER...

The battle against the Shadow King might be over, but that's not the end of Nova's story.

If you're not ready to say goodbye to Nova and the guys then books 7-9, Blood, Ice, and Snow are available now.

LOVE FIRE BIRD?

If you enjoyed Fire Bird, I would be incredibly grateful if
you'd leave a review so that others can discover it too!

As an independent author, reviews are one of the most
important tools we have to help spread the word about our
books.

Even if it's short, it will be *hugely* appreciated.

You can leave reviews on Amazon, Goodreads, or Storygraph
- just search for The Phoenix Prophecy and hit 'leave a
review'.

THANK YOU

Thank you for reading Nova by Cara Clare. If you are looking for more books to get lost in please check out our other published titles at;

www.apbeswickpublications.com.
A.P Beswick Publications
Oswaldtwistle Mills Business Centre
Clifton Mill
Pickup Street
Accrington
BB53AP

ABOUT CARA

If you love why-choose romance, magic, super-hot mages, and even hotter RH scenes, then we're destined to be friends.

I mean it when I say I love keeping in touch with my readers. Come say hi over on TikTok.

www.caraclare.com

[a] amazon.com/Cara-Clare/e/B09ZQRV4QG
[♪] tiktok.com/@caraclareauthor
[○] instagram.com/caraclareauthor

The Ocean Plague

THE OCEAN PLAGUE

or,

A Voyage to Quebec in an Irish Emigrant Vessel.

Embracing

A Quarantine at Grosse Isle in 1847. With notes illustrative of
the ship-pestilence of that fatal year.

BY A CABIN PASSENGER.

[Robert Whyte]

"To throw starving and diseased paupers under the rock
at Quebec, ought to be punishable as murder."—LORD
SYDENHAM.

BooksUlster

First published in Boston in 1848 by Coolidge and Wiley. This new edition published by Books Ulster in 2019.

ISBN 978-1-910375-37-2

Front cover image is from the painting 'An Emigrant Ship, Dublin Bay, Sunset' by Edwin Hayes (1820-1904).

Editor's Introduction

Dire poverty and the threat of starvation that faced large swathes of the peasantry were great recruiting sergeants for emigration agents in mid-Nineteenth Century Ireland. Not without justification, North America particularly was seen by the Irish poor as the epitome of freedom, 'a land flowing with milk and honey', and full of opportunity for those willing to grasp it, so it was naturally and by far the principal choice of destination for the Irish emigrant. Asenath Nicholson, an American widow who travelled through Ireland in 1844 and 1845 expressed it in this way in her *Ireland's Welcome to the Stranger* (1847):

> "But America is all the theme by the laboring class of Ireland; glad was I, that, notwithstanding her abominable slavery, yet here is a little green spot, where I could rest and look my enemies in the face undaunted. The free states of my own country have ever been an asylum to the foreigner, and the reward of his labor has been given him. The ragged laborer has soon exchanged his tatters for decent apparel, the bare feet of the cabin girl have been covered, and the basket has been taken from the back of the peasant woman. I would acknowledge with gratitude that, throughout the length and breadth of Ireland, the poor have required no letter of introduction, but the name of America."

Although Canada and America most certainly offered hope of a better future, leaving the woes of old Ireland behind to begin again in the New World was fraught with its own dangers and, to all intents and purposes, ultimate success was quite literally a case of the survival of the most fortunate and fittest. Many Irish emigrants would be pitted against the perils of both Man and Nature and would unhappily be made completely destitute or die before the promised land was ever reached. In *The Language of the Walls* (1855), James Dawson Burn describes how conmen

would travel on ships sailing from Irish ports to Liverpool in order
to ingratiate themselves with would-be emigrants and have them
fleeced by associates on arrival. The author outlines some of the
many scams that the rogue gangs employed to part the travellers
from their few possessions and little money, stating that it was
unlikely that many of the victims would have been able to leave
the country as a consequence. For him, it begged the question,

> "… how is it that these heartless ruffians prefer victimising their own
> poor country-men? In our opinion the reason is quite plain. An un-
> sophisticated Irishman is the most credulous and open-hearted be-
> ing in existence; a kindly expression or a benevolent act is sufficient
> to make poor Paddy turn himself inside out. And none understand
> his character better than his own villanous country-men who are
> located about the Pool. None but those who understand the Irish
> character can form any idea of the methods those fellows employ to
> circumvent and rob the poor emigrants. It may appear somewhat
> strange to many of our readers that such a wholesale system of rob-
> bery should be allowed to exist in a town like Liverpool."

Neither was there any shortage of crooks waiting on the other side
of the Atlantic to take advantage of the Irish who actually made
it that far. John Francis Maguire in *The Irish in America* (1868)
described the situation there as follows:

> "As voracious fish devour the smaller and helpless of the finny tribe,
> so did a host of human sharks and cormorants prey upon the unhap-
> py emigrant, whose innocence and inexperience left him or her com-
> pletely at their mercy; and scant was the mercy they vouchsafed their
> victims. These bandits—for such they literally were, notwithstand-
> ing that they did not exactly strike down their victims with pistol
> or with poignard—assumed many forms, such as brokers, runners,
> boarding-house keepers, commission agents, sellers of 'bogus' tick-
> ets, and others; and from their number and audacity they appeared
> to set all law and authority at defiance."

As bad as they were, the unscrupulous fraudsters who lay waiting to pounce in major ports and beyond did not pose the greatest threat to the emigrant. It was on the passage across the Atlantic that emigrants were in danger of losing their very lives. Fever and disease spread contagiously in the crammed holds of what came to be known as "coffin ships" because so many died on board them.

What follows is an account of one such voyage, from Dublin to Quebec, undertaken in 1847. In *The Ocean Plague*, first published in 1848, we read of the horrific symptoms of disease that so many passengers and members of the crew succumbed to. We hear of the decimation of families, the orphaning of children, the practicalities of disposing of the dead, and the callous indifference of many to the suffering of others. And, soberingly, the conditions aboard the unnamed vessel in question were without doubt better than those that many Irish emigrants had to endure in other ships. For here, at least, was a captain and his wife who showed genuine concern for those in their care and did what little they could to alleviate the distress of the sick and bereaved.

The author was evidently a man of reasonable means and good education. He had his own berth and dined with the ship's captain and his wife. However, although Robert Whyte did not have to suffer the same deprivation and misery as his compatriots in the hold, his view of the many dreadful events that befell them is seen through a lens of religious compassion and social conscience, and his diary is nevertheless invaluable eyewitness testimony to the hardship and tragedy experienced on board an Irish emigrant ship in the mid-Nineteenth Century.

Derek A. Rowlinson

Contents

CHAPTER V.

CHAPTER VI.

CHAPTER VII.

CHAPTER VIII.

CHAPTER IX.

CHAPTER X.

CHAPTER XI.

CHAPTER XII.

CHAPTER XIII.

CHAPTER XIV.

APPENDIX.

Introduction

Men judge by the complexion of the sky,
The state and inclination of the day:
So may you by my dull and heavy eye,
My tongue hath but a heavier tale to say.
I play the torturer by small and small
To lengthen out the worst that may be spoken.
—SHAKSPEARE.

Emigration has for a long time been considered by British political economists the most effective means of alleviating the grievous ills under which the Irish peasantry labor. It is not our province to inquire into its expediency; but viewing the subject with the single eye of common-sense, it is difficult to see the necessity of expatriating the superfluous population of a country wherein hundreds of thousands of acres of land susceptible of the highest culture, lie waste,—whose mines teeming with wealth remain unworked,—and which is bordered by more than two thousand miles of sea coast, whose banks swarm with ling, cod, mackerel, &c., while salt-fish is largely imported from Scotland.

Many years previous to legislators taking up the matter, emigration from Ireland existed, and that of a class of persons which could be badly spared from the already impoverished island; consisting as it did of small but substantial farmers, who perceiving but a gloomy prospect before them, sold off their land, and, turning their capital into cash, availed themselves of the opportunities that existed to find comfort and independence by settling in America.

The majority of these adventurers being successful in their undertakings, they induced their relatives and friends to follow them; and thus a strong tide of emigrants, whose number gradually increased each season, set toward the West.

This progressive and natural system of emigration, however, gave place within the last few years to a violent rush of famished, reckless human beings, flying from their native land, to seek food in a distant and unknown country.

The cause of this sudden change is easily ascertained. Every one is familiar with the wretched lot of the Irish peasantry,—obliged to work for a miserable pittance, their chief reliance was upon the crop of potatoes grown by each family in the little patch of ground attached to their hut; a poor dependence indeed, not only as regards the inferiority of the potato as the sole diet of a people, but from the great uncertainty always attending its propagation. The consequences of even a partial failure—an event of common occurrence—being of the most serious nature.

In the year 1822, the deficiency was so general that the price quadrupled, and the peasantry of the south and west were reduced to actual starvation. To alleviate the distress a committee was formed in London, and sub-committees throughout England; and such was the benevolence of individuals, that large funds were in a short time at their disposal. By the end of the year subscriptions had been raised in Great Britain amounting to £350,000; to which parliament added a grant of £300,000; while the local collections in Ireland were £150,000,—making altogether 800,000,—a large sum, but how inadequate to meet the wants of some three or four millions of starving people?

This serious warning it should be supposed would have opened the eyes of the country to the necessity of having something else as a resource under a similar emergency; but a plentiful season lulled them into forgetfulness of what they had suffered, and apathy concerning the future.

So abundant was the produce of the seasons 1842 and 1843, that the poorest beggar refused potatoes, and they were commonly used to manure the land.

But the blight of the crop of 1845, and the total destruction of

that of 1846, brought the country to the lowest ebb, and famine with its attendant, disease, stalked through the land.

Charity stretched forth her hand from far and near. America giving liberally of her abundance. But all that could be done fell far short of the wants of the dying sufferers. The government stepped forward, and advanced funds for the establishment of public works; this was attended with much advantage and mitigated a great deal of distress; but unfortunately, all the money had to be returned in the shape of onerous taxation upon the landowners.

The gentry became seriously alarmed, and some of them perceiving that the evil was likely to increase year after year, took into their consideration what would be the surest method of terminating it.

At length it was discovered that the best plan would be to get completely rid of those who were so heavy a burthen upon them, by shipping them to America; at the same time publishing to the world, as an act of brotherly love and kindness, a deed of crafty, calculating selfishness,—for the expense of transporting each individual was less than the cost of one year's support in a workhouse.

It required but little argument to induce the prostrated people to accede to their landlords' proposal, by quitting their poverty-stricken country for "a land flowing with milk and honey,"—poor creatures, they thought that any change would be for the better. They had nothing to risk, every thing to gain. "Ah! Sir," said a fellow-passenger to me, after bewailing the folly that tempted him to plunge his family into aggravated misfortune,—"we thought we could'nt be worse off than we war; but now to our sorrow we know the differ; for sure supposin we were dyin of starvation, or if the sickness overtuk us. We had a chance of a doctor, and if he could do no good for our bodies, sure the priest could for our souls; and then we'd be buried along wid our own people, in the ould church-yard, with the green sod over us; instead of dying like rotten sheep thrown into a pit, and the minit the breath is out of our bodies, flung into the sea to be eaten up by them horrid sharks."

It cannot excite the least surprise that these wretched beings should carry with them the seeds of that plague from which they were flying; and it was but natural that these seeds should rapidly germinate in the hot-bed holds of ships crammed almost to suffocation with their distempered bodies. In short, nothing was wanted to encourage the speedy development of the direst disease and misery; but alas! every thing that could check their spread was absent.

My heart sickens when I think upon the fatal scenes of the awfully tragic drama enacted upon the wide stage of the Atlantic ocean, in the floating lazar houses that were wafted upon its bosom during the never-to-be-forgotten year 1847.

Without a precedent in history, may God grant that the account of it may descend to posterity without a parallel.

Laws for the regulation of passenger ships were in existence; but whether on account of difficulty arising from the vast augmentation of number, or some other cause, they (if at all put in force) proved quite ineffectual.

What a different picture was presented by the Germans who migrated in large bodies? who,—although the transmission of human beings from Fatherland must always be attended by more or less pain and trouble,—underwent none of those heart-rending trials reserved exclusively for the Irish emigrant.

Never did so many souls tempt all the dangers of the deep, to seek asylums in an adopted country; and, could we draw a veil over the sad story of the ship pestilence, "this migration of masses, numbering of late years more than 100,000 annually, now to nearly 300,000 annually, not in the warlike spirit of the Goths and Vandals who overran the Roman Empire, and destroyed the monuments of art and evidences of civilization, but in the spirit of peace, anxious to provide for themselves and their children the necessaries of life, and apparently ordained by Providence to relieve the countries of the old world, and to serve great purposes

of good to mankind,—is one of the most interesting spectacles the world ever saw."*

The reader must not expect to find any thing more in these pages than a faithful detail of the occurrences on board an emigrant vessel. The author has no desire to exaggerate, were it possible to do so. And he who wishes to arrive at any conclusion as to the amount of suffering, must calculate, from the affliction that I have faintly portrayed upon a small scale, what must have been the unutterable "weight of woe" in ships whose holds contained five or six hundred tainted, famished, dying mortals.

The following extract from the London Times newspaper presents a faithful and graphic review of the dire tragedy.

"The great Irish famine and pestilence will have a place in that melancholy series of similar calamities to which historians and poets have contributed so many harrowing details and touching expressions. Did Ireland possess a writer endued with the laborious truth of Thucydides, the graceful felicity of Virgil, or the happy invention of De Foe, the events of this miserable year might be quoted by the scholar for ages to come, together with the sufferings of the pent-up multitudes of Athens, the distempered plains of northern Italy, or the hideous ravages of our own great plague. But time is ever improving on the past. There is one horrible feature of the recent, not to say present visitation, which is entirely new. The fact of more than a hundred thousand souls flying from the very midst of a calamity across a great ocean to a new world, crowding into insufficient vessels, scrambling for a footing on a deck, or a berth in a hold, committing themselves to these worse than prisons, while their frames were wasted with ill fare and their blood infected with disease, fighting for months of unutterable wretchedness against the elements without and pestilence within,

---

* *Immigration into the United States.* By J. Chickering. Boston, 1848. [Author's note]

giving almost hourly victims to the deep, landing at length on shores already terrified and diseased, consigned to encampments of the dying and the dead, spreading death wherever they roam, and having no other prospect before them than a long continuance of these horrors in a still farther flight across forests and lakes under a Canadian sun and a Canadian frost—all these are circumstances beyond the experience of the Greek historian or Latin poet, and such as an Irish pestilence alone could produce.

"By the end of the season there is little doubt that the emigration into Canada alone will have amounted to 100,000; nearly all from Ireland. We know the condition in which these poor creatures embarked on their perilous adventure. They were only flying from one form of death. On the authority of the Montreal Board of Health we are enabled to say that they were allowed to ship in numbers two or three times greater than the same vessels would have presumed to carry to an United States port.

"The worse horrors of that slave-trade which it is the boast or the ambition of this empire to suppress, at any cost, have been reenacted in the flight of British subjects from their native shores. In only ten of the vessels that arrived at Montreal in July, four from Cork and six from Liverpool, out of 4,427 passengers, 804 had died on the passage, and 847 were sick on their arrival; that is, 847 were visibly diseased, for the result proves that a far larger number had in them the seeds of disease. 'The *Larch*,' says the Board of Health, on August 12th, 'reported this morning from Sligo, sailed with 440 passengers, of whom 108 died on the passage, and 150 were sick.

"'The *Virginius* sailed with 596; 158 died on the passage, 186 were sick, and the remainder landed feeble and tottering; the captain, mates, and crew, were all sick.'

"The Blackhole of Calcutta was a mercy compared to the holds of these vessels. Yet simultaneously, as if in reproof of those on whom the blame of all this wretchedness must fall, foreigners, Ger-

mans from Hamburg and Bremen are daily arriving, all healthy, robust, and cheerful.

"This vast unmanageable tide of population thus thrown upon Montreal, like the fugitives from some bloody defeat, or devastated country, has been greatly augmented by the prudent, and, we must add, most necessary precautions adopted in time by the United States, where most stringent sanitary regulations, enforced by severe penalties, have been adopted to save the ports of the Union from those very horrors which a paternal government has suffered to fall upon Montreal. Many of these pest ships have been obliged to alter their destination, even while at sea, for the St. Lawrence.

"At Montreal a large proportion of these outcasts have lingered from sheer inability to proceed. The inhabitants of course have been infected.

"A still more horrible sequel is to come. The survivors have to wander forth and find homes. Who can say how many will perish on the way, or the masses of houseless, famished, and half-naked wretches that will be strewed on the inhospitable snow when a Canadian winter sets in?

"Of these awful occurrences some account must be given. Historians and politicians will some day sift and weigh the conflicting narrations and documents of this lamentable year, and pronounce with or without affectation, how much is due to the inclemency of heaven, and how much to the cruelty, heartlessness or improvidence of man. The boasted institutions and spirit of the empire are on trial. They are weighed in the balance.

"Famine and pestilence are at the gates, and the conscience-stricken nation will almost fear to see the 'writing on the wall.'

"We are forced to confess that, whether it be the fault of our laws or our men, this new act in the terrible drama has not been met as humanity and common-sense would enjoin. The result was quite within the scope of calculation, and even of care."

Miscalculation, and want of care, are terms far too mild to apply

to such wanton negligence as resulted in the immediate sacrifice of upwards of 25,000 souls, four fifths of whom fell upon their way to Canada. From the report issued at the end of the season, it appears that, of the 98,105 (of whom 60,000 were Irish) that were shipped for Quebec,

There died at sea,	5,293
At Grosse Isle and Quebec,	8,072
In and above Montreal,	7,000
Making	20,365,

besides those who afterwards perished, whose number can never be ascertained. Allowing an average of 300 persons to each, 200 vessels were employed in the transmission to Canada of Irish emigrants alone; and each of these vessels lost one third of her living cargo ere she again set sail upon her return to Europe.

If we suppose those 60,000 persons to be an army on their way to invade some hostile power, how serious would appear the loss of one third of their number before a battle was fought? Yet the 40,000 who landed upon the Canadian shores had to fight many a deadly battle before they could find peace or rest. Or, in order to make the matter sensible to those who know the value of money better than of human life, let us multiply 20,000 by 5, the cost in pounds sterling of the passage of each individual, and we perceive a loss of £100,000, or $500,000 dollars.

But it may be thought that the immolation of so many wretched starvelings was rather a benefit than a loss to the world. It may be so. Yet—untutored, degraded, famished, and plague-stricken, as they were; I assert that there was more true heroism, more faith, more forgiveness to their enemies, and submission to the Divine Will, exemplified in these victims, than could be found in ten times the number of their oppressors.

Chapter I.

Each moment plays
His little weapon in the narrower sphere
Of sweet domestic comfort, and cuts down
The fairest bloom of sublunary bliss.
Bliss—sublunary bliss;—proud words and vain,
Implicit treason to divine decree,
A bold invasion of the rights of heaven,
I clasp'd the phantoms, and I found them air.
O, had I weighed it ere my fond embrace,
What darts of agony had miss'd my soul.—Young.*

May 30th, 1847.

Many and deep are the wounds that the sensitive heart inflicts upon its possessor, as he journeys through life's pilgrimage; but on few occasions are they so acutely felt, as when one is about to part from those who formed a portion of his existence; deeper still pierces the pang as the idea presents itself that the separation may be for ever; but when one feels a father's nervous grasp,—a dear sister's tender, sobbing embrace; and the eye wanders around the apartment drinking in each familiar object, until it rests upon the vacant chair which she who nursed his helpless infancy was wont to occupy, then the agony he wishes to conceal becomes insupportable. But as the skilful surgeon tears off the bandage which the hand of affection gently withdraws from the wound,—thereby

---

* From *The Complaint*, or *Night Thoughts on Life, Death and Immortality* by Edward Young (1683–1765).

unconsciously inflicting greater pain; so it is better not to linger upon the affecting scene; but rush suddenly away.

It was a charming morning on which I left dear old Ireland;— the balmy new-born day, in all the freshness of early summer, was gladdened by the beams of the sun which rose above the towers of the city, sunk in undisturbed repose. It was a morning calculated to inspire the drooping soul with hope; auguring future happiness.

Too soon I arrived at the quay, and left my last footprint on my native land. The boat pushed off, and in a few minutes I was on board the brig that was to waft me across the wide Atlantic.

There was not a soul on deck; but presently the grizzled head of the captain was protruded from the cabin; and from the uninviting aspect of his face I feared that he would prove an unsocial companion for a long voyage. He received me as kindly as his stubborn nature would allow; and I was forced to admire the manly dignity of the rude tar, when, from the bent attitude he was obliged to assume while ascending the companion ladder, he stood upright on the deck. The sailors now issued from the forecastle, and the mate came up and introduced himself to me.

The captain having given the word to weigh anchor, a bustle immediately arose throughout the vessel; the seamen promptly proceeded to their work, with apparent pleasure; although (being the Sabbath) they did not accompany the action with the usual chant. The chain having become entangled in the cables of some fishing boats, it was a considerable while before the anchor was hoisted. At length, the top-sails were unreefed, and our bark glided through the beauteous bay.

In a short time we rounded the promontory of Howth; having taken the north channel as the wind was southerly.

The captain then led me down to the cabin for breakfast, and introduced me to his wife, who, he informed me, always accompanied him to sea, and whom I shall for the future designate as the mistress,—as by that term she was known to both crew and

passengers. Feeling an inclination towards squeamishness, and being much more sick at heart, I retired to my state-room! and lying down upon the berth, fell into a dreamy slumber, in which I remained until aroused; when I found it was late in the afternoon, and tea was ready. I felt somewhat revived by the grateful beverage; and accompanied the captain on deck. We were off Carlingford, and the mountains of Mourne. The passengers were cooking their evening meal at their fires upon the fore-deck; and the sailors discussing their coffee in the forecastle. I endeavored to enter into conversation with the captain, but he was provokingly taciturn; however, we were soon joined by the mistress, who was not unwilling to make up for her husband's deficiency. The sun set; and twilight subsided into darkness; a cold night breeze also told that it was time to go below.

Monday, May 31st.

I rose early, and inhaled the fresh morning air. We made good progress during the night, and the bold cliffs of the coast of Antrim were visible on one hand, the Scotch shore on the other. At 8, A. M., the bell rang for breakfast, and I took my seat opposite the captain. The mistress sat in an arm-chair, and the mate on a stool next me, completing the cabin circle. We were attended by Simon the cabin-boy, whom at first sight I took to be a "darky."

His face was coated with smoke and soot, streaked by the perspiration that trickled from his brow, which was surmounted by a thicket of short, wiry black hair, standing on end; his lustreless brown eyes I cannot better describe than by borrowing a Yankee illustration: they were "like two glass balls lighted by weak rush lights;"—his lips were thick, straight, and colorless; his complexion, (when unveiled) was a grimy yellow;—and the expression of his wide flat face, idiotic. He wore a red flannel shirt, and loose

blue pilot trowsers; but neither shoes, nor stockings; his movements were slow, except at meals, when he seemed to regain his
suspended animation; and it was a goodly sight to see him gulping
coffee, bolting dodges of fat pork, and crunching hard biscuit, as
ravenously as a hungry bear.

No two specimens of human nature could possibly present more
striking contrasts than Simon and his fellow-apprentice Jack. The
latter was about 15 years of age, remarkably small and active.
Squirrel never climbed tree more nimbly than Jack could go aloft;
and in the accomplishments of chewing and smoking he might
compete with the oldest man aboard; his fair skin was set off by
rosy cheeks; and his sparkling blue eyes beamed with—devilment.
He was a favorite of every one except the mistress, with whom
his pranks did not pass, being therefore exempt from the menial
offices of cabin boy, which devolved upon Simon; his principal
amusement consisted in persecuting that genius.

The mate was a very little man, not more than five feet high;
but in excellent condition, as seamen generally are; he was lame
in one leg; which deformity he took great pains to hide; causing a
constrained limp that was extremely ludicrous; he was well-look-
ing, and sported a capacious pair of black whiskers, the outline
of which he frequently altered. He had been a "captain," but
unfortunately, loving the bottle, he lost his "caste." There existed
little confidence between him and the captain; and both being of a
warm temperament, there were occasional symptoms of collision;
but they were prevented from ending in open rupture by the
timely interference of the mistress, on whom the captain would
let loose his wrath, which though expressed in no gentle terms,
she bore with exemplary patience.

The mistress was small, ruddy, and sun-burnt; having seen some
sixty winters, forty of which she had spent at sea,—generally in
the home trade; but varied occasionally by a voyage to Russia,
or to America. She was in the habit of keeping a private log, in

which she noted the incidents of her travels. I was allowed to look into this interesting production, which amused me no less by the originality of the orthography, than its elegance of diction. Being a native of Cumberland, her pronunciation was not particularly euphonious; she also, when addressing her husband, the mate, and all familiar acquaintances, used the terms "thee" and "thou," invariably reversing their grammatical order.

Tuesday, June 1st.

After breakfast, the mate invited me to see the depot of provisions. I accordingly followed him, descending by a ladder into an apartment partitioned off from the hold, and dividing it from the cabin.

By the light from the lantern I perceived a number of sacks, which were filled with oatmeal and biscuit. The mate having proceeded to prepare the passengers' rations for distribution, I sat down upon one of the sacks, from beneath which suddenly issued a groan. I jumped up, quite at a loss to account for the strange sound, and looked at the mate, in order to discover what he thought of it. He seemed somewhat surprised; but in a moment removed two or three sacks; and lo! there was a man crouched up in a corner. As he had not seen him before, the mate at once concluded that he was a "stowaway," so giving him a shake to make him stand upright, he ordered him to mount the ladder, bestowing a kick upon the poor wretch to accelerate his tardy ascent.

The captain was summoned from below, and a council immediately held for the trial of the prisoner, who confessed, that not having enough of money to pay for his passage, he bribed the watchman employed to prevent the possibility of such an occurrence. He had been concealed for three days, but at night made his way into the hold, through a breach in the partition: his presence was therefore known to some of the passengers. He had

no clothes but the rags he wore; nor had he any provisions. To decide what was to be done with him was now the consideration, but the captain hastily terminated the deliberation, by swearing that he should be thrown overboard. The wretched creature was quite discomfited by the captain's wrath, and earnestly begged for forgiveness. It was eventually settled that he should be landed upon the first island at which we should touch; with which decision he appeared to be quite satisfied. He said that he was willing to work for his support; but the captain swore determinedly that he should not taste one pound of the ship's provision. He was therefore left to the tender mercies of his fellow-passengers.

In consequence of this discovery, there was a general muster in the afternoon, affording me an opportunity of seeing all the emigrants; and a more motley crowd I never beheld;—of all ages, from the infant to the feeble grandsire and withered crone.

While they were on deck, the hold was searched, but without any further discovery, no one having been found below but a boy, who was unable to leave his berth, from debility. Many of them appeared to me to be quite unfit to undergo the hardship of a long voyage; but they were inspected and passed by a doctor, although the captain, as he informed me, protested against taking some of them. One old man was so infirm, that he seemed to me to be in the last stage of consumption.

The next matter to be accomplished was to regulate the allowance of provisions to which each family was entitled. One pound of meal or of bread being allowed for each adult,—half a pound for each individual under fourteen years of age,—and one third of a pound for each child under seven years. Thus, although there were 110 souls, great and small, they counted as 84 adults. That was, therefore, the number of pounds to be issued daily. On coming on board, provisions for a week were distributed; but as they wasted them most improvidently, they had to be served again to-day. The mate consequently determined to give out the day's rations every morning.

Wednesday, June 2nd.

We made but little progress during the night, and were still in the channel, within sight of the Mull of Cantire, and the northern shore of Ireland.

Having but a few books with me, I seized upon a greasy old volume of sundry magazines, which I found in the cabin. I also commenced the study of a book of navigation. These, varied with the Book of books, Shakspeare, and Maunder's Treasuries, kept me free from ennui. When tired of reading, I had ample scope for observation.

The mistress spent the forenoon fishing, and the afternoon in curing the mackerel and gurnet she caught. We had some at tea, when I met with a deprivation I had not anticipated;—there was no milk! and I did not at all relish my tea without it. One cup was quite enough for me; but I soon became habituated to it. Having rounded the long promontory of Donegal, the outline of the shore became indistinct; and making our calculations not to see land again for some time, the mate took his "departure" from Malin Head.

Chapter II.

Roll on, thou dark and deep blue ocean, roll!

—Byron.

June 3d.

When I came on deck this morning, I found that we were sailing upon the bosom of the broad Atlantic, no object being visible to relieve the vast expanse of water and sky, except the glorious sun; and as I turned my eyes from the survey of the distant horizon, and fixed them upon the little bark that wafted us, a sensation akin to that of the "Ancient Mariner" possessed my mind.

"Alone, alone, all, all alone,
Alone on a wide, wide sea."

As the boy who was unable to attend the muster still continued ill, and was reported to be feverish, the mistress and I reviewed the medicine chest. We found it to contain a jar of castor oil, epsom salts, laudanum, hartshorn, &c.; also a book of directions, which were by no means explicit, and they so perplexed the mistress, even with the aid of her spectacles, that as she was nothing the wiser of the study, she resolved to trust to her own experience in the concoction of a dose. The mate took his first observation at noon; and as he stood peering through the eye-hole of the quadrant, he reminded me forcibly of poor old uncle Sol's little midshipman.*

---

*   A reference to the wooden midshipman referred to in Chapter 19 of Charles Dickens' *Dombey and Son.*

The passengers' fire-places, upon either side of the fore-deck, furnished endless scenes, sometimes of noisy merriment, at others of quarrels. The fire was contained in a large wooden case, lined with bricks and shaped something like an old-fashioned settee; the coals being confined by two or three iron bars in front. From morning till evening they were surrounded by groups of men, women and children; some making "stirabout,"† in all kinds of vessels, and others baking cakes upon extemporary griddles. These cakes were generally about two inches thick, and when baked were encased in a burnt crust coated with smoke, being actually raw in the centre. Such was the unvaried food of the greater number of these poor creatures. A few of them, who seemed to be better off, had herrings, or bacon. The meal with which they were provided was of very bad quality;—this they had five days; and biscuit, which was good, two days in the week.

Friday, June 4th.

The sailors and apprentices were (as the mate expressed it in his log) variously employed,—mending sails, tarring ropes, spinning yarns, &c. Sailors sit and sew very differently from tailors; instead of doubling up their legs under them, they stretch them out straight before them as they sit upon the deck. Their thimble is also peculiar, not being worn on the top of the finger, but upon the ball of the thumb, to which it is fastened by a leather strap, buckled round the wrist. I was surprised at the expedition and neatness with which they sewed, with their coarse needles and long threads.

---

† A porridge of Irish origin that consisted of (usually) oatmeal stirred into boiling water or milk.

Jack created some diversion by daubing a "gossoon's"* face with tar, and shaving him with a rusty knife. It was exhilarating to hear the children's merry laughter;—poor little things, they seemed quite reconciled with their situation! I learned that many of these emigrants had never seen the sea nor a ship, until they were on board. They were chiefly from the county Meath, and sent out at the expense of their landlord, without any knowledge of the country to which they were going, or means of livelihood, except the labor of the father of each family. All they knew concerning Canada was, that they were to land in Quebec, and to go up the country; moreover, they had a settled conviction that the voyage was to last exactly three weeks. In addition to these there were a few who were going to try their fortunes on their own account. One of the latter was a Connaught "boy," who having lived upon the coast and spent his time partly in fishing, made himself useful about the brig, and thereby ingratiated himself into favor with the captain, and the consequent jealousy of his fellow-passengers, who, thinking him rather soft, took pleasure in teasing him. Two young men from Kilkenny, and one from the county Clare, completed the list. The former used to astonish the Meath-men with the triple wonders of their native city.

Saturday, June 5th.

As the passengers had a great inclination to infringe upon the after-deck, the captain drew a line, the penalty for crossing which was the stoppage of a day's water.

I observed the sea to be crowded with myriads of slimy looking objects, which the sailors called "slobbs." They varied in size, form, and color; some of them resembling a lemon cut in half. How

---

*   An often patronising term for a young boy or lad.

beautiful also was the luminous appearance of the water at night, which I delighted to watch, as we glided through the liquid fire.

Nor was it less pleasing to observe the "Portuguese men of war," with their tiny sails set to the breeze, and surmounting the crests of the rolling billows. I had a rummage through the charts, and enjoyed a practical lecture upon them, with illustrative lectures by the mistress, enlivened, by way of episode, with occasional contradictions by the captain, who with rule and compass traced our progress daily upon the great chart of the North Atlantic ocean. We had two ships in company with us all the day; but they were too distant to distinguish their names. One of the passengers having thrown the Connaughtman's hat overboard, the captain gave him a blue and white striped night-cap, with which on his head he strutted about, much to the amusement of the youngsters, one of whom attached a rope to the tail of his coat; this he dragged after him for some time, until Jack changed the scene by cutting the tail off. When Paddy discovered his loss, he was outrageous, and made a grievous complaint to the mate, who doctored the coat by abstracting the other tail, thereby transforming the garment into a jacket. When the matter came to the captain's ears, he presented Paddy with an old pilot jacket, which made a great coat for him; he was therefore no loser by the affair.

Sunday, June 6th.

The favorable breeze that carried us out of the channel having forsaken us, the little progress we made was gained by tacking, which kept the sailors constantly employed. The passengers were dressed in their best clothes; and presented a better appearance than I expected. The sailors also donned their holiday toggery in the afternoon.

A group of young men being at a loss for amusement, began to

wrestle and play "pitch and toss;" but the mate soon put a stop to their diversions; at which they grumbled, saying that "they did'nt think that Mr. Mate would be so hard."

Very few of them could read; neither did they seem to have any regard for the sanctity of the Sabbath. In the evening they had prayers in the hold; and were divided into two parties,—those who spoke Irish, and those who did not; each section having a leader, who gabbled in his respective language a number of "Paters and Aves," as quickly as the devotees could count their beads.

After these religious exercises they came upon deck, and spent the remainder of the day jesting, laughing, and singing.

We had a clear and beautiful sunset; from which the captain prognosticated an easterly wind.

Chapter III.

Thou shalt not be afraid for any terror by night, nor for the arrow that flieth by day; for the pestilence that walketh in darkness, nor for the sickness that destroyeth in the noon-day.—PSALMS OF DAVID.

June 7th.

The passengers elected four men to govern their commonwealth, the principal of whom had the title of "Head committee." The other three being inactive, the sole authority was wielded by him, much to the terror of the little boys, who were often uproarious, and to keep whom in order he frequently administered the "cat."*

The other duties of this functionary consisted in seeing that the hold was kept clean; in preventing smoking below, settling differences, &c. He was also the medium of communication with the "other house," he and Paddy alone being permitted to go aft.

Tuesday, June 8th.

We steered a southward course, but gained very little longitude.

The two ships were again in sight; one was the *Tamerlane* of Aberistwyth; the other the *Virginius* of Liverpool; both fine vessels, with passengers.

The head committee reported that two women were ill; they were therefore dosed according to the best skill of the mistress, who was desirous of going into the hold to see them; but the captain peremptorily desired her upon no account to do so; and kept a sharp lookout, that she might not visit them unknown to him.

---

* I.e., the 'cat o' nine tails', a rope whip with nine knotted cords.

The boy, whom nothing ailed but sea-sickness and fatigue, had recovered. I saw him upon deck,—a miserable looking little animal, with a huge misshapen head, sallow, lantern-jaws, and glassy eyes;—apparently about twelve years of age; but his father said that he was twenty. I could scarcely credit him, but was assured of the fact by his neighbours, who said that he always had the same emaciated appearance, although he never before complained of illness. He went by the name of "The little shoemaker."

Wednesday, June 9th.

As we were seated at dinner, in the cabin, discussing a savory dish of "Lobscouse"* made by the mistress, we were alarmed by the shouting of men, and screaming of women.

We hurried on deck, thinking that some one was overboard, and judge of our terror, when we saw the fore part of the brig in a blaze. All hands having assisted, a plentiful supply of water in a short time subdued the fire, which extended no further than the caboose;† it arose from the negligence of Simon, who fell asleep, leaving a lighted candle stuck against the boards. This was the only brilliant act of which he was guilty during the voyage, and as a reward for which the mate bestowed upon him a rope's end.

Thursday, June 10th.

The only incidents of the day were, breakfast, dinner, and supper,—the meridional observation, and the temporary stir con-

---

*   A type of lamb or beef stew, once extremely popular in seaports such as Liverpool.

†   I.e., the ship's galley or kitchen.

sequent on the captain coming upon deck after a "snooze," and shouting out "'bout ship." Some more cases of illness were reported; and the mistress was kept busy mixing medicine, and making drinks; hoping that by early attention the sickness might be prevented from spreading.

Friday, June 11th.

As I was pacing the deck in the afternoon, I observed one of the passengers,—a well looking man, with fine brown eyes, timidly approach me. After looking about him, to assure himself that the captain was below, he doffed his hat and addressed me as follows: "I beg your honor's pardon, but I hope it's no offence." Having told him that he had given me none, he proceeded,—"Well then master, is'nt it mighty quare intirely, and how can the likes of us know the differ; but I hope your honor it's all right?" I replied that I was not aware of any thing being wrong, and desired him to say what was the danger he feared, which caused him to ask; "Aragh! why thin are we goin back to ould Ireland?" I demanded his reason for such a supposition; when after scratching his head, and casting a glance towards the cabin, looking rather perplexed, he went on, "That little gossoon of mine, your honor,—a mighty smart chap he is too, and a great scholiar entirely, he tould us,— but faith! I dunno how to believe him,—though he got his larnin at the national school, and can cast up figures equal to the agint, and can read the whole side of a book without stoppin,—he says sir,—that the sun, God bless it, sets in the wist." Here he paused and looked earnestly at me, as if for a confirmation of the fact. I therefore said that the boy's knowledge was pretty accurate. Seeming encouraged, he continued—"Moreover than that, he says that Ameriky, where we all are goin to, if the Almighty God spares us, (here he crossed himself) glory be to his name! it's in the wist of

the world too." He again paused, and looked enquiringly. "Well," said I, "he is pretty right there also, America is west from Ireland." "Then master, here's what we want to come at, you see. If Ameriky is in the wist, musn't the sun set in it,—then why is it, your honor, that instead of followin it, we're runnin away from it as hard as we can lick?" Such was the fact,—a fresh northerly breeze compelling us to bear to the south-east. I now saw the nature of the problem he wished to have solved, and explained the matter as explicitly as I possibly could; but it was some time before he comprehended me. At length he seemed to become enlightened on the subject, for, giving his thigh a slap of his open palm, he exclaimed, "Och! by the powers, I see it all now; it's as plain as a pike-staff; and I'm sure I'm obleeged to your honor, and so is the gossoon too.—Oh, that divil's clip,—Jack; wait till I ketch him. If I don't murder him it's no matter. What do you think your honor, he tould the little chap, when he axed him all about it? 'Why,' says he, 'sure we're goin back again for the mistress' nittin needles, that she forgot.' So as he wouldn't tell him, nor none of the sailors, I made bould to ax your honor, as the little chap was loth to make so free."

On the conclusion of the dialogue, Jack,—who was over our heads, in the shrouds,—burst into a hearty fit of laughter. In which I could not but participate, when I noticed the comicality of the arch sailor-boy's appearance, and the simplicity of my interlocutor, who, hearing the captain's heavy step coming up the ladder, hastily retired, vowing vengeance upon Jack.

Saturday, June 12th.

I amused myself taking a sketch of the cabin "interior." It was about ten feet square, and so low that the only part of it in which the captain could stand upright, was under the skylight. At either

side was a berth; both of which were filled with the mistress' boxes, the captain's old clothes, old sails, and sundry other articles, which were there stowed away, and concealed from view by chintz curtains, trimmed with white cotton fringe. The ceiling was garnished with numerous charts rolled up, and confined by tapes running from beam to beam; from one of which,—carefully covered by a cotton handkerchief,—was suspended the captain's new hat. A small recess above the table contained a couple of wine glasses, one of them minus the shank; also an antique decanter, resting upon an old quarto prayer-book, and guarded by a dangerous looking blunderbuss, which was supported by two brass hooks, from one of which hung a small bag containing the captain's spectacles, rule, pencil, and compass. At each side of this recess was a locker: one of them containing a crock of butter, and another of eggs, besides tobacco and soap; the other held a fine Cheshire cheese, a little keg of sprats, and other articles too numerous to mention. An unhappy canary, perched within a rusty cage, formed a pendant from the centre of the sky-light, but a much more pleasing picture decorated one of the panels,—a still-life, admirably delineating an enormous flitch of bacon, which daily grew—less. A small door led into the captain's state-room; the ceiling of which was tastefully ornamented by several bunches of dipt candles; while the narrow shelves groaned under the weight of,—jars of sugar, preserves, bottled porter, spices and the other usual necessaries for a long voyage. I was disturbed in the progress of my portraiture by the mistress, who came down to warm a drink at the stove, for some of the sick folks. The two women who first became ill, were said to show symptoms of bad fever; and additional cases of illness were reported by the Head committee. The patients begged for an increased allowance of water; which could not be granted, as the supply was very scanty; two casks having leaked.

Sunday, June 13th.

The reports from the hold became very alarming; and the mistress was occupied all day attending the numerous calls upon her. She already regretted having come the voyage; but her kind heart did not allow her to consult her ease. When she appeared upon deck, she was beset by a crowd of poor creatures, each having some request to make; often of a most inconsiderate kind, and few of which it was in her power to comply with. The day was cold and cheerless; and I occupied myself reading in the cabin.

Monday, June 14th.

The Head committee brought a can of water to show it to the captain: it was quite foul, muddy, and bitter from having been in a wine cask. When allowed to settle it became clear, leaving considerable sediment in the bottom of the vessel; but it retained its bad taste. The mate endeavoured to improve it by trying the effect of charcoal, and of alum; but some of the casks were beyond remedy, and the contents, when pumped out, resembled nauseous ditch water. There were now eight cases of serious illness;—six of them being fever and two dysentery;—the former appeared to be of a peculiar character, and very alarming: the latter disease did not seem to be so violent in degree.

Tuesday, June 15th.

The reports this morning were very afflicting, and I felt much, that I was unable to render any assistance to my poor fellow-passengers. The captain desired the mistress to give them every thing out of his own stores that she considered would be of service to

any of them. He felt much alarmed; nor was it to be wondered at that contagious fever,—which under the most advantageous circumstances, and under the watchful eyes of the most skilful physicians, baffles the highest ability,—should terrify one having the charge of so many human beings, likely to fall a prey to the unchecked progress of the dreadful disease; for once having shown itself in the unventilated hold of a small brig, containing one hundred and ten living creatures, how could it possibly be stayed,—without suitable medicines, medical skill, or even pure water to slake the patient's burning thirst?

The prospect before us was indeed an awful one; and there was no hope for us but in the mercy of God.

Wednesday, June 16th.

The past night was very rough, and I enjoyed little rest. No additional cases of sickness were reported: but there were apparent signs of insubordination amongst the healthy men, who complained of starvation, and the want of water to make drinks for their sick wives and children. A deputation came aft to acquaint the captain with their grievances, but he ordered them away, and would not listen to a word from them. When he went below, the ringleader threatened that they would break into the provision store.

The mate did not take any notice of the threat, but repeated to me, in their hearing, an anecdote of his own experience when a captain; showing with what determination he suppressed an outbreak in his vessel. He concluded by alluding to cutlasses, and the firearms in the cabin. And in order to make a deeper impression on their minds, he brought up the old blunderbuss, from which he fired a shot, the report of which was equal to that of a small cannon. The deputation slunk away, muttering complaints.

If they were resolute, they might easily have seized upon the provisions. In fact, I was surprised how famished men could so patiently bear with their own, and their starved children's sufferings; but the captain would willingly have listened to them if it were in his power to relieve their distress.

Thursday, June 17th.

Two new cases of fever were announced, and from the representation of the mate,—the poor creatures in the hold were in a shocking state. The men who suffered from dysentery were better; the mistress's prescription—flour porridge with a few drops of laudanum—having given them relief. The requests of the friends of the fever patients were most preposterous;—some asking for beef, others wine. They were all desirous of laudanum being administered to them in order to procure sleep; but we were afraid to dispense so dangerous a remedy, except with extreme caution. Our progress was almost imperceptible, and the captain began to grow very uneasy, there being at the rate of the already miserable allowance of food, but provisions for fifty days. It also now became necessary to reduce the complement of water, and to urge the necessity of using sea water in cookery.

Friday, June 18th.

The fire-places were the scenes of endless contentions. The sufferings they endured appeared to embitter the wretched emigrants one against another. Their quarrels were only ended when the fires were extinguished, at 7 o'clock, P. M.; at which time they were surrounded by squabbling groups, preparing their miserable evening meal. They would not leave until Jack mounted the

shrouds of the fore-mast, and precipitated a bucket full of water on each fire; when they snatched up their pots and pans, and, half blinded by the steam, descended into the hold, with their half cooked suppers. Although Jack delighted in teasing them, they never complained of his pranks, however annoying.

Chapter IV.

I saw the seven angels which stood before God; and to them were
    given seven trumpets……
And the seven angels which had the seven trumpets prepared them-
    selves to sound……
And the seventh angel sounded……
And the sea gave up the dead which were in it; and death and hell de-
    livered up the dead which were in them: and they were judged
    every man…

—Revelations.

June 19th.

A shark followed us all the day, and the mate said it was a certain
forerunner of death. The cabin was like an apothecary's shop,
and the mistress a perfect slave. I endeavoured to render her every assistance in my power. The mate also was indefatigable in
his exertions to alleviate the miserable lot of our helpless human
cargo. Not having seen the "stowaway" on deck for some time,
upon inquiring after him, I learned that he was amongst the
sick, and was very bad; but he was kindly attended by the young
man from the county Clare, who devoted himself to attending
the afflicted, some of whom the members of their own families
neglected to take care of.

Sunday, June 20th.

Having hinted to the captain the propriety of having divine service read upon the Sabbath, he said that it could not be done.

Indeed, the sailors seldom had a spare moment, and as to the mate, I often wondered how he got through so much work. This day, therefore, had no mark to distinguish it from any other. The poor emigrants were in their usual squalid attire; neither did the crew rig themselves out as on former Sundays.

All were dispirited, and a cloud of melancholy hung over us.

The poor mistress deplored that she could not get an opportunity of reading her Bible. I pitied her from my heart; knowing how much she felt the distress that surrounded us, and her anxiety to lighten the affliction of the passengers.

Monday, June 21st.

I was surprised at the large allowance of food served out to the sailors. They had each 1 1-2 lbs. of beef, or pork, daily, besides coffee, and as much biscuit as they pleased; but it being a temperance vessel, they had no grog,—in lieu of which they got lime-juice. However, there was a little cask of brandy in a corner of the cabin; but the captain was afraid to broach it, knowing the mate's propensity. I noticed the latter often casting a wistful glance at it as he rose from dinner; and he did not fail to tell me that it was the best possible preventive against the fever.

Tuesday, June 22nd.

One of the sailors was unable for duty, and the mate feared he had the fever.

The reports from the hold were growing even more alarming, and some of the patients who were mending, had relapsed. One of the women was every moment expected to breathe her last, and her friends,—an aunt and cousins,—were inconsolable about her;

as they persuaded her to leave her father and mother, and come with them. The mate said that her feet were swollen to double their natural size, and covered with black putrid spots. I spent a considerable part of the day watching a shark that followed in our wake with great constancy.

Wednesday, June 23d.

At breakfast I inquired of the mate after the young woman who was so ill yesterday, when he told me that she was dead; and when I remarked that I feared her burial would cause great consternation, I learned that the sad ordeal was over, her remains having been consigned to the deep within an hour after she expired. When I went on deck I heard the moans of her poor aunt, who continued to gaze upon the ocean as if she could mark the spot where the waters opened for their prey. The majority of the wretched passengers, who were not themselves ill, were absorbed in grief for their relatives; but some of them, it astonished me to perceive, had no feeling whatever, either for their fellow creatures' woe, or in the contemplation of being themselves overtaken by the dreadful disease. There was a further addition to the sick list, which now amounted to twenty.

Thursday, June 24th.

Being the festival of St. John, and a Catholic holiday, some young men and women got up a dance in the evening, regardless of the moans and cries of those who were tortured by the fiery fever. When the mate spoke to them of the impropriety of such conduct, they desisted and retired to the bow, where they sat down and spent the remainder of the evening singing. The monotonous

howling they kept up was quite in unison with the scene of desolation within, and the dreary expanse of ocean without.

Friday, June 25th. 43 deg. 24 min. N. lat., 40 deg. 4 min. W. lon.

This morning there was a further accession to the names upon the sick roll. It was awful how suddenly some were stricken. A little child who was playing with its companions, suddenly fell down, and for some time was sunk in a death-like torpor, from which, when she awoke, she commenced to scream violently, and writhed in convulsive agony. A poor woman who was warming a drink at the fire for her husband, also dropped down quite senseless, and was borne to her berth.

I found it very difficult to acquire precise information respecting the progressive symptoms of the disease, the different parties of whom I inquired disagreeing in some particulars; but I inferred that the first symptom was generally a reeling in the head, followed by a swelling pain, as if the head were going to burst. Next came excruciating pains in the bones, and then a swelling of the limbs, commencing with the feet, in some cases ascending the body, and again descending before it reached the head, stopping at the throat. The period of each stage varied in different patients; some of whom were covered with yellow, watery pimples, and others with red and purple spots, that turned into putrid sores.

Saturday, June 26th. 44 deg. 21 min. N. lat., 41 deg. 36 min. W. lon.

Some of those who the other day appeared to bid defiance to the fever, were seized in its relentless grasp; and a few who were on the

recovery, relapsed. It seemed miraculous to me that such subjects could struggle with so violent a disease without any effective aid.

Sunday, June 27th. 44 deg. 9 min. N. lat., 42 deg. 10 min. W. lon.

The moaning and raving of the patients kept me awake nearly all the night; and I could hear the mistress stirring about until a late hour. It made my heart bleed to listen to the cries for "Water, for God's sake some water." Oh! it was horrifying; yet, strange to say, I had no fear of taking the fever, which, perhaps, under the merciful providence of the Almighty, was a preventive cause. The mate, who spent much of his time among the patients, described to me some revolting scenes he witnessed in the hold; but they were too disgusting to be repeated. He became very much frightened, and often looked quite bewildered.

Monday, June 28th.

The number of patients upon the list now amounted to thirty, and the effluvium of the hold was shocking.

The passengers suffered much for want of pure water, and the mate tried the quality of all the casks. Fortunately he discovered a few which were better, and this circumstance was rather cheering.

Tuesday, June 29th. 43 deg. 24 min. N. lat., 46 deg. 37 min. W. lon.

The wind kept us to the south, but though occasionally becalmed, we were slowly gaining longitude.

I could not keep my mind fixed upon a book, so I was obliged to give over reading, and spent the day watching the rolling of the dolphin, the aerial darts of the flying-fish, with the gambols of numbers of porpoises that danced in the waters around the prow. It being the mate's watch, I remained upon deck until midnight, listening to his yarns. Some of them were rather incredible, and upon expressing such to be my opinion, he was inclined to take offence. Being the hero of some of his stories himself, I could not doubt the veracity of them, though they were not the least marvellous. Although a well informed and intelligent man, he was very superstitious. But it is not uncommon for sailors to be so.

Wednesday, June 30th. 43 deg. 48 min. N. lat., 48 deg. 6 min. W. lon.

Passing the main hatch, I got a glimpse of one of the most awful sights I ever beheld. A poor female patient was lying in one of the upper berths—dying. Her head and face were swollen to a most unnatural size; the latter being hideously deformed. I recollected remarking the clearness of her complexion when I saw her in health, shortly after we sailed. She then was a picture of good humor and contentment; now, how sadly altered! Her cheeks retained their ruddy hue, but the rest of her distorted countenance was of a leprous whiteness. She had been nearly three weeks ill, and suffered exceedingly until the swelling set in, commencing in her feet, and creeping up her body to her head. Her afflicted husband stood by her holding a "blessed candle" in his hand, and awaiting the departure of her spirit. Death put a period to her existence shortly after I saw her. And as the sun was setting, the bereaved husband muttered a prayer over her enshrouded corpse, which, as he said "Amen," was lowered into the ocean.

Thursday, July 1st. 44 deg. 36 min. N. lat., 48 deg. 38 min. W. lon.

The wind was still unfavorable, but we gained a little by constant-ly tacking, and were approaching the banks of Newfoundland. Some new cases were announced, making thirty-seven now lying. A convalescent was assisted on deck, and seemed revived by the fresh air. He was a miserable object. His face being yellow and withered, was rendered ghastly by the black streak that encircled his sunken eyes.

Chapter V.

About midnight the shipmen deemed that they drew near to some country, and sounded.—Acts of the Apostles.

Friday, July 2nd.

We were enveloped in a dense fog, and had a horn sounding constantly. One of the patients, who was represented to be dying, sent for the mate, and giving him the key of his box, in which there was a small sum of money, requested him to take charge of it, and, upon his return to Ireland, send it to his (the sick man's) mother.

The mate promised to do so, but did not consider the poor fellow as bad as he himself feared he was.

Saturday, July 3d.

Any idea I ever formed of complete horror, was excelled by the stern reality of the frightful picture which the past night presented. The gloom spread around by the impenetrable fog was heightened by the dismal tone of the foghorn, between each sound of which might be heard the cries and ravings of the delirious patients, and occasionally the tolling of a bell, warning us of the vicinity of some fishing-boat, numbers of which were scattered over the banks.

The mate being unable to make an observation, we were obliged to depend upon his "dead reckoning."

Sunday, July 4th.

We enjoyed a favorable breeze, and the fog having cleared off at noon, the mate had an observation, by which we were in 45° 11' N. lat., 51° 40' W. lon. No new cases of sickness were reported, but some of the patients were said to be very bad.

We spoke* a bark† and a brig, both homeward bound; and differed but little in longitude. There was something exciting in listening to the friendly voice from the deep toned speaking-trumpet, and in beholding the board marked with the longitude. In a few moments the ensigns were lowered, and each pursued its course.

The day was exceedingly cold; so much so, that the captain supposed that we were in the neighbourhood of icebergs; and I hoped to see one of these castellated floating masses, lifting its pinnacles on high, and glittering in the rays of the sun.

Monday, July 5th. 45 deg. 21 min. N. lat., 53 deg. 52 min. W. lon.

The morning was foggy, and we were near running into a French fishing-boat.

The captain having given orders for sounding, Jack was sent to find the reel and line, which he brought up from the depths of the lazaretto. This receptacle for all sorts of commodities was situated below the cabin; and it afforded me some amusement to see the boy, by the faint light of the lantern, groping among beef casks, pork barrels, paint and tar pots, spars, and rusty irons. The sails having been put aback, so that the brig stood motionless upon the bosom of the water, the reel was held by a man at the stern, and the line being uncoiled, was drawn outside the ropes of the

---

* *Speak* being a nautical term meaning to manoeuvre alongside another ship generally for the purpose of exchanging greetings and news.

† A *barque* is a sailing vessel of three or more masts, with all masts but the sternmost square-rigged, the sternmost being fore-and-aft-rigged.

rigging, until it reached the bow. The lead was then attached, and carried by a seaman to the point of the bowsprit, where the sailor sat swinging the weight, like a pendulum, until, upon the order to heave, he cast it forth upon its mission. Bottom having been found at thirty-four fathoms, the line was placed upon a pulley and drawn up; when there was found imbedded in the grease with which the lead was filled, fine white sand, as laid down in the chart.

The sails were again set to the breeze, and we were once more gliding through the water, the momentary commotion soon settling down into the usual inanity.

Tuesday, July 6th. 45 deg. 37 min. N. lat., 54 deg. 53 min. W. lon. 7 deg.

During the past night there was a heavy fall of rain, which left the atmosphere clear and cool.

Two men (brothers) died of dysentery, and I was awakened by the noise made by the mate, who was searching for an old sail to cover the remains with. In about an hour after, they were consigned to the deep, a remaining brother being the solitary mourner. He continued long to gaze upon the ocean, while a tear that dropped from his moistened eye told the grief he did not otherwise express. I learned in the afternoon that he was suffering from the same complaint that carried off his brothers.

Wednesday, July 7th.

The phosphorescent appearance of the ocean at night was very beautiful. We seemed to be gliding through a sea of liquid fire. We passed a great number of fishing-boats, chiefly French, from the isles Miquelon and St. Pierre.

They were anchored at regular intervals, for the purpose of catching cod-fish, which, allured by the vast numbers of worms found upon the bottom, abound upon the banks. The vessels generally are large sloops, and have a platform all round, with an awning over the deck. When a fish is taken, it is immediately split and cleaned; then it is thrown into the hold; and when the latter is full, the fishermen return home, and land their cargo, to be dried and saved.

Owing to these processes being sometimes too long deferred, the bank fish, though larger, is considered inferior to that taken along the coast of Newfoundland.

Great variety of opinion exists respecting the nature and origin of these submarine banks, but none of them appears to me so natural as this:—The stream which issues from the Gulf of Mexico, commonly called the "Florida gulf stream," being checked in its progress by the southern coast of Newfoundland, deposits the vast amount of matter held in suspension. This by accumulation formed the Banks, which are still increasing in extent. The temperature of the water upon the Banks is higher than that of the Gulf of St. Lawrence, and of the ocean; and its evaporation causes the fog that almost perpetually prevails.

The afternoon was clear, with a gentle breeze, which formed a ripple on the surface of the water, and gave a beautiful appearance to the reflection of the declining sun, looking like jets of gas bursting from the deep.

Thursday, July 8th. 45 deg. 24 min. N. lat., 57 deg. W. lon.

Another of the crew was taken ill, thereby reducing our hands when they were most required. The captain had a great dread of the coast of Newfoundland, which being broken into deep bays, divided from each other by rocky capes, is rendered exceedingly

perilous; more especially, as the powerful currents set towards this inhospitable shore.

We kept a lookout for some vessel coming from the gulf, in order to learn the bearings of land, but did not perceive one during the day.

Friday, July 9th. 46 deg. N. lat., 58 deg. W. lon.

A few convalescents appeared upon deck. The appearance of the poor creatures was miserable in the extreme. We now had fifty sick, being nearly one half the whole number of passengers. Some entire families being prostrated, were dependent on the charity of their neighbours, many of whom were very kind; but others seemed to be possessed of no feeling. Among the former, the Head-committee was conspicuous. The brother of the two men who died on the sixth instant, followed them to-day. He was seized with dismay from the time of their death, which no doubt hurried on the malady to its fatal termination. The old sails being all used up, his remains were placed in two meal-sacks, and a weight being fastened at foot, the body was placed upon one of the hatch battens, from which, when raised over the bulwark, it fell into the deep, and was no more seen. He left two little orphans, one of whom, a boy seven years of age, I noticed in the evening, wearing his deceased father's coat. Poor little fellow! he seemed quite unconscious of his loss, and proud of the accession to his scanty covering. The remainder of the man's clothes were sold by auction, by a friend of his who promised to take care of the children. There was great competition, and the "Cant," as they called it, occasioned jibing and jesting, which it was painful to listen to, surrounded as the actors were, (some of whom had just risen from a bed of sickness) by famine, pestilence and death.

Chapter VI.

The floods are risen, O Lord, the floods have lifted up their voice; the floods lift up their waves. The waves of the sea are mighty and rage horribly: but yet the Lord who dwelleth on high is mightier.—DAVID.

July 10th, 46 deg. 36 min. N. lat., 59 deg. 36 min. W. lon.

We spoke a wherry which was conveying cattle from Nova Scotia to Newfoundland, and learned from the steersman the bearings of St. Paul's Island. We shortly afterwards passed a large fleet, coming from the gulf, and in the afternoon descried Cape North.

The passengers expressed great delight at seeing land, and were under the impression that they were near their destination, little knowing the extent of the gulf they had to pass, and the great river to ascend. Early in the evening we saw Isle St. Paul, and indistinctly the point of Cape Ray, between which and Cape North is the passage into the Gulf of St. Lawrence. St. Paul's Island lies about ten miles to the north of the latter cape, in latitude 47° 14' north, and longitude 60° 11' 17" west. It is a huge rock, dividing at top into three conical peaks. Rising boldly from the sea, there is a great depth of water all round it, and vessels may pass at either side of it. It has been the site of numerous shipwrecks; many vessels, carried out of their reckoning by the currents, having been dashed against it when concealed by fog, and instantly shattered to atoms.

Human bones and other memorials of these disasters are strewed around its base. We passed the light of this dangerous island, at 10 P. M., entering into the "goodly, great gulf, full of islands, passages, and entrances, towards what wind soever you please to bend."*

---

*   Cartier. [Author's note]

This gulf was first explored by John Cabot, in 1497, who called the coast of Labrador *Primavista*. The Portuguese afterwards changed the name of that desert region to Terra Coterealis; and the gulf they designated as that of the "Two Brothers," in memory of Gaspar and Michael Cotereal, the first named of whom not having returned from the second expedition he commanded, the latter went in search of him; but neither of them were afterwards heard of.

Jaques Cartier having entered it upon the festival of St. Lawrence, gave to the gulf and the river flowing into it the name they still retain.

Sunday, July 11th.

We had a fair wind, and were going full sail at 7 knots an hour. At noon we passed the Bird Islands, which are low ledges of rocks, and swarm with gannets, numbers of which were flying about. They were as large as geese, and pure white with the exception of the tips of the wings, which were jet black. Some of Mother Carey's chickens† were following in our wake, and it was highly amusing to watch the contentions of the little creatures for bits of fat thrown to them.

We had a distant view of the Magdalen Islands, which, although lying nearer to Nova Scotia, are considered as belonging to Canada; and form a portion of the circuit within the district of Gaspé, a court being held at Amherst harbor annually, from 1st to 10th of July. The largest of the group are Bryon, Deadman's, Amherst, Entry, and Wolf islands, which are inhabited by a hardy race of fishermen. The huge walrus may at times be seen upon their shores.

---

† Another name for the storm petrel.

Monday, July 12th.

In the morning we were becalmed, the water being smooth as glass, and of a beautifully clear, green hue.

A breeze sprung up at 12 o'clock, and the captain having provided himself and me with lines, we spent the afternoon fishing for mackerel, which were so plenty that I caught seventy in about two hours, when I had to give over, my hands being cut by the line. The captain continued, and had a barrel full by evening. They were the finest mackerel I ever saw, and we had some at tea, which we all enjoyed as a delicious treat after six weeks of salt beef and biscuit diet. Many of the passengers having noticed our success, followed our example, and lines were out from every quarter; all the twine, thread, &c. that could be made out, being put into requisition, with padlocks and bolts for weights, and wire hooks. Even with such rude gear, they caught a great number; but their recreation was suddenly terminated, a young man who was drawing in a fish having dropped upon the deck quite senseless, and apparently dead. He was carried below and put into his berth, there to pass through the successive stages of the fever.

Tuesday, July 13th.

We were again becalmed during the forenoon, but a breeze that soon became a gale arose about one o'clock, P. M., and lasted until evening, being accompanied by thunder and lightning, and followed by a heavy shower of rain. The clouds cleared away at sunset, when we were within 10 or 12 miles of the eastern point of the island of Anticosti, which when the captain perceived, he gave the order to sheer off on the other tack. This island is particularly dangerous, being surrounded by sunken reefs. It is of considerable extent, being 130 miles in length from east to west,

and 30 miles across its greatest breadth. Its surface is low and level, and covered with a pristine forest, through which prowls the bear, undisturbed, except when hunted by Indians, who periodically resort hither for that purpose.

The sterility of its soil offering no inducement to the white man, it is uninhabited, except by the keepers of the lighthouses, to which are attached small establishments for the purpose of affording relief to shipwrecked mariners. The name Anticosti is probably a corruption of Natiscotee, which it is called by the aborigines. Cartier named it "L'isle de l'Assumption."

Wednesday, July 14th.

We had the bold headlands of capes Gaspé and Rosier on our left, and had entered the majestic river St. Lawrence, which here, through a mouth ninety miles in width, after a course of upwards of 2,000 miles, disgorges the accumulated waters of the great lakes, swollen by the accession of hundreds of tributaries, (some of them noble rivers,) draining an almost boundless region.

The reports of the sufferings in the hold were heartrending. Simon and Jack were both taken ill.

Thursday, July 15th.

Last night I was suddenly wakened by the captain, shouting "get up! get up! and come on deck quickly." Somewhat alarmed, I obeyed the summons as speedily as possible, and was well recompensed for the start, by the magnificence of the glorious scene I beheld. The northern portion of the firmament was vividly illuminated with a clear though subdued light, while across it shot fiery meteors from different directions; now rushing against

each other as if engaged in deadly warfare; again gliding about in wanton playfulness.

Disappearing for a while, and leaving behind a faintly luminous trail, they would again burst forth upon their stage, lighted up by a sudden flash for the igneous performers. I watched with delight until the lustrous picture was finally enshrouded in darkness, when I returned to bed.

There was a birth on board this morning, and two or three deaths were momentarily expected. The mate's account of the state of the hold was harrowing. It required the greatest coercion to enforce any thing like cleanliness or decency; and the Head committee had no sinecure office. I spent the greater part of the day upon deck, admiring the numberless jets d'eau of the bottle-nosed whales that plunged about in the water. The poor mistress was greatly grieved about Jack and Simon; and the captain was savage for lack of assistance.

Friday, July 16th.

We were tacking about all day, which though tedious I enjoyed, as it afforded an opportunity of seeing both shores of the noble river. That to the north is indescribably grand; rugged mountains rising precipitously from out the water, and indented by sweeping bays, in which are numerous islets. Towards evening we were in view of Seven Islands bay, lovely though desolate. No human eyes behold this region of unbroken solitude, save now and then those which can but lightly appreciate its grandeur. I cannot describe the effect produced by the mist that sometimes completely hides the mountains—rolling up their sides, and resembling gracefully festooned drapery.

The sailors who could work were greatly harassed by being obliged to tack repeatedly. The mate, especially, was one moment

down in the hold waiting on some dying fellow-creature; the next, perhaps, stretched across a yard, reefing a top-sail. Although lame, he was surprisingly active, and used to astonish the emigrants, one of whom said to me, "Och! your honor, isn't Mister Mate a great bit of a man?"

Saturday, July 17th.

The morning was fine, and shortly after breakfast I was upon deck admiring the beauty of the pine-clad hills upon the southern shore of the river, when the captain came up from the cabin, and after looking about gave the word to "double reef top-sails and make all snug." Not long after, the sky, which had been quite clear, became black, and a violent gale arose, lashing the water into tremendous waves, which tossed us mercilessly about; one moment borne up by an angry billow; the next, plunging into a deep abyss. The roaring wind was drowned by the tremendous noise of successive peals of thunder, while the forked lightning played about in zig-zag lines, and the rain descended in torrents.

At 5, P. M., the wind abated, and the waves began to subside. About an hour after, the leaden clouds parted, and, as if in defiance of the contending elements, the sun set in gorgeous splendor. The poor passengers were greatly terrified by the storm, and suffered exceedingly. They were so buffetted about that the sick could not be tended; and after calm was restored a woman was found dead in her berth.

Chapter VII.

So frequent death,
Sorrow he more than causes, but confounds;
For human sighs, his rival strokes contend,
And make distress, distraction.—YOUNG.

Sunday, July 18th.

I was enchanted with the extraordinary beauty of the scenery I beheld this morning, when I came on deck.—The early beams of the sun played upon the placid surface of the river, here forty miles wide, the banks on either hand being moderately elevated, and covered with firs. On the north was Cape des Monts, terminating in a low point, on which stood a light-house and diminutive cottage. On the south Cape Chat rose to a considerable height; the outline of its summit being broken by sudden gaps, giving to it a character that to me was unique.

An unbroken stillness reigned around, as if nature were at rest after the storm of the previous day; and our brig lay almost motionless upon the water.

I occupied myself again and again noting, so as to impress upon my mind, the peerless beauty I am unable to portray, and in reading the Acts of the Apostles. I felt a renewed interest in the account of St. Paul's voyages, as I could now appreciate by experience the force and accuracy of their description. We made no way, and it was with difficulty we retained our position against the current.

Monday, July 19th.

Another death and burial. A few who had been ill, again appeared on deck, weak, and weary. The want of pure water was sensibly felt by the afflicted creatures, and we were yet a long way from where the river loses its saltness. In the morning there came alongside of us a beautiful little schooner, from which we took a pilot on board. When he found that we had emigrants, and so much sickness, he seemed to be frightened and disappointed; as he had avoided a large ship, thinking we had not passengers. However, he could not nor dare he retreat. The first thing he did was to open his huge trunk, and take from it a pamphlet, which proved to be the quarantine regulations; he handed it to the captain, who spent a long time poring over it. When he had read it I got a look at it—one side was printed in French, the other in English. The rules were very stringent, and the penalties for their infringement exceedingly severe; the sole control being vested in the head physician, the power given to whom was most arbitrary. We feared that we should undergo a long detention in quarantine, and learned that we could hold no communication whatever with the shore until our arrival at Grosse Isle.

The pilot was a heavy, stupid fellow—a Canadian, speaking a horrible patois, and broken English; he was accompanied by his nephew and apprentice, Pierre, a fine lad.

The wind favored us for some hours, and towards evening we saw Mount Camille upon the southern bank, rising above the surrounding hills to a height of 2036 feet.

Tuesday, July 20th.

Our course lying more to the southern bank of the river, I could observe minutely the principal objects upon that side. Many

charming tributary streams rolled along sweet valleys, enfolded in the swelling hills, whose sides were clothed with verdure. I would fain explore each of these enchanting vales; but too soon we passed them, and some jutting cape would hide from view the little settlements at each embouchure. The most considerable of these, was that upon Point aux Snellez, near the mouth of the river Metis, about 200 miles from Quebec. Here commences the Kempt road, which terminates at Cross point on the river Restigouche,—a distance of 98 miles. A new road, connecting this with Grande Nouvelle on the Bay of Chaleur, completes the communication with Halifax.

Wednesday, July 21st.

A thick fog concealed every object from view, at times so low as only to hide the hulls of vessels, by whose rigging we could perceive them tacking like ourselves; the sky being unclouded. A strong wind blew down the river, which together with the forcible current kept us back. One of the sick sailors reappeared upon deck, but was too weak to resume duty; the other man was still very bad; as were also Simon and Jack.

Simon got up from his berth in a delirious fit, and ran down to the cabin, where his wild appearance nearly frightened the life out of the mistress. It was with difficulty he was laid hold of; and he resisted violently while he was carried back to his hammock, in the forecastle, where he was strapped down.

Thursday, July 22nd.

Soon after retiring to my berth last night, I heard a grating noise, accompanied by a tremulous motion of the brig, and felt alarmed,

fearing that we had grounded upon some bank; but my anxiety was relieved, by learning that it was caused by the dropping of the anchor, it being useless to contend against both wind and current. The latter here being strengthened by the vast body of water discharged from the river Saguenay. When I came on deck this morning, I found that we were anchored off the village of Trois Pistolles, with Cape L'Orignal to the east, and Basque Isle on the west. Being the first Canadian village I had seen, I was delighted by the rural aspect of the pretty white cottages with red roofs, scattered over the sloping bank, each surrounded by a small garden. The captain was impatient, and though the pilot said it would only tend to harass the sailors, we weighed anchor at noon, and after beating about all the day, again came to, near the same spot as before. A child, one of the orphans, died and was buried in the evening, no friend being by to see the frail body committed to its watery grave. The water could not be used by the wretched emigrants, and but half a cask of that provided for the cabin and crew remained; they were therefore obliged to use the saline water of the river.

Friday, July 23d.

We remained at anchor all day, a fresh breeze blowing down the river. Some of the recovered patients who were slowly regaining strength, had relapsed into the most violent stages, and three new cases were announced, showing exceedingly virulent symptoms.

The wind abated at noon, and it was quite calm for about an hour. During this period I was upon deck, and on looking across the river was greatly astonished at perceiving something resembling an island, which I had not before noticed. It was circular, and quite black. I spent some time in conjecturing what it could be; the captain could not tell; and the pilot was asleep. At length

two vessels sailing down the river, when they came near this object, assumed a similar appearance, from which I immediately inferred that it was a ship at anchor, transformed by mirage.

As the vessels sailed along, they underwent extraordinary meta-morphoses—sometimes the bow and stern were turned up like those of a Chinese junk; at others the hulls were up in the air and the masts seemingly in the water; the latter being twisted and curved. A cottage upon the north bank stood apparently upon the surface of the river, and the light-house on Bic island had a duplicate of itself perched upon it, the copy being inverted, lantern down and base up. The illusions occurred only within certain limits, which were defined by an appearance distinct from the surrounding atmosphere. The difference being something like that presented by clear water and the empty space within a half filled vial.

Chapter VIII.

These are miracles, which man,
Cag'd in the bounds of Europe's pigmy plan,
Can scarcely dream of; which his eye must see,
To know how beautiful this world can be.—MOORE.*

Saturday, July 24th.

We once more weighed anchor this morning, and beat about all the day between Trois Pistolles and the mouth of the river Escamin, which discharges itself nearly opposite, upon the north shore. We had a large fleet of ships, barques, and brigs in company, two of which were transports with troops. It was a pleasing sight to see such a number of vessels, continually passing each other, and each evidently endeavoring to gain upon the rest, every tack.

In the afternoon a brig hoisted her ensign as a signal of recognition, and upon the next tack we passed near enough to speak; when the captain turned out to be a particular friend of our captain and the mistress. They kept up a regular conversation the rest of the day, every time we met, which was pretty often; each inquiring of the other, the number of deaths?—what sickness?—how many days out?—from what port? &c. &c. We learned, much to our surprise, that she had a greater number of deaths than we; and this news was very consoling to the mistress. Towards evening the wind abated, and we were in hope that it was about to change. It died away altogether, and the vessels that before shot past one another, were now almost motionless, and scattered over the surface of the river, which here is twenty-five miles wide. At sunset we lay at the

---

* Extract from a poem by Thomas Moore (1779–1852) written 'From the Banks of the St. Lawrence.'

north side, and could almost reach the trees covering the bank. I have seen many a beautiful sunset, but all fade before the exquisite beauty of that which I witnessed this evening. The glorious luminary sunk behind the dark blue hills, upon the summits of which seemed to rest the border of heaven's canopy, dyed in crimson sheen, softening down to a light orange tint, that imperceptibly blended with the azure sky, which was here and there hid by fleecy vermilion clouds. Cape L' Orignal was clothed in a vesture of purple, of every shade, from violet to that of the deepest hue, o'ershadowing the village of Trois Pistolles. There was not a ripple upon the water, but gentle undulations heaved its bosom, decked in a tissue of carmine, ultramarine, and gold. Such vividness and variety of colors I never before conceived, or since experienced. Oh! thought I, why is not Danby* here to fix them upon imperishable canvass? As night came on the pilot grew uneasy, there not being good anchorage at that side; however, a slight breeze from the old quarter wafted us across, to the very spot where we before lay, and where we again dropped anchor in the midst of our consorts.

Sunday, July 25th.

We lay at anchor all day, the wind blowing strongly against us. It was exceedingly trying to be detained here within a few miles of the tidal influence, having once gained which, we would be independent of the wind. The poor patients, too, were anxiously looking out for the quarantine station, where they hoped to find some alleviation to their sufferings. The mistress and mate were uneasy, as the cabin water was nearly out, and they feared to let the captain know of it. I was obliged to remain below, the effluvia from the hold being quite overpowering. I could hear the tolling of the village church-bell, and its sweet tone induced me

---

*   Francis Danby (1793–1861), landscape painter.

to go on deck for a few moments, where I was charmed with the appearance of the showily dressed Canadians, some standing in groups, talking; others seated upon benches, while caleshes† were momentarily arriving with "habitans"‡ from distant settlements, who, after tying up their horses under a shed close by the "pres-bytere," joined the chatting parties until the bell ceased, when all retired within the church.

Monday, July 26th.

The wind was not so strong, and the effluvia not quite so un-pleasant. I was therefore not so much confined to the cabin. The captain was desirous of sailing, but the pilot would not consent; and the latter proved to be right, as two of the vessels weighed anchor in the morning, and after beating about for a couple of hours were obliged to come to. A pretty stream,—the mingled waters of the Abawisquash and Trois Pistolles rivers,—flows into the St. Lawrence, adjacent to the village. Like all the tributaries upon the southern side, it is of inconsiderable length, the hills in which they have their sources lying at no great distance from the bank. But many of those which empty themselves at the north side, as the Manicouagan, Bustard, Belsiamites, Portneuf, &c., are fine rivers, rising in the elevated ridge that divides Canada from the Hudson's Bay territory; and in their courses through the untrodden forests expanding into large lakes. After dinner the mistress carried the baby that was born on board, down to the cabin. The captain at first was very angry; but a smile upon the face of the little innocent, softened his heart, and he soon ca-ressed it with all the endearments he was in the habit of lavishing

---

† Two or four-wheeled light horse-drawn vehicles, often with folding tops.

‡ I.e., inhabitants.

upon the canary; when tired of which amusement, he opened the locker and took therefrom an egg, which he held up to the light and looked through, to see if it were good. Not being satisfied on that point, he tried another, and then another, until he got one to please him. He next got some salt, and opening the infant's little hand, placed it upon the palm, and gently closed the tiny fingers upon it. He then performed a similar operation upon the other, enclosing a shilling in lieu of salt. The egg he handed to the mistress to send to the mother, and acquaint her that he wished the child to be called "Ellen," after her.

The mistress, kind to all, was particularly so to the little children, about twenty of whom we had aboard. One poor infant, whose father and mother (neither of whom were twenty years of age) were both ill and unable to take care of it, she paid a woman for nursing; and I could not believe it to be the same child when I saw it clean and comfortably covered with clothes she made for it. Jack came upon deck. Poor fellow! he was sadly altered. Simon also was reported to be better, but unable to leave his hammock. The mate began to complain, and the brandy cask, (which had been broached,) supplied his remedy.

Tuesday, July 27th.

The wind veered about five o'clock last evening, and the vessels, one by one, sailed away. Our pilot saying that it would again change in a short time, was not inclined to weigh anchor, but the captain insisted upon doing so. At 6 P. M. we were once more in motion, and in a few minutes were in full sail, going seven knots an hour. Basque island was soon left behind, and stemming the dark waters discharged by the Saguenay, as day was fading, we were before Tadousac, a settlement at the mouth of that grand river. The Saguenay ranks second amongst the tributaries of the

St. Lawrence; indeed, although its course is not so long, it is supposed to convey a larger body of water than the Ottawa. At its juncture with the St. Lawrence it is about a mile wide; but in some parts it expands to three. At a distance of one hundred and forty miles it receives the waters of lake St. John, which is the reservoir of numerous rivers, some of which are precipitated into it by magnificent rapids and falls. This lake, which is about one hundred miles in circumference, is remarkable for its shallowness, from which cause the navigation of it is frequently dangerous; as the least wind produces a ground swell and breakers. Its water is said to be tepid, and it abounds with a variety of fish, great quantities of which are taken at the mouth of the Ouiatchouan river, where there is a station, at which they are salted and packed for traffic. The climate is very salubrious, and the soil of the great valley that borders the lake is susceptible of the highest culture. A few Indians wander over this fine tract of country, which it is the intention of the provincial government to open to French Canadians, whose laws acknowledging no right of primogeniture, they have overpopulated many of the old settlements. The Indians call this fine sheet of water, "Piegougamis," signifying "the flat lake." First-class ships can ascend the Saguenay to Chicoutimi, a distance of sixty-eight miles. There is a small settlement here, the communication between which and the lake, being broken by rapids, can only be overcome by experienced "voyageurs" in canoes. At Ha-Ha Bay, eighteen miles below Chicoutimi, there is a pretty large settlement, and here the river assumes its grand and romantic feature, passing for the remainder of its course between almost perpendicular cliffs, from one thousand to fifteen hundred feet in height. Its great depth is another characteristic; bottom not being found near the mouth with a line of three hundred and thirty fathoms while the depth of the St. Lawrence at the junction is but two hundred and forty feet. However, its great rapidity renders it impossible accurately to learn its soundings.

Chapter IX.

But soft! the tinges of the west decline,
And night falls dewy o'er these banks of pine.
Among the reeds in which our idle boat
Is rock'd to rest, the wind's complaining note
Dies, like a half breath'd whispering of flutes.
Along the waves the gleaming porpoise shoots,
And I can trace him like a wat'ry star,
Down the steep current, till he fades afar
Amid the foaming breakers' silvery light,
Where yon rough rapids sparkle through the night.—MOORE.

July 27th.

Feeling somewhat excited by the sudden acceleration of our progress, I determined to remain on deck until the turn of the tide would compel us to come to an anchor. There was something also most enchanting in being wafted by both wind and tide, at the rate of ten knots an hour, watching the lights upon the different islands, and the myriads of bright stars that studded the firmament, and were reflected in the darkened surface of the broad river, which upon the north side was overshadowed by the mountainous banks, while the southern shore might be traced by a continuous line of flickering lamps within the cottages upon its border. We soon left Green island behind us; then Hare island and Riviere du Loup, upon which is a large settlement with a population of about fifteen hundred. There are some large saw-mills here, and a "portage" leading through Madawaska to the lower provinces. After passing the Pilgrims, a group of rocky islets, I went below,

and had not long "turned in" when I heard and felt the dropping of the anchor.

In the morning I found that we lay off Kamouraska, which is charmingly situated in a rich district, at the base of a chain of hills that rise behind the village, and stretch far beyond it. This lovely spot, being one of the healthiest places in Lower Canada, attracts many visitors during the summer season. It is also enriched by the fisheries established upon the numerous islands that lie immediately in front, supplying abundance of shad, salmon, herrings, &c. Directly opposite, upon the other side of the river, is Murray Bay, into which flows the Malbaie River, upon whose banks reside the descendants of Wolfe's highlanders, many of whom settled there, after the campaign. The bay is environed by an amphitheatre of majestic hills, cultivated to the very summits, their sloping sides being dotted over with comfortable abodes.

We weighed anchor at noon, and gently glided through a scene of indescribable loveliness. The noble river here unbroken by islands, presented a lake-like expanse, bounded by the lofty Cap Diable, and Goose Cape. Village succeeded village upon the south shore; and the gigantic hills upon the north were adorned by sweet alpine cots, surrounded by cleared patches of land, embosomed by the dark green pines. The weather was very warm, and nature basked in uninterrupted sunshine. Oh! what a contrast to this magic beauty was presented within our floating pest-house; not that matters were worse than they had been; there was rather an abatement in the violence of the fever, and I perceived some faces, that I with difficulty recognized, so changed were they since I saw them, before their illness. Simon and Jack were both on deck, the former being deprived of memory, and partially deranged in his mind. Poor fellow! having, the previous voyage, fallen from the topsail yard, and injured his head, his intellect was thereby impaired, and the fever confirmed the insanity, which had not left him when I quitted the brig, some three weeks after. Being

now in fresh water the passengers were relieved of one calamity, and the women who were able, were busy washing; two or three men were also similarly engaged, their wives being unable; and we endeavoured to impress upon them the fact, that the length of our detention in quarantine would greatly depend on the cleanliness of their persons, and of the hold. There were still some very bad cases, and the poor Head committee was in great trouble about his wife, who was dying. The mate still kept up, being afraid of going to hospital, but it was quite evident that he was very ill indeed.

We passed two steamers that were going down the river to tow up ships. We also had a Scotch brig, the "Delta," in company.

At 6 P. M., the tide being on the ebb, we once more anchored, opposite to the Isle aux Coudres, which lies in front of St. Paul's bay. This beautiful island was so named by Cartier, who found upon it a profusion of filberts. A smaller island lies inside of it, whose origin is thus accounted for in a manuscript belonging to the Jesuit college of Quebec; which relates the effects of the earthquake felt throughout Canada in 1663:—"Near St. Paul's bay (fifty miles below Quebec, on the north side,) a mountain about a quarter of a league in circumference, situated on the shore of the St. Lawrence, was precipitated into the river; but, as if it had only made a plunge, it rose from the bottom and became a small island, forming with the shore a convenient harbour, well sheltered from all winds." The same authority says, "Lower down the river, towards Point Alouettes, an entire forest of considerable extent was loosened from the main bank, and slid into the river St. Lawrence, where the trees took fresh root."

The rivers Du Gouffre and Des Marees empty themselves into St. Paul's bay, flowing through luxuriant valleys, intervening between the detached mountains.

Delightfully located upon an eminence, on the south bank, stands the village of St. Anne, at the head of a bay of the same name, into which flows the river Ouelle. It is large, and has a

Catholic College, and some handsome churches.

The surrounding country is highly cultivated, presenting every feature of softness and beauty that can adorn a landscape.

The evening was a charming one,—clear and still,—the water smooth as a mirror, in which gleamed the reflection of the tin covered roofs and spires, that glittered in the rays of the setting sun; while occasionally a huge snow-white porpoise rose above the surface, plunging again beneath the water, which closing, formed circles, becoming larger and larger, until the unwieldy creature again appeared and formed them anew. I remained on deck long after all had retired to rest, and watched the gray twilight creeping over day, until it was illumined by the pale moon, which soon smiled upon one of earth's most beauteous pictures.

I retired to my berth, and took a short repose; which was broken shortly after midnight by the weighing of the anchor. As I wished not to lose the sight of the least part of the river (which I loved to look upon by night as well as by day), I hurried on deck.

We passed through the Traverse—an intricate channel, marked by floating lights—and by the Pillars, a group of dangerous rocks on one of which is a revolving light. At day-break we were passing Goose island, which at low water is connected with Crane island, on the northern extremity of which is the handsome residence of the seigneur. The southern bank presented the same charming features, and in the distance I discerned the chain of hills claimed by the United States as the boundary of the State of Maine. In a short time we arrived before the village of St. Thomas, picturesquely situated on the banks of Riviere du Sud, in which were anchored some vessels which were being freighted with lumber from the several saw-mills. The soil in this neighbourhood is exceedingly productive, and is well cultivated; on which account it is called the granary of the lower province. The village is of considerable extent, and is composed of white houses, clustering around a pretty church. A few miles further sail brought us among a number of

beautiful islets—so beautiful that they seemed like a fairy scene; their verdant turf was almost level with the blue water that wound amongst them, submerging not a few, so that the firs that grew upon them appeared to rise from the river. A vast fleet of vessels lying at anchor told that we had arrived at Grosse Isle; and after wending our way amongst isles and ships, we dropped anchor in the ground allotted for vessels upon arrival, and hoisted our ensign at the peak, as a signal for the inspecting physician to board us.

Chapter X.

And when I looked, behold, an hand was sent unto me; and, lo, a roll of a book was therein;

And he spread it before me; and it was written within and without; and there was written therein, lamentations, and mourning, and woe.—EZEKIEL.

Grosse Isle, July 28th.

By 6. A. M., we were settled in our new position before the quarantine station. The passengers that were able to be up were all busy, cleaning and washing, some clearing the hold of filth, others assisting the sailors in swabbing the deck. The mistress herself washed out the cabin last evening, and put every thing in order.

The captain commenced shaving himself at 7, and completed the operation in about an hour and a half. The mate was unable to do anything, but kept repeatedly calling to the mistress for brandy, and requested that his illness should be kept from the doctor, as he was sure he had not fever. Breakfast was speedily despatched, and anxiety was depicted on every countenance. At 9 o'clock a boat was perceived pulling towards us, with four oars and a steersman with a broad leafed straw hat and leather coat, who the pilot told us was the inspecting physician. In a few minutes the boat was alongside, and the doctor on deck. He hastily enquired for the captain, and before he could be answered was down in the cabin where the mistress was finishing her toilet. Having introduced himself, he enquired if we had sickness aboard?—Its nature?—How many deaths?—How many patients at present? These questions being

answered, and the replies noted upon his tablet, he snatched up his hat,—ran up the ladder,—along the deck,—and down into the hold. Arrived there, "ha!" said he, sagaciously, "there is fever here." He stopped beside the first berth in which a patient was lying,—felt his pulse,—examined his tongue,—and ran up the ladder again. As he passed by me he handed me some papers to be filled up by the captain, and to have ready "tomorrow or next day." In an instant he was in his boat, from which, while the men were taking up their oars, he shouted out to me that I was not obliged to remain in quarantine, and might go up to Quebec when I pleased. I brought the papers to the captain, who remained in the cabin, supposing that the doctor would return thither, in order to give directions for our guidance; and when he learned that that gentleman had gone, he was desperately enraged. The mistress endeavored to pacify him by suggesting that it was likely he would visit us again in the course of the day, or at least that he would send a message to us. When I acquainted the mistress that I was at liberty to leave the brig, she looked at me most pitifully, as if she would say, "Are you too going to desert us." But I had no such intention, and was determined to remain with them, at all events until they reached Quebec. The poor passengers expecting that they would be all reviewed, were dressed in their best clothes, and were clean, though haggard and weak. They were greatly disappointed in their expectations, as they were under the impression that the sick would be immediately admitted to the hospital, and the healthy landed upon the island, there to remain until taken to Quebec by a steamer. Indeed, such was the procedure to be inferred from the book of directions given to the captain by the pilot, when he came aboard.

When the mistress appeared on deck, I scarcely knew her. She usually wore a black stuff gown, a red worsted "bosom friend," which she told me (at least once a day,) was knit for her by her neice;—with a cap having three full borders, which projected

beyond the leaf of the little straw bonnet, covered with the ac-cumulated stains and smoke of many a voyage. Now, she had on a new fancy striped calico dress, as showy as deep reds, yellows, blues and greens could make it,—a black satin bonnet, with no lack of red ribands, and a little conservatory of artificials around her good natured face,—not forgetting her silver spectacles. All day long we kept looking out for a message from shore, and in watching the doctor's boat, going from vessel to vessel; his visit to each occupying about the same time as to us, which was exactly five minutes. We sometimes fancied that he was making for us, but the boat the next moment would be concealed by some large ship; then we were sure we would be the next; but no, the rowers pulled for shore. The day wore away before we gave up hope.

I could not believe it possible, that here within reach of help we should be left as neglected as when upon the ocean;—that after a voyage of two months' duration, we were to be left still enveloped by reeking pestilence, the sick without medicine, medical skill, nourishment, or so much as a drop of pure water; for the river although not saline here, was polluted by the most disgusting objects, thrown overboard from the several vessels. In short, it was a floating mass of filthy straw, the refuse of foul beds, barrels containing the vilest matter, old rags, and tattered clothes, &c., &c. The Head committee was greatly grieved for his wife, whose death he momentarily expected. He had looked anxiously forward to the time when we should arrive here, hoping that at least the doctor would see her; but his hopes, as well as those of others, were suddenly blasted. The brig that arrived with us sailed for Quebec immediately after the doctor's visit, possibly not having had any sickness: five other vessels also were discharged. How long they were detained, we could not tell; but the captain was so provoked, that he vowed he would sail without permission. The pilot, who did not well understand his hasty disposition, ventured to remonstrate with him, and fell in for a hurricane of curses and

abuse; to which, though ignorant of many of the expressions, he replied in French, not finding himself sufficiently eloquent in the English tongue.

Four vessels arrived with the evening tide, and hoisted their signals, but were not visited. Several sailed by us without stopping, not having passengers, and a vast number went down the river during the day. Two huge steamers also arrived, and in the afternoon brought off hundreds of human beings from the island.

Thursday, July 29th.

This morning a boat was perceived making towards us, which at first was thought to be the doctor's; but when it approached nearer there appeared but two persons in it, both of whom were rowing. In a few minutes more the boat was alongside, and from the cassocks and bands of the two gentlemen we learned that they were Canadian priests. They came on deck, each carrying a large black bag. They inquired for the captain, who received them courteously, and introduced them to the mistress and to me, after which they conversed awhile in French with the pilot, whom they knew; when, having put on their vestments, they descended into the hold. They there spent a few minutes with each of the sick, and administered the last rites to the dying woman and an old man, terminating their duties by baptizing the infant. They remained in the hold for about an hour, and when they returned complimented the captain on the cleanliness of the vessel. They staid a short time talking to us upon deck, and the account they gave of the horrid condition of many of the ships in quarantine was frightful. In the holds of some of them they said, that they were up to their ancles in filth. The wretched emigrants crowded together like cattle, and corpses remaining long unburied, the sailors being ill, and the passengers unwilling to touch them.

They also told us of the vast numbers of sick in the hospitals, and in tents, upon the island, and that many nuns, clergymen and doctors, were lying in typhus fever, taken from the patients. They were exceedingly intelligent and gentlemanly men, and telling us that we had great cause of thankfulness in having escaped much better than so many others, they politely bowed, and got into their little boat, amid the blessings of the passengers, who watched them until they arrived beside a distant ship.

The Head committee expressed himself satisfied that his wife saw a priest before her death, which occurred about an hour after; and as the pilot said that the remains should not be thrown into the river, there being a burial ground upon the island, the corpse lay in the hold until the next day.

The mate continued to grow worse, and the mistress was un-ceasing in her attention to him. The day was exceedingly hot and sultry, and I could not have remained on deck, but the captain spread an awning over it, which kept the cabin cool. We lay at some distance from the island, the distant view of which was ex-ceedingly beautiful. At the far end were rows of white tents and marquees, resembling the encampment of an army; somewhat nearer was the little fort, and residence of the superintendent physician, and nearer still the chapel, seaman's hospital, and lit-tle village, with its wharf and a few sail boats; the most adjacent extremity being rugged rocks, among which grew beautiful fir trees. At high water this portion was detached from the main island, and formed a most picturesque islet. But this scene of natural beauty was sadly deformed by the dismal display of human suffering that it presented;—helpless creatures being carried by sailors over the rocks, on their way to the hospital,—boats arriving with patients, some of whom died in their transmission from their ships. Another and still more awful sight, was a continuous line of boats, each carrying its freight of dead to the burial-ground, and forming an endless funeral procession. Some had several corpses,

so tied up in canvass that the stiff, sharp outline of death was easily traceable; others had rude coffins, constructed by the sailors, from the boards of their berths, or I should rather say, cribs. In a few, a solitary mourner attended the remains; but the majority contained no living beings save the rowers. I could not remove my eyes until boat after boat was hid by the projecting point of the island, round which they steered their gloomy way. From one ship, a boat proceeded four times during the day; each time laden with a cargo of dead. I ventured to count the number of boats that passed, but had to give up the sickening task.

The inspecting doctor went about from vessel to vessel, six of which came in each tide, and as many sailed.

We expected him to visit us every moment; but he did not come near us.

In the afternoon a boat made for our brig, and the mistress, who was on deck, was greatly delighted to find that it contained two "captains," one of whom was her nephew. One arrived the day before we came; the other a day previous. They were as ignorant of the course of proceeding as we; and before they went away it was agreed on, that they, our captain, and I, should wait on the superintendent physician the next day.

Chapter XI.

As from the wing no scar the sky retains,
The parted wave no furrow from the keel,
So dies in human hearts the thought of death.
E'en with the tears which nature shed
O'er those we love, we drop it in their graves.—YOUNG.

Friday, July 30th.

This morning, when I came on deck, a sailor was busily employed constructing a coffin for the remains of the Head committee's wife; and it was afflicting to hear the husband's groans and sobs accompanying each sound of the saw and hammer, while with his motherless infant in his arms he looked on. About an hour after, the boat was lowered, and the bereaved husband, with four rowers, proceeded to the burial ground to inter the corpse; and they were followed by many a tearful eye, until the boat disappeared behind the rocky point.

At 10, A. M., we descried the doctor making for us, his boatmen pulling lustily through the heavy sea; a few minutes brought him alongside and on board, when he ran down to the cabin and demanded if the papers were filled up with a return of the number of deaths at sea? how many cases of sickness? &c. He was handed them by the captain; when he enquired,—how many patients we then had; he was told there were twelve; when he wrote an order to admit six to hospital; saying that the rest should be admitted when there was room; there being 2500 at that time upon the island, and hundreds lying in the various vessels before it. The

order written, he returned to his boat, and then boarded a ship lying close to us, which lowered her signal when he approached. Several other vessels that arrived in the morning, had their ensigns flying at the peak, until each was visited in turn.

Immediately after the doctor left us, the captain gave orders to have the patients in readiness. Shortly after, our second boat was launched, and four of the passengers volunteered to row; the sailors that were able to work, being with the other. O God! may I never again witness such a scene as that which followed;—the husband,—the only support of an emaciated wife and helpless family,—torn away forcibly from them, in a strange land; the mother dragged from her orphan children, that clung to her until she was lifted over the bulwarks, rending the air with their shrieks; children snatched from their bereaved parents, who were perhaps ever to remain ignorant of their recovery, or death. The screams pierced my brain; and the excessive agony so rent my heart, that I was obliged to retire to the cabin, where the mistress sat weeping bitterly.

The captain went in the boat, and returned in about an hour; giving us a frightful account of what he witnessed upon the island.

The steamers returned, and all the afternoon were engaged, taking the *healthy* passengers out of some of the vessels; they went alongside several until their cargo was complete, when they sailed for Montreal, their decks thickly crowded with human beings; and most extraordinary to relate, each of them had a fiddler, and a dancing party in the prow.

Early in the evening the captain's nephew came to take us in his boat, on shore. After a long pull through a heavy swell, we landed upon the Isle of Pestilence; and climbing over the rocks passed through the little town, and by the hospitals, behind which were piles upon piles of unsightly coffins. A little further on, at the edge of a beautiful sandy beach, were several tents, into one of which I looked, but had no desire to see the interior of any

others. We pursued our way, by a road cut through a romantic grove of firs, birch, beech, and ash, beneath the shade of which grew and blossomed charming wild flowers, while the most curious fungi vegetated upon odd, decayed stumps. The path led us into a cleared lawn, passing through which, we arrived in front of the superintendent physician's cottage, placed upon a sloping bank at the river's side, on which were mounted two pieces of ordnance guarded by a sentinel. The view from this spot was exquisitely beautiful;—upon the distant bank of the broad river were the smiling, happy-looking Canadian villages, backed by deep, blue hills, while the agitated water in front tossed the noble vessels that lay at anchor, and which were being swung round by the turning tide.

The doctor not being within, we walked about until his return; when he invited us into his cottage and heard what the captains had to say; after which he promised to discharge our friend the next day, and that he would send a steamer to take our passengers. He also gave the captain an order for the admission of the mate to the seaman's hospital. Our mission having been so successful, we thanked the doctor and departed. Upon our return we called at the store licensed to sell provisions upon the island. It was well stocked with various commodities, among which were carrion beef, and cattish mutton, bread, flour, cheese, &c. Although the captain wished to treat the mistress to fresh meat, he declined purchasing what we saw, and merely bought some flour. The storekeeper did not lack better customers, however, for there was a vast concourse of mates, stewards, seamen, and boys, buying his different articles, and stowing them away in their boats. The demand for bread was very great; and several batches were yielded from a large oven, while we remained.

Hearing the music of a fiddle accompanied by the stamping of feet in time with the tune, I walked up to the shed from which it issued. There were two men dancing a jig; one of them a Cana-

dian, the other a sailor,—both fine fellows, who were evidently
pitted against each other, in a trial of skill. The former wore huge
boots coming above the knees, and drawn over his gray trowsers
composed of "etoffe du pays,"—a light blue flannel shirt confined
at the waist by a scarlet scarf, whose parti colored ends hung at
one side. On his head was a woollen "bonnet rouge," whose tassel
jumped about with the wearer's movements. His brilliant black
eyes lighted up his sallow visage, and his arms were as busily
engaged as his legs. The sailor was rigged out in pumps, white
trowsers, blue jacket, and straw hat with streaming black ribands;
his ruddy face glowing with the exercise. The fiddler's costume was
similar to that of his brother Canadian, except that his "bonnet"
was blue; he stood upon a barrel; and around the dancers was a
circle of "habitans" and sailors, who encouraged them by repeated
"bravos." I did not remain long, nor could I enjoy the amusement
in such a place; and therefore joined my companions in the boat;
where we were detained a few moments, while one of the men
returned for lime, which the captain had forgotten to procure.
He soon returned, and again ploughing through the waves, we
shortly arrived beneath the "Leander;" after examining which
noble ship, the captain and I returned to the brig, and acquainted
the mistress with the issue of our adventure.

Our boat returned, just at the same time; the men having been
away all the day. It appeared that they could not find the burial
ground, and consequently dug a grave upon an island, when as
they were depositing the remains they were discovered, and obliged
to decamp. They were returning to the brig, when they perceived
several boats proceeding in another direction, and having joined
them, were conducted to the right place. The wretched husband
was a very picture of desperation and misery, that increased the
ugliness of his countenance;—for he was sadly disfigured by the
marks of small pox, and was blind of an eye. He walked moodily
along the deck, snatched his child from a woman's arms, and went

down into the hold without speaking a word. Shortly after, one of the sailors who was with the boat told me, that after the grave was filled up, he took the shovels and placing them crosswise upon it, calling heaven to witness said, "By that cross, Mary, I swear to revenge your death; as soon as I earn the price of my passage home, I'll go back, and shoot the man that murdered you, and that's the landlord."

Saturday, July 31st.

It was with great reluctance the mate consented to go to hospital, and as he went into the boat he charged the captain, the mistress, and me with cruelty. The captain went with him, and gave him in charge of a doctor.

In consequence of the superintendent's promise to send a steamer to take our passengers, and to give us clean bills if the vessel were well whitewashed between decks, the passengers' births were all knocked away, and the filthy boards thrown into the river; after which four men worked away cleaning and whitening all the day; but no steamer arrived that day. One which lay over night, took 250 passengers from the captain's nephew, who sailed not long after. Vessels were arriving with every tide; two ships from Bremen came in the morning and were discharged at once, having no sickness; some others sailed up with the evening tide, after which there were more than thirty in quarantine. Boats were plying all day long, between the several vessels and the island; and the sea being high the miserable patients were drenched by the spray; after which they had to clamber over the slimy rocks, or were carried by sailors. There was also an almost unbroken line of boats carrying the dead for interment; then there was the doctor's boat unceasingly shooting about; besides several others containing captains of ships, many of whom had handsome gigs with six oars,

and uniformly-dressed rowers. It was indeed a busy scene of life and death. To complete the picture, the rigging of the vessels was covered over with the passengers' linen, hanging out to dry; by the character of which as they fluttered in the breeze, I could tell with accuracy from what country they came; alas! the wretched rags of the majority told but too plainly that they were Irish.

Chapter XII.

O the tender ties,
Close twisted with the fibres of the heart,
Which broken break them, and drain off the soul
Of human joy; and make it pain to live.—YOUNG.

Sunday, August 1st.

The passengers passed a miserable night, huddled up, as they were without room to stretch their weary limbs. I pitied them from my soul, and it was sickening to see them drink the filthy water. I could not refuse to give one or two of them a mouthful from the cask upon the quarter deck, which fortunately was filled lower down the river. They asked for it so pitifully, and were so thankful; but I could not satisfy all and regretted the disappointment of many.

They had on their best clothes, and were all clean, with the exception of one incorrigible family. The doctor came on board in the forenoon, to inspect the passengers, who were all called on deck, but those who were unable. Placing himself at a barrier, he allowed each to pass, one by one; making those he suspected of being feverish, show their tongues. This proceeding lasted about a quarter of an hour; when the doctor went into the hold to examine those below, and to see if it were clean; he then wrote out the order to admit the six patients to hospital, and promised to send the steamer to take the remainder; after which we should have clean bills. When he had gone, the patients were lowered into the boat amid a renewal of the indescribable woe that followed the

previous separations. Two of them were orphan sisters, who were sent for by a brother in Upper Canada. Another was a mother, who had tended all her family through illness,—now careworn, and heartbroken, she became herself a prey.

In the early part of the voyage, I observed the unfilial conduct of a boy, who frequently abused, and even cursed his mother, following the example set by his wretched father. On one occasion, his hand was raised to strike her, when his arm was arrested by a bystander; but the poor woman begged of the man not to punish him, and wept for the depravity of her son. It was she who was now being carried to the boat; while the boy who cursed and would have stricken her, clung to her, crying, and imploring her blessing and forgiveness; but she was unable to utter a word, and by an effort raised her arm feebly and looked sadly upon the afflicted boy, who seized her hand and bathed it with his tears, until he was torn away, and she dropped into the boat, which a moment after rowed off. I felt much for the poor fellow, who was conscious that he should never again see his mother; for there was no hope of her recovery; and I little thought that any one could be so heartless as to aggravate his sufferings, as did two or three women who surrounded him, one of them saying, "Ha! you villain, there's the mother you abused, and cursed, you rascal! you may now take your last look at her." He followed the boat with his eyes, until it reached the shore; when he beheld the inanimate figure borne to the hospital. It was evident from the poignancy of his sorrow, that his heart was not depraved, but that his misconduct arose from education. The morning was fine, clear and warm, and many of the vessels were decorated with their flags, giving a cheerful aspect to the scene, which alas, was marred by the ensigns of two ships (one on either side of us), which were hoisted half-mast high, the captain of one, and the chief mate of the other, being dead. While the captain was away with the boat the steamer came alongside of us to take our passengers. It did not take very long to transship

them, as few of them had any luggage. Many of them were sadly disappointed when they learned that they were to be carried on to Montreal, as those who had left their relatives upon Grosse Isle, hoped, that as Quebec was not far distant, they would be enabled by some means to hear of them, by staying there. Each of them shook hands with the mistress, and all heaped blessings upon her head; and as to the captain, one of them remarked that "though he was a divil, he was a gintleman."

The steamer pushed off, amid the cheers of her motley freight, and was soon out of sight. The mistress was quite overcome by the expressions of the poor creatures' gratitude for her unceasing, and otherwise unrequited attention, and benevolence. The captain returned, and after dinner he and I went ashore for our clean bills of health. We saw Dr. Douglass, who informed us that the inspecting physician, Dr. Jaques, had them, and that he was going his rounds among the vessels; with the intention of calling at the brig. But as we considered that it would probably be late before he would reach her, we pulled for a barque, beside which we descried the well known boat. Before we were half way, it was gone and making for a ship some distance off; however, we still followed, and again were disappointed. We determined not to give up the chase, and at length caught the doctor on board a German emigrant vessel. He was inspecting the passengers, of whom there were 500,—all of them (without a single exception,) comfortably and neatly clad, clean, and happy. There was no sickness amongst them, and each comely fair haired girl laughed as she passed the doctor, to join the group of robust young men who had undergone the ordeal.

Although it was pleasing to see so many joyous beings, it made me sad when I thought of the very, very different state of my unfortunate compatriots; and I had become so habituated to misery, disease, and death, that the happiness that now surrounded me was quite discordant with my feelings. The doctor having com-

pleted his task, countersigned our clean bills, and handed them to
the captain; we therefore thanked him and took our leave. Before
returning to the brig, we called to see the mate, who was lying
with his clothes on, upon a bed; the next one to which contained
a figure writhing in torture, and, as the face was turned towards
me, I recognized to my great surprise and dismay, the sailor, who,
but the evening but one before, was dancing with the Canadian.
When the mate perceived us, he rose from the bed, and taking the
captain by one arm, and me by the other, walked us both out of
the hospital, to the porch; saying that we had no business there,
as there was fever upon all sides of us. The hospital was a large
chapel, transformed to its present use, and was exceedingly clean
and well ventilated, the large windows were all open, causing a
draught of air that was agreeable; the evening being very sultry.

We did not remain long with the mate, who raved consider-
ably in his conversation, though he said he was quite well; so,
the captain giving him in charge of the attendant, with pressing
injunctions to have every attention paid to him, and saying that
he hoped he would be able to join the brig upon his return, we
departed. As we got into the boat, we made a signal to the pilot
(who was desired to be on the lookout,) to weigh anchor, so as
not to lose the tide by any unnecessary delay. As we repassed the
German ship, the deck was covered with emigrants, who were
singing a charming hymn, in whose beautiful harmony all took
part; spreading the music of their five hundred voices upon the
calm, still air, that wafted it around. The vessel being discharged,
began to move almost imperceptibly, so that we quickly passed
her; but she gradually gained speed, and was ahead of us by the
time we reached the brig, and as the distance between us increased,
the anthem died away, until it became inaudible. It was the finest chorus I ever heard,—performed in a theatre of unrivalled
magnificence.

The mistress was delighted when she learned that we were free,

and all were glad to leave behind the Isle of Death, though we regretted leaving the mate there. The sailors that had been ill, still continuing very weak, the captain induced two young men to remain, in order to assist in working the vessel. At 7 P. M. the anchor was weighed, the sails unreefed, and we glided slowly along.

Chapter XIII.

Sail on, sail on, thou fearless bark,
    Wherever blows the welcome wind;
It cannot lead to scenes more dark,
    More sad, than those we leave behind.—Moore.

Monday, August 2d.

It was indeed with gratefulness to the Almighty for having pre-
served me scathless in the midst of the dread pestilence, that I
left Grosse Isle; and a more beautiful panorama I never beheld,
than the country through which we passed,—the churches of
St. Thomas' and St. Pierre's, surrounded by handsome cottages
and beautiful fields; on our right Isle Madame, the largest of the
numerous islands that clustered in the centre of the river, embosomed in the mighty stream, beyond which rose Cap Tourment,
with the village of St. Joachim at its base. And Mount St. Anne,
sheltering its village also; both of these lofty hills being of a deep
purple hue. At sunset we had reached the eastern extremity of
the Isle of Orleans; and an hour after, dropped anchor before St.
Francois,—a sweet village composed of quaint looking cottages,
whose walls were as white as snow; with red roofs, bright yellow
doors, and green Venetian window blinds. Such was the universal
style, all of them appearing as if they had been newly painted.

    We again set sail, soon after day-break this morning, with a
breeze against us, which compelled us to tack about. I did not
regret this, as I had many near views of the southern bank of
the river, and of the beautiful shore of Orleans island, with its
luxuriant orchards and well cultivated farms, sloping down to

the water's edge; and dark forest upon the crest of its elevated interior. This fine island, which is 20 miles in length, and five in width, is divided into five parishes, and has a population of 5000 Canadians. While it is an object of the greatest beauty, it is at the same time of great usefulness, affording shelter to the harbor of Quebec on the east side, and producing large supplies of fruits and vegetables of the finest description. The northern shore consists of low and marshy beaches, that abound with game. It is surprising that there is no regular communication between the island and the city, during the summer season; but in winter it is easy of access, over the frozen river, when the inhabitants convey their produce to market. When Cartier visited it in the year 1535, the island was covered with vines, on which account he called it the Isle of Bacchus. It was on it, also, that Wolfe took up his quarters previous to the attack upon Quebec. At 8 A. M. we passed St. Vallier and St. John's; the latter upon the island, consisting of entirely white cottages, which are chiefly inhabited by the branch pilots, upwards of 250 of whom find lucrative employment in the river navigation during the season, enabling them and their families to live comfortably through the long winter, in which they are unemployed.

At noon, we dropped anchor again, before St. Michel's, where we lay until 6 P. M., when we once more renewed our tacks, passing the sheltered cove called Patrick's hole, in which a fine ship rode, previous to leaving port for sea. This little natural harbour is very valuable, as it securely shelters vessels that arrive before the winter's ice is sufficiently broken up to allow them to gain the city.

At Anse au Maraud,—which is adjacent, there were launched in the year 1824, two enormous ships—the *Columbus* and the *Baron of Renfrew*, which were built with the intention of being broken up in England, the projectors thinking thereby to save the duty on the timber of which they were constructed: but their object was frustrated by the decision that a voyage should previously be

made out of an English port. The *Columbus* traversed the Atlantic, and returned in safety; but was wrecked upon her second voyage. The *Baron*, in whose construction six thousand tons of timber were consumed, was 309 feet long, and of proportionate breadth.

She sailed for London on the 25th of August, 1825, with a cargo (it is said of 10,000 tons) of lumber, her four masts crowded with sails, and followed down the river by a fleet of steamers and pleasure yachts. After a voyage of fifty days, she arrived at Dover, where she took on board both Deal and river pilots; but her draft of water being thirty feet, she could not be taken through the queen's channel, which is safe for ships of war. She was therefore obliged to remain outside of the Goodwin sands, near the entrance of the king's channel. Having encountered a violent gale, she grounded upon the Long sands, but was got off on the following day. She safely rode out a second gale upon the 19th of October, but successive storms, and strong northerly winds, eventually drove her upon the Flemish banks, and after being buffeted for several weeks by the waves, she was shattered to atoms; the fragments of the wreck and her cargo being wafted along the coast from Calais to Ostend.

Such was the history of these monster ships, whose ill fortune deterred Canadian builders from again constructing such unwieldly vessels.

We next passed Beaumont, where the south bank becomes elevated, increasing in height to Point Levi, the tin spire of whose church was visible; and on Orleans Island, St. Famille.

The magnificent fall of Montmorenci then was revealed to view, in a sheet of tumbling snow-white foam, set between the dark green banks, covered with fir and other trees. As we approached nearer, the low thundering sound of the "many waters" broke on the ear, which died away as we sailed upon the other tack; and night spread its curtain over the splendid picture, when we reached the mouth of the river St. Charles, where we dropped anchor.

Tuesday, 3d August.

I was charmed with the splendid prospect I enjoyed this morning when I came on deck.

The harbour was thickly covered with vessels, many of them noble ships of the largest class.

The city upon the side of Cape Diamond, with its tin covered dome and spires sparkling in the morning sun, and surrounded by its walls and batteries bristling with cannon, was crowned by the impregnable citadel, while a line of villages spread along the northern shore, reaching to Beauport and Montmorenci. The lofty Mount St. Anne bounding the view upon the east. Opposite the city lay Point Levi, with the village of D'Aubigné; crossing the river were steam ferry-boats, horse-boats, and canoes; and up the stream,—far as the eye could reach, the banks were lined by wharves, and timber ponds, while the breeze wafted along a fleet of batteaux, with great white sails; and numberless pilot boats were in constant motion.

We could not go ashore, neither dare any one come on board, until we were discharged from quarantine by the Harbour Master, and Medical Inspector. These functionaries approached us in a long six-oared boat, with the Union Jack flying in her stern. When they came on board, they demanded the ship's papers, and clean bills of health, which the captain gave them; in return for which he received a release from quarantine. Soon after they left us, a butcher brought us fresh meat, milk, eggs and vegetables, to which we did ample justice at breakfast; when I went with the captain on shore.

I remained with the brig during her stay in Quebec harbour, and sailed in her for Montreal, on the evening of Thursday, 5th August. We were towed up the river by a steamboat; and by daylight the following morning were passing the mouth of the river Batiscan.

The sail during the day was extremely pleasing; true, the St.

Lawrence did not present the same grand features as below Quebec, but there was something of exceeding interest or beauty to be seen every moment. The banks varied in height, but did not gain any great elevation, and were lined by an almost unbroken chain of settlements, with villages upon either side at intervals of about ten miles. At noon we sailed by Trois Rivieres, upon the river St. Maurice, which divides into three branches before it empties itself into the St. Lawrence, forming two pretty islands, connected with each other and the main land by three handsome bridges. A couple of hours brought us into Lake St. Peter, which is an extension of the river, and of intricate navigation, affording but a narrow channel, which is marked out by buoys and beacons; towards its western extremity it is full of low marshy islands, surrounded by rushes, between which lies the winding passage. At sunset we had a charming view of Sorel, upon the eastern bank of the Richelieu, which discharges the waters of lakes George and Champlain.

The river again narrowed, and presented similar features as below the expansion. We anchored for the night, and early next morning were forcing our way through the rapids called current St. Mary, passing the village of Longueil, and the charming isle St. Helens. Montreal then opened to our view, and by 8 A. M. we were moored to its fine quay. The brig having completed her cargo, sailed for London, on the 19th of August, when I bade the captain and the mistress adieu, and followed them some distance down the river; until the favorable breeze that filled her sails, wafted the brig out of sight. I have represented these worthy people just as they appeared to me, and if I have spoken too plainly, I would crave their pardon, should they ever recognize their lineaments in these sheets, (which I do not think probable). Indeed, I should much regret causing their displeasure, having received from them every attention; their conduct towards me extending even to unwonted kindness, and for which I shall never cease to feel grateful. I was anxious to learn if the mate recovered, and in compliance with

my desire the captain wrote to me from Quebec, and also from Green Island. The first of these letters was dated August 23d, and the following is an extract from it:

"I got doun hear on satterday and saled all the way down which was a great saving to me it was bubful sale we Ankered all night and saled in the day which gave hus opertunety of seeing every Curisity we went on Shore and got Eags and milk and sead a little of the Contry this Mornning I am gowing on Shore if there be any Letters for you I will foward them to you I have not heard of my Mate Ariving hear yet which Disapoints me Greatly I wish you had bean with hus Yesterday we had a Drive in the Countrey 9 Miles which was a plesent drive and toke tea in the Countrey a long with Cpt —. I will sale on Tusday Morning My Wife Joyns me in Cinde Regards to you." In justice I must also quote the postscript, "you must Excuse this as I am in a hury."

The second letter was written on August 27th. In it the captain says, "I am sorey to inform you of my Mate being so hill I coled at Gruss Ile for him and went on shore and it would have hurt you much to have sean him he was mostly but a Skellitan, but though as hill as he was, I should have brought him on Boord if the Docter would Aload me, I have not any hopes of him, he got nerely well, and mite have come up to the ship but as I told you made two frea with is self putting Bottel to is head Docter to my Wife and me we are all well at present which I hope you cape your Helth, my Wife Joyns me in Cind regards to you."

I learned with satisfaction that the brig arrived at her destination in safety, but of the mate's fate I still remain ignorant.

Of the passengers I never afterwards saw but two, both of them young men, who got employment upon the Lachine canal. The rest wandered over the country, carrying nothing with them but disease; and that but few of them survived the severity of the succeeding winter, (ruined as their constitutions were,) I am quite confident.

Chapter XIV.

Of comfort no man speak.
Let's talk of graves, of worms, and epitaphs;
Make dust our paper, and with rainy eyes
Write sorrow on the bosom of the earth.
Let's choose executors, and talk of wills;
And yet not so,—for what can we bequeath,
Save our deposed bodies to the ground?—SHAKSPEARE.

That the system of quarantine pursued at Grosse Isle afforded but a very slight protection to the people of Canada, is too evident from the awful amount of sickness, and the vast number of deaths that occurred amongst them during the navigable season of 1847. From the plan that was adopted, of sending the majority of the emigrants from the island directly up to Montreal, Quebec did not suffer so much as that city. However, during the three days I was there, in the month of August, too many signs of death were visible; and upon a second and more prolonged visit, later in the season, it presented an aspect of universal gloom; the churches being hung in mourning, the citizens clothed in weeds; and the newspapers recording daily deaths by fever contracted from the emigrants. To their honor and praise be it spoken, these alarming consequences did not deter either clergymen or physicians from the most unremitting zeal in performing their duty, and it is to be lamented that so many valuable lives were sacrificed. A paper of the month of September contained the following paragraph:—"Quarantine Station—Grosse Isle. The Rev. J. Butler, missionary at Kingsey, went down on tuesday morning, to take his turn in attendance upon the sick at the quarantine station.

"The Rev. Richard Anderson and Rev. N. Gueront came up

on the evening of the same day. The former felt indisposed, and thought it prudent to remain in town for the benefit of medical advice. If he should have an attack of fever, the precaution thus early taken will, it is hoped, prevent its proving severe. We regret to say that the Rev. C. J. Morris, recently returned from the station, is now seriously ill with Typhus Fever." The death of the last gentleman is recorded as follows: "Died, this morning at the private hospital at Beauport, of typhus fever, the Rev. Charles J. Morris, A. M., missionary of the church of England, at Portneuf in this district. Mr. Morris contracted the disease which has thus proved fatal to him, in his ministrations to the sick at Grosse Isle. The funeral will take place in the Cathedral church, to-morrow afternoon, at 3 o'clock."

The Rev. Mr. Anderson also died, within a few days of the same period; and that the mortality continued to a late part of the season, appears by the following, from the Boston Journal of December 1st. "We learn from Quebec that Drs. Painchaud and Jackson, and seven or eight Nuns of the Hotel Dieu* were sick with the ship fever. One of the Quebec physicians says that mortality among the physicians during the past season has been greater than it was during the Cholera." On Sunday, October 10th, I had the pleasure of listening to a discourse delivered in St. Patrick's chapel by Rev. Mr. McMahon, before he commenced which, he read a list of the names of several persons, (emigrants) who were separated from their families, and who took this method of endeavoring to find them out; the Rev. Gentleman also

---

* The Hotel Dieu convent in Montreal was at the heart of a seismic scandal when the *Awful Disclosures of Maria Monk* was published in 1836. Monk claimed to have been a nun there and made many shocking allegations against the superior and visiting priests, including of torture, rape and murder of nuns. Her account was republished in 2017 by Books Ulster (ISBN 978-1-910375-59-4)

acknowledged having received several sums of money remitted from parties in Ireland to friends in Canada, amongst which he said were some without signatures, and one of these was directed "To my Aunt Biddy," upon which his Reverence remarked that people should be more particular where money was concerned.

Although (as I have already stated) the great body of emigrants were sent out to Montreal by steamers, all of them could not be so transferred, and many were detained in Quebec, where the Marine and Emigrant Hospital contained during the season, several hundreds, the number that remained upon October 2nd, being 443, of whom 93 were admitted during the week previous, and in which time there were discharged 132, and 46 died.

One of the first objects that appeared to my view upon my arrival in Montreal, was the Emigrant Hospital, upon Point St. Charles, a low tract of ground cut off from the city by the Lachine canal, and on which the Indians were in the habit of encamping every summer before it was turned to its present purpose. On the day I arrived, August 7th, it contained 907 patients, 16 having died during the last 24 hours. An official return of burials in the city was furnished up to the same day, by which it appeared, that during the previous nine weeks the number was 1730, of which 924 were residents, and 806 were emigrants. Exclusive of these there died in the sheds, 1510 emigrants, making a total of 3,240, being 2,752 more than occurred during the corresponding period of the preceding year. Upon August 23rd the emigrant sheds contained 1330, 27 having died during twenty-four hours; and so late as October 11th, there remained 746 patients in them.

Montreal lost many of her most valuable citizens in consequence of the contagion, among whom were Dr. Cushing, and the mayor. Neither was the pestilence stayed here, for the inhabitants of Kingston, Bytown, Toronto, and other places were infected, and a great number died of the fever, amongst whom was the Rev. Dr. Power, R. C. Bishop of Toronto, who contracted the disease

in the discharge of his sacred functions among the sick. The following extract, taken from the Toronto Standard, serves to show the manner in which the people of Canada suffered, and their sympathy for those who brought so much woe amongst them. "The health of the city remains in much the same state as it did several weeks ago. The individual cases of fever have abated nothing of their violence, and several families have caught the infection from having admitted emigrants into their houses. The greatest caution should be observed in this respect, as it does not require contact alone, to infect a healthy person with the deadly virus of the fever. Breathing the same atmosphere with the infected, or coming under the influence of the effluvia rising from their clothes is, in some states of the healthy body, perfectly sufficient for effecting a lodgment of the disease in the human frame. On Monday evening last, the report of the Finance Committee, on the subject of erecting a House of Refuge for the destitute persons who have sought refuge in our City, was received by the Council. This committee report in favor of erecting immediately such a building as would shield those gers from the severities of winter, and recommend that a sum not exceeding £5,000 should be expended for that purpose, and that this sum should be put under the joint superintendence of the Board of Works and the Finance Committee, so that now we have from the praiseworthy benevolence and alacrity of the Council, an assured hope, that the emigrants will not be exposed to any hardships which it is in the power of the city authorities to ward off."

The reader will bear in mind, that the above relates to the city of Toronto, in Western Canada, at a distance of upwards of 500 miles from the Quarantine station, whose stringent regulations were intended to protect the country from contagion.

It now only remains for me to say a few words respecting the people that endured and reproduced so much tribulation.

The vast number of persons who quitted Europe, to seek new

homes in the western hemisphere, in the year 1847, is without a precedent in history. Of the aggregate I cannot definitely speak, but to be within the limits of truth, they exceeded 350,000.

More than one half of these emigrants were from Ireland, and to this portion was confined the devouring pestilence. It is a painful task to trace the causes that led to such fatal consequences; some of them may, perhaps, be hidden, but many are too plainly visible. These wretched people were flying from known misery, into unknown and tenfold aggravated misfortune. That famine which compelled so many to emigrate, became itself a cause of the pestilence. But that the principal causes were produced by injustice and neglect, is plainly proved. Many, as I have already stated, were sent out at the expense of their landlords; these were consequently the poorest and most abject of the whole, and suffered the most. No doubt the motives of some landlords were benevolent; but all they did was to pay for the emigrants' passage—this done, these gentlemen washed their hands of all accountability, transferring them to the shipping agent, whose object was to stow away the greatest possible number between the decks of the vessels chartered for the purpose. That unwarrantable inducements were held out to many, I am aware, causing some to leave their homes, who would not otherwise have done so. They were given to understand that they would be abundantly provided for during the voyage, and that they were certain of finding immediate employment upon their arrival, at a dollar per day. Another serious injury was done many families, who had previously experienced the blessings of temperance, from being, upon their arrival at the different ports where they were to embark, obliged to lodge in public houses of the worst description; whose proprietors, knowing that they possessed a little stock of money, seduced them to violate their "pledge," under the specious pretext that they were no longer bound by its obligations, and that whiskey was the very best preventive of sea-sickness. After a detention—often of many days,

the vessel at length ready for sea, numbers were shipped that were quite unfit for a long voyage. True, they were inspected, and so were the ships, but from the limited number of officers appointed for the purpose, many oversights occurred. In Liverpool, for instance, if I am rightly informed, there was a staff of but five or six men to inspect the mass of emigrants, and survey the ships, in which there sailed from that port 107,474. An additional heavy infliction was their sufferings on ship-board, from famine, the legal allowance for an adult being one pound of food in twenty-four hours; but perhaps the most cruel wrong was in allowing crowds of already infected beings to be huddled up together in the confined holds, there to propagate the distemper, which there was no physician to stay. The sufferings consequent upon such treatment, I have endeavoured to portray in the previous narrative, which alas! is but a feeble picture of the unmitigated trials endured by these most unhappy beings. Nor were their sufferings ended with the voyage. Oh! no, far from it. Would that I could represent the afflictions I witnessed at Grosse Isle! I would not be supposed to think, that the medical officers situated there did not exercise the greatest humanity in administering their disagreeable duties, which consisted—not in relieving the distress of the emigrants; but in protecting their country from contamination. Still it was most afflicting, that after combatting the dangers of the sea, enduring famine, drought, and sickness, the wretched survivors should still have to lie as uncared for as when in the centre of the Atlantic Ocean.

The inefficacy of the quarantine system is so apparent, that it is needless to particularize its defects, neither need I repeat the details of the grievous aggravations of their trials, heaped by it upon the already tortured emigrants. My heart bleeds when I think of the agony of the poor families who as yet undivided had patiently borne their trials, ministering to each other's wants—when torn from each other. Painful as it was to behold the bodies of those

who died at sea, committed to the deep, yet the separation of families was fraught with much greater misery. And as if to reach the climax of endurance, the relatives and friends of those landed upon the island were at once carried away from them to a distance of 200 miles. On their way to Montreal, many died on board the steamers. There, those who sickened in their progress were received into the hospital, and the survivors of this second sifting were sent on to Kingston,—180 miles further; from thence to Toronto, and so on,—every city and town being anxious to be rid of them. Nor were there wanting villains, who preyed upon these stricken people.—The Montreal Herald of October 13th thus writes. "The rapid closing of the season of course diminishes the number of arrivals of emigrants, and thus the hospitals and asylums are less crowded than they have been at an earlier period of the year. The statements are, however, still extremely distressing. An assertion has been made in the Common Council, and is generally believed to be true, that considerable sums have been brought here by some of these people, and consigned by them, in their last moments, to persons who have in many instances appropriated the money to their own use. An Alderman named Tully, who is known to have the means of information, calculates the average of the sums brought to Canada by emigrants at £10 each—we suppose heads of families."

In a tour which I made through Upper Canada, I met in every quarter some of my poor wandering fellow-country people. Travelling from Prescott to Bytown, by stage, I saw a poor woman with an infant in her arms, and a child pulling at her skirt, and crying as they went along. The driver compassionately took them up, and the wayfarer wept her thanks. She had lost her husband upon the voyage, and was going to Bytown to her brother, who came out the previous year, and having made some money by lumbering in the woods, remitted to her the means of joining him; she told her sad tale most plaintively, and the passengers all sympathized

with her. The road being of that description called "corduroy," and the machine very crazy, the latter broke down within five miles of our destination, and as she was unable to carry her two children, the poor creature was obliged to remain upon the road all the night. She came into Bytown the following morning, and I had the satisfaction to learn that she found her brother.

A large proportion of the emigrants who arrived in Canada crossed the frontiers, in order to settle in the United States. So that they were to be seen in the most remote places. At St. Catherine's, upon the Welland canal, 600 miles from Quebec, I saw a family, who were on their way to the western part of the state of New York. One of them was taken ill, and they were obliged to remain by the wayside; with nothing but a few boards to protect them from the weather. There is no means of learning how many of the survivors of so many ordeals were cut off by the inclemency of a Canadian winter, so that the grand total of the human sacrifice will never be known but by "Him who knoweth all things."

As I cannot so well convey my sentiments in my own language, I will conclude with the following quotation from England's most popular writer, and would that his suggestions uttered five years before the commencement of the tragic drama, had been attended to in time: if they had, much evil had been spared humanity. "The whole system of shipping and conveying these unfortunate persons is one that stands in need of thorough revision. If any class deserve to be protected and assisted by the government, it is that class who are banished from their native land in search of the bare means of subsistence. All that could be done for those poor people by the great compassion and humanity of the captain and officers, was done, but they require much more. The law is bound, at least upon the English side, to see that too many of them are not put on board one ship; and that their accommodations are decent, not demoralizing and profligate. It is bound, too, in common humanity, to declare that no man shall be taken on

board without his stock of provisions being previously inspected by some proper officer, and pronounced moderately sufficient for his support upon the voyage. It is bound to provide, or to require that there be provided a medical attendant; whereas in these ships there are none, though sickness of adults and deaths of children on the passage are matters of the very commonest occurrence. Above all, it is the duty of any government, be it monarchy or republic, to interpose and put an end to that system by which a firm of traders in emigrants purchase of the owners the whole 'tween-decks of a ship, and send on board as many wretched people as they can get hold of on any terms they can get, without the smallest reference to the conveniences of the steerage, the number of berths, the slightest separation of the sexes, or any thing but their own immediate profit. Nor is this the worst of the vicious system; for certain crimping agents of these houses, who have a per centage on all the passengers they inveigle, are constantly travelling about those districts where poverty and discontent are rife, and tempting the credulous into more misery, by holding out monstrous inducements to emigration which never can be realized."*

---

*   Dickens. *American Notes.* [Author's note]

Appendix.

Immediately a place
Before his eyes appear'd, sad, noisome, dark;
A lazar-house it seem'd; wherein were laid
Numbers of all diseased; all maladies
Of ghastly spasm, or racking torture, qualms
Of heart-sick agony, all feverous kinds,
Marasmus, and wide-wasting pestilence,
Dropsies, and asthmas, and joint-racking rheums,
Dire was the tossing, deep the groans: Despair
Tended the sick, busiest from couch to couch;
And over them triumphant Death his dart
Shook, but delay'd to strike, though oft invoked
With vows, as their chief good, and final hope.
Sight so deform what heart of rock could long
Dry eyed behold?—MILTON.

The intention of this appendix is, by the means of a few extracts from newspapers, hospital returns, reports, &c., to furnish some further general information respecting the ship pestilence.

But as the previous narrative is not designed to present a history of that sad subject, so neither will this sequel supply complete statistics regarding it. The extracts go no further back than the beginning of August; but will be found sufficient to elucidate the events from that time until the termination of the season.

"Grosse Isle.—Il y avait samedi dernier à la Grosse Isle 2148 malades; du 1er au 6 août 130 personnes sont mortes."—*La Reveu Canadienne.*

"Monday Afternoon, August 9.
"Since my last, the wind has been blowing fresh from the north-

east, and severat vessels have arrived in port, the names of which you will find enclosed. Four have just arrived, but are not yet boarded. I make out the names of three, viz:—Bark Covenanter, Bark Royal Adelaide, and Schooner Maria, of Limerick. The Zealous has not yet made her appearance.

"The accounts from Grosse Isle since my last, are not of a favorable nature, and the number of deaths is much the same. The building of the new sheds there is advancing rapidly.

"A letter was received this forenoon, from the mate of the bark Naparima, with passengers, from Dublin, dated off Bic, last Friday, announcing that the Captain, Thomas Brierly, died on the 3d instant, and was buried on the same day. She was then fifty days out, and short of provisions,—about 20 of the passengers were sick, but were recovering when the mate wrote, and he intended to put into some convenient place for supplies. There was a pilot on board, and every exertion would be made to get her up to the Quarantine Station as soon as possible."—*Quebec Correspondence of the Montreal Herald.*

"We are in possession of the latest news from Grosse Isle. The hospital statement yesterday, the 9th, was 2240. There is a large fleet of vessels at the station, and amongst them some very sickly, as it may be seen from the following statement:—

		Passengers.	Deaths.	Sick.
Bark Ellen Simpson,	Limerick,	184	4	—
Brig Anna Maria,	„	119	1	1
Bark Amy,	Bremen,	289	—	—
Brig Watchful,	Hamburg,	145	—	—
Ship Ganges,	Liverpool,	393	45	80
Bark Corea,	„	501	18	7
Bark Larch,	Sligo,	440	108	150

Bark Naparima,	Dublin,	226	7	17
Bark Britannia,	Greenock,	386	4	25
Brig Trinity,	Limerick,	86	all well.	—
Bark Lilias,	Dublin,	219	5	6
Bark Brothers,	„	318	6	—

"A full rigged ship just coming in—not yet boarded.

"The hospitals have never been so crowded, and the poor creatures in the tents (where the healthy are), are dying by dozens! Eleven died on the night of the 8th, and one on the road to the hospital yesterday morning.

"Captain Read, of the Marchioness of Breadalbane, died in hospital on the 7th. The Captain of the Virginius died the day after his arrival at Grosse Isle.

"We regret to learn that the Rev. Mr. Paisley is in a critical state. He was dangerously ill this morning.

"Since writing the above we learn that 60 new cases were admitted into hospital, and 300 more, arrived on the 8th and 9th, remain to be admitted!"—*Quebec Mercury, August* 10th, 1847.

"The Steamer St. George arrived from Grosse Isle yesterday afternoon, but brought nothing of importance. The cool temperature of the last few days has had a favorable effect on the sick in the tents, and fewer cases of fever had appeared.

"The Ship Washington from Liverpool, 9th of July, had arrived at the station yesterday. She has one cabin, and 305 steerage passengers, had 22 deaths and 20 sick. She reports 15 vessels with passengers in the Traverse.—*Quebec Chronicle.*

"*Hospital return—Grosse Isle, September* 14th, 1847.
        Remaining on 14th,   1386,
        Died 12th to 13th inst.,   41."

"Hospital return—Grosse Isle, from 19*th to* 25*th of Sept.*

Remaining on 19th,	1196,	Discharged,	234,
Admitted since,	436,	Died,	121,
	1632		355
	355		
	1277		

"Deaths at the sheds, where the healthy passengers are landed, during the same period—10.

"There are 1240 cases of fever, and 37 cases of small pox. Two men died whilst being landed from the Emigrant, and 162 cases were admitted into hospital from the same vessel."

"Hospital statement to the 28*th:*

Men,	473
Women,	441
Children,	349
Total,	1263

Grosse Isle.—Return of sick in hospitals 1*st October.*

		Discharged.	Died.	Remaining.
Men,	414	103	7	304
Women,	412	156	3	253
Children,	326	109	1	216
	1152	368	11	773

(Signed) I. M. Douglass, *Med. Sup.*

"About 400 convalescents went up to Montreal in the Canada on Thursday last, and 35 came up to Quebec in the Lady Colborne on Friday.

"This has enabled the Medical Superintendent to close another

hospital; and this day the services of two more medical men, with their staff of orderlies and nurses will be dispensed with."

"*Hospital statement, 5th October.*
"Men, 230—Women, 124—Children, 150—Total, 504.
"There were then three vessels with emigrants at the station."

"A Melancholy Tale of Woe.

"On Saturday last, 30th October, the Lord Ashburton, from Liverpool, 13th September, with general cargo and passengers, arrived at Grosse Isle in a most wretched state.

"When sailing she had 475 steerage passengers, and before her arrival at the Quarantine Station, she had lost 107 by dysentery and fever; and about 60 of those remaining were then ill of the same complaints. So deplorable was the condition of those on board that five of the passengers had to remain to work the ship up from Grosse Isle."—*Quebec Mercury.*

"Emigration from Liverpool.

"The amount of emigration from Great Britain and Ireland has this year far surpassed that of any previous year, as will be seen from the following returns, made up on the 6th instant, of emigration from this port alone:—

United States,	77,403
Canada,	27,666
New Brunswick,	1,479
Nova Scotia,	171
Prince Edward's Isle,	444
Other places,	311
Total,	107,474

"Of this vast number of emigrants, two thirds were Irish, and of the remaining one third, two fifths were Scotch and English,

and one fifth German, of whom a larger number than formerly left this port during the past season."

Reports of the following vessels upon their arrival at Grosse Isle; namely,

		Passengers.	Deaths.	Sick.
Sir Henry Pottinger,	Cork,	399	98	112
Bark Wellington,	Liverpool,	435	26	30
Bark Sir Robert Peel,	„	458	24	12
Schooner Jessie,	Limerick,	108	2	16
Bark Anne Rankin,	Glasgow,	332	7	3
Bark Zealous,	London,	120	1	5

"We are glad to learn that the *Sœurs Grises*,* amongst whom sickness and death have made such fearful havoc, during their self-immolating ministrations to the dying emigrants, are again pursuing their charitable labors at the Sheds at Point St. Charles. We are happy to learn, also, that the sickness in Griffintown is rapidly on the decrease."—*Montreal Pilot.*

The following advertisement is a specimen of many of a similar nature, that daily appeared in the newspapers; and requires no comment.

"Information wanted of Abraham Taylor, aged 12 years, Samuel Taylor, 10 years, and George Taylor, 8 years old, from county Leitrim, Ireland, who landed in Quebec about five weeks ago—their mother having been detained at Grosse Isle. Any information respecting them will be thankfully received by their brother, William Taylor, at this office."—*Montreal Transcript*, September 11th, 1847.

---

* The Gray Sisters, a community of charitable Nuns. [Author's note]

"The 'Quebec Chronicle' having obtained permission to copy them from the official records, has commenced the publication of the names of all the unfortunates who have died in the hospital at Grosse Isle, with their ages and the names of the vessels in which they came to Canada, as well as the date of the decease. The 'Chronicle' deserves well of the community, for thus affording the relatives of the poor sufferers the means of knowing what has become of them."—*Montreal Courier*.

"The immigration commissioners report that 94 vessels have landed in the Province of New Brunswick, the present season, 15,269 passengers. The deaths at sea on board these vessels, were six hundred and sixty two."

"The schooner Victoria, from Quebec, with 20 passengers, anchored at the Quarantine ground on Tuesday last. She had three cases of typhus fever on board. The passengers and crew were landed on Middle Island this morning, the captain securing the maintainance of the healthy passengers and crew until discharged."—*Miramichi Gleaner*, 27*th July*.

"*Emigration to New York.*—We have received from Senator Folsom a printed copy of the report forwarded to the Legislature by the Commissioners of Emigration at this port. It is dated October 1st, 1847. The board of Commissioners having been organized on the 8th May last, Robert Taylor being appointed agent, and William F. Havemeyer, president—proceeded immediately to take charge of the sick and destitute emigrants. Having filled the Quarantine hospitals, all the spare rooms connected with the City Almshouse department were hired at a dollar per week for each destitute emigrant, and a dollar and a half per week for the sick. But the introduction of fever patients at the Almshouse was attended with too much risk, and buildings were erected for their

accommodation on Staten Island. These being still inadequate, the buildings on the Long Island Farms were leased, but the fear of contagion so alarmed the neighborhood, that the buildings were burned by incendiaries.

The United States Government at once granted their warehouses at Quarantine for the accommodation of the sick. They were soon filled, as all the principal hospitals, public and private, to which the Commissioners had to resort. At this crisis, a large stone building was leased on Ward's Island, which with buildings subsequently added to it, afforded ample accommodation for the thousands dependent upon their benevolent undertaking.

"Many were destitute of clothing, and from May to September, ten thousand three hundred and eight articles of dress were made at Ward's Island and furnished to them, by direction of the Commissioners. Hundreds have been provided with employment in the interior of the state, and many forwarded West at the expense of the Commissioners.

"The number of passengers who arrived from May 5th to Sept. 30th, inclusive, and for whom commutation money was paid, or bonds given, was 101,546, of whom only 25 were bonded.

"Of said passengers there were natives of

Germany,	43,208
Ireland,	40,820
England and Wales,	6,501
Holland,	2,966
France,	2,633
Scotland,	1,856
Switzerland,	1,506
Norway,	881
Belgium,	478
West Indies,	265
Italy,	130

Sweden,	119
Spain,	72
Denmark,	51
Portugal,	31
Poland,	21
East Indies,	6
Turkey,	1
South America,	1
Total,	101,546

Of which number there were

Forwarded from the city.	427.
Temporarily relieved.	217.
Sent to Hospitals.	5,148.
Sent to Alms house.	713.

Total, 6,505, of whom were Irish 3,792.

"Adding to the above 256 emigrants who were in Hospital at the time the Commissioners entered upon their duties, we have 6,761, the total number under their care up to the date of this report.

"Of these, seven hundred and three died between the 8th of May and the 1st October. The names, ages, and places of birth, of the dead, are not given. This is an oversight which ought to be corrected.

"It seems, also, that no provision was made for the erection of any memorial over their graves."—*New York Paper.*

"*Ship Fever.*—The British ship India, Gray, (late Thompson), arrived yesterday from Liverpool, after a passage of 57 days. Captain Thompson died of the ship fever on the 14th inst., (January, 1848) and during the passage 39 of the passengers died of the same disease. The chief officer of the ship, and a large number of the passengers are now sick. When the India left Liverpool she had two hundred and seventy passengers."—*New York Express.*

"The British Ship Viceroy, arrived at New Orleans on the 5th instant, with 286 immigrants.

"Fourteen had died on the passage, and many others were very sick, and sent to the Charity Hospital. The Orizaba, which arrived from Liverpool on the 31st ult., had shipped 170; 24 of whom died, and most of the rest were sent to the Hospital."—*Boston Mail, Jan. 19th*, 1848.

"*Report of Deer Island Hospital, Boston, for the week ending January 26th*, 1848.

Number remaining as per last week's report,	311	
Admitted since,	28	
Total,	—	339
Discharged,	36	
Died,	13	49
Remaining,		290
Whole number admitted to this date,		2,230
Whole number buried on the Island,		347
Of whom were brought from the ship dead,		20
Died the day of their reception,		8
In carriage,		2"

—Boston Journal.

"Foreign Emigrants.—A communication from the State Department was laid before the House of Representatives on Friday last, reporting the number of passengers who arrived from foreign countries on shipboard, during the year ending the 30th of September last. The number of males was 139,166; females, 99,325; sex not reported, 989; total, 239,480. The prospect is that the number will be much larger the present year.

"Of the above number of passengers, 145,838 landed in New York; 20,848 in Massachusetts; 5,806 in Maine; 14,777 in Pennsylvania; 12,018 in Maryland; 34,803 in Louisiana, and 3,873 in Texas."—*Boston Journal.*

Abstract statement of payments on account of the expenses attending emigration, in the Province of Canada, during the season 1847. Taken from the Inspector General's report.

Amount paid for the erection of Hospital Sheds.

At Grosse Isle,	£10,609,	11, 7
At Quebec,	1,120,	0, 0
At Montreal,	15,914,	17, 5
	£27,644,	9, 0
For transport of emigrants inland, including cost of provisions,	35,450,	0, 0
For Boards of Health.		
Canada, East and West,	60,220,	19, 7
Expenses at Quarantine Station,	15,465,	17, 6
Emigration Agent for transport,	10,502,	4, 5
Board of Health, and Emigrant Hospital at Quebec,	8,000,	0, 0
Total,	£157,283	10, 6

Table showing the comparative number of emigrants to the ports designated, viz:

	1846	1847	Increase 1847
Quebec,	32,753	98,105	65,352
New York,	97,843	145,890	48,047
New Orleans,	22,148	40,442	18,294
Boston,	14,079	20,745	6,666
Philadelphia,	7,236	14,763	7,527
Baltimore,	9,327	12,018	2,691
	183,386	331,963	148,577

"Emigration to British North America.

"Emigration returns just issued by order of her Majesty, state that the numbers who embarked in Europe, in 1847, for Canada, was 98,006. Viz:

From England,*	32,228
From Ireland,	54,329
From Scotland,	3,752
From Germany,	7,697
	98,006

Of the whole number 91,882 were steerage passengers, 634 cabin, and 5541 infants. Deducting from this aggregate the Germans and the cabin passengers, the entire number of emigrants who embarked at British ports was 89,738, of whom 5,293 died before their arrival, leaving 84,445 who reached the colony. Of these it is estimated that six sevenths were from Ireland. Of the 84,445 who reached the colony alive, no less than 10,037 died after their arrival. Of the remainder no less than 30,265 were admitted into Hospital for medical treatment. Up to the 12th of November last, the number of destitute emigrants forwarded from the agency at Montreal to Upper Canada was 38,781."—*New Orleans Price Current.*

As the conduct of Irish landlords has been severely commented upon, in the foregoing pages, it is but just to inform the reader of a most honorable exception; and which it affords the author extreme gratification to be enabled to do, by transcribing the following article from the "British Canadian."

"Last Season's Emigration.

"Among the landlords who last summer were desirous of pro-

---

* It may be necessary to remark that many of the Irish emigrants sailed from English ports. [Author's note]

viding an asylum for a portion of their tenantry, was one who was actuated by far other motives than merely getting rid of so many people. We trust there were others urged by similar motives, but there were some not very creditable exceptions. Steven E. De Vere, Esq., a gentleman of fortune, and the proprietor of some estates in the South of Ireland, having heard a great deal about the evils and benefits of emigration to this Province, and hearing also of the sufferings of many poor people who had been sent from the country, determined to try the experiment himself. This he came to the conclusion to do, not by making arrangements for the transport of so many hundreds of thousands of his tenantry, and remaining at home to hear as much, or as little as might be, of their fate; but he would see for himself. He accordingly picked some dozen volunteers from among the numbers who would gladly have accompanied him, and with them took shipping for Quebec, in the steerage of one of the regular passenger ships. Landlord and Tenant fared alike, the former taking careful notes of the events of the passage. Of the voyage we need say nothing more than that it was of the average character—there was all the disease, ill usage, and wretchedness of which our readers have often been made perfectly aware;—the state of things which imported the fever that carried off many of our most valued friends and citizens. At Quebec, proceedings were commenced against the Captain, which were ultimately compounded upon his paying a certain amount for the benefit of the suffering Emigrants. Mr. De Vere proceeded to Upper Canada, and closely observed the whole process of transportation, to the very last destination—the graves of the fever-stricken people. In Toronto this philanthropic gentleman attended the emigrant office, and rendered much assistance to the lamented and indefatigable agent, Mr. McElderly, boarding with him every steamer filled with the wretched cargoes, and transmitting to the "proper authorities" the result of his laborious experience. He was well pleased with the management

of our hospitals; but shocked, as every one was, with the mode of transporting the poor people hither. Some of the steamboat cargoes were sufficient to recall to the mind the horrors of the sea voyage. Mr. De Vere's people suffered from fever, but recovered, receiving his constant personal attendance. The fact of this gentleman's investigations being laid before the Colonial Secretary, and some members of the House of Lords, coming as they did from one well known, and who could not possibly have any interest in writing, but the benefit of his countrymen, has had a good effect, and he merits well of the people of this Province, as well as the emigrating population of the mother country.

Few men are found to act from such pure disinterestedness in these days, and it is gratifying to observe the result of such labors.

Mr. De Vere returns shortly to England, and, by making his views public, will, we hope, be the means of obtaining further improvements, as those already made are by no means sufficient. One fact is certain, his information may be implicitly relied upon by government; for he has obtained it himself, on the spot, and by the most careful, and indeed dangerous investigation, as the above mentioned facts fully show."

It was the author's intention to confine himself to the occurrences of the year 1847; but as the publication of the foregoing narrative has been delayed longer than was anticipated, it may here be observed that he had strong hopes that judicious precautions would have been taken to prevent the repetition this season, of the tragic scenes of the last.

Some legislative enactments for the further regulation of Emigrant ships have been passed by Great Britain, during the last session of Parliament; but it is much to be feared that they will prove quite inefficient. It is painful to observe the very unfavorable accounts from some of the Ports of the United States, as well as of New Brunswick and Nova Scotia.

As regards Canada the prospect is exceedingly gloomy, to judge from the conduct of the executive government *in forbidding the publication, or issue of any reports from the Quarantine Station*, respecting the state of things there.

Were not the trials of the wretched emigrant already sufficiently great, that he must

"To such unsighty sufferings be debased?"

The Press has boldly taken up the matter, and it is to be hoped that the appearance and repetition of such articles as the following will tend to the repeal of the obnoxious and cruel edict.

"GROSSE ISLE INTELLIGENCE.

"The executive government have forbidden the transmission of any news or statements from the island, except, we suppose, to head quarters, that is, to themselves. This is a proceeding as arrogant as it is absurd and mischievous. Last year full reports were given to the public of the state of the island and the proceedings there, as well from official as from private sources. Why then interdict the publication this year, when more than ever a faithful return of the health and sickness prevailing at the quarantine station is most desirable?

If the prohibition be intended to prevent alarm, it is founded upon false premises, as, in the absence of authentic information, wild and exaggerated rumors obtain credence. The public have a right to be informed of what is passing at Grosse Isle."—*Kingston Chronicle*, 17th June, 1848.

It is unnecessary to bring forward any further evidence of the popular indignation so warmly expressed against such despotic cruelty. How long will

"Oppression, with her heart
Wrapp'd up in triple brass, besiege mankind?"

THE END.

IRELAND'S
WELCOME
TO THE STRANGER

ASENATH NICHOLSON

ISBN 978-1910375624

ISBN 978-1910375631

ASENATH NICHOLSON

in 1847, 1848 and 1849

IRELAND

FAMINE IN

ANNALS OF THE

ISBN 978-1910375594

Maria Monk & Rebecca Theresa Reed

IN A CONVENT
OR, SIX MONTHS' RESIDENCE

& THE NUN

MARIA MONK

AWFUL DISCLOSURES OF

The

SCOTCH-IRISH IN AMERICA

Henry Jones Ford

ISBN 978-1910375495

45842213R00069